'A complete original' *Saturday Review*

'An artist in both line and words . . . with talents of gold.' *Observer*

'The singularity of Bemelmans, whether he draws or writes, is his double capacity to see freshly like a child and comment shrewdly like a grown-up. The product is a wry wisdom, the wisdom of a reflective innocent who is surprised at nothing and delighted with everything.' Clifton Fadiman

'Witty, festive and picturesque . . . Ludwig Bemelmans' gifts are brilliant, visual simile and an eye for the rascality of his onetime trade.' V S Pritchett

'Mr Bemelmans is always pricking bubbles, discreetly, appreciatively, out of a sense of duty rather than a desire to shock, and the process is delightful.' *The Times*.

'A note of expensive cosmopolitanism is brilliantly sustained. There are stories here that could hardly be done better.' *New Statesman*

'Very entertaining . . . an excellent story-teller.' *Sunday Times*

'I know of no other writing that pleases the mental palate as pungently, sw   Mr Bemelmans.' Elizabeth Bowe

'One reads Bem   ous novelist but for the sheer n   his evocation of atmosphere and mood.' *Punch*

About the Author

Ludwig Bemelmans – author and illustrator of over 40 books – was born in the Austrian Tyrol in 1898. A rebellious child, Bemelmans never finished his formal education and was apprenticed out to his Uncle Hans, a prosperous hotelier. After being dismissed from a series of hotels, he shot a headwaiter after a dispute and was given a choice between reform school and emigration to America. The 16-year-old Bemelmans left for New York in 1914 sporting two pistols with which to fend off hostile Indians. He had letters of introduction to managers of several large hotels and began working as a waiter. He enlisted in the US Army in 1917 and became naturalized in 1918. After the war he continued to work in the New York hotel and restaurant trade and honed his skills as an artist. He didn't turn to writing until 1934, when a friend in publishing saw his paintings and suggested he write a children's book. His first effort, *Hansi*, was followed by 15 other children's books including his greatest success *Madeline*. His adult writings began with *My War with the United States*, about his army experiences, in 1937. Other writings include several humorous volumes on hotel life: *Life Class* (1938), *Small Beer* (1939), *Hotel Splendide* (1941) and *I Love You, I Love You, I Love You* (1942). Bemelmans married in 1935 and settled down to life as a bon viveur. He contributed to the *New Yorker* and a host of other magazines. He designed sets for Broadway, wrote for Hollywood and kept his hand in in the restaurant business. He died in New York City on 1 October, 1962. Bemelmans always claimed to have no imagination and that all his books were a product of his own life experience. Yet his writings always inhabited a uniquely enchanted world somewhere between fiction and autobiography.

HOTEL
BEMELMANS

Ludwig Bemelmans

By the same author

HOTEL BEMELMANS

Ludwig Bemelmans

Introduction by
Anthony Bourdain

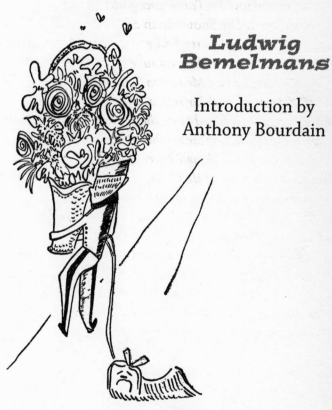

EBURY
PRESS

1 3 5 7 9 10 8 6 4 2

First published in 1956
Copyright © Barbara Bemelmans and Madeleine Bemelmans

Introduction © 2002 Anthony Bourdain

Portions of this book are from the author's earlier volumes: *Life Class*, *Hotel Splendide*, *Small Beer* and *I Love You, I Love You, I Love You*

First published 2002 by Ebury Press,
An imprint of Random House,
20 Vauxhall Bridge Road, London SW1V 2SA
www.randomhouse.co.uk

Random House Australia (Pty) Limited
20 Alfred Street, Milsons Point, Sydney,
New South Wales 2061, Australia

Random House New Zealand Limited
18 Poland Road, Glenfield, Auckland 10, New Zealand

Random House South Africa (Pty) Limited
Endulini, 5a Jubilee Road, Parktown 2193, South Africa
The Random House Group Limited Reg. No. 954009

www.randomhouse.co.uk

Typeset by SX Composing DTP, Rayleigh, Essex
Printed and bound in Great Britain by Cox & Wyman Ltd, Reading, Berkshire

A CIP catalogue record for this book is available from the British Library.

Cover designed by Keenan
Cover illustrations by Ludwig Bemelmans

ISBN 0 09188 787 9

Contents

Introduction
by Anthony Bourdain

He was the original bad boy of the New York hotel/restaurant subculture, a waiter, busboy and restaurateur who 'told all' in a series of funny and true (or very near true) autobiographical accounts of backstairs folly, excess, borderline criminality and madness in the grande Hotel Splendide – a thinly disguised double for the author's one-time employer, the Ritz Carlton. He was a legendary bon viveur, hustler/operator, raconteur and man about town, known best as the author and illustrator of the wildly successful *Madeline* children's books and for his whimsical and occasionally biting *New Yorker* cover illustrations. He was also, at various times, a set designer on Broadway, a painter, decorator, Hollywood screenwriter and the author of over 200 titles in scores of languages. He was a man of many parts and much mystery. His murals which still decorate the walls of the eponymous Bemelmans Bar at the Hotel Carlyle in Manhattan are inspired and witty, but reveal little of a complicated, adventurous – sometimes desperate – but always fascinating life spent travelling the world.

Ludwig Bemelmans was born in the Austrian Tyrol in 1898 to a family of hoteliers and quickly distinguished himself as a bad seed. He was expelled from one school after another for reasons of being 'unruly, impertinent, never serious, always late and keeping bad company'. Packed off to apprentice with his Uncle Hans, he fared no better in the Austrian hotel business and was fired again and again for insolent, drunken and destructive behaviour. When he shot a busboy after an argument (for this reason alone many chefs should love him), the family had had enough and promptly exiled their problem child to America.

Bemelmans is said to have set off for New York with two pistols in his pockets, anticipating imminent conflict with Indians. Employed as a busboy then as a waiter, he bounced around the New York restaurant hotel underbelly, working his way up over the next two decades to jobs in first-class hotels, all the while remaining a keen observer of both the backstage manoeuvrings, tribal customs, practices and degradations of the serving class – the cooks, maitre d'hotels, waiters and scullions who he worked with – and the lusts, vanities and peculiarities of the wealthy clientele out front. He moved easily between the two worlds, it seems, relying on his skills as a hardened professional in the back of the house, while entertaining those outside the cloistered world of the hotel business with his storytelling, his artistry and his larger than life personality.

The kind of über-snob only a lifetime waiter can be, he used his knowledge of languages, food, wine and the complex hierarchy of the upper classes to cow, entertain, manipulate and enchant while careening through life seeking pleasure in all its forms, leaving an amazing body of work, many friends and a trail of unpaid bills behind. Long esteemed for the justifiably famous *Madeline* books and his artwork, he is, sadly, less well known for his bitingly funny and true stories of his travails in the hotel/restaurant underbelly. This reprinting of *Hotel*

INTRODUCTION

Bemelmans sets that right. A compendium of 24 stories redacted from other books and articles, and two unpublished elsewhere, illustrated with 73 of his drawings, this collection presents between two covers what is probably the most important work of a genre begun by Orwell in his account of his misadventures as a dishwasher 'plongeur' at the 'Hotel X' in *Down and Out In Paris and London* and continued through Nicolas Freeling's *The Kitchen* and my own lurid reminisces of a chequered career as a chef. *Kitchen Confidential* – as I learned recently, reading these pages for the first time – was nothing new at all. Bemelmans got there first, more frequently and better, describing brilliantly the whole world of kitchens, back passageways, pilfered foods, dining rooms and banquet halls – a strange, fabulous and sometimes terrible world populated by rogues, con-men, geniuses, craftsmen, lunatics, gypsies, tramps and thieves. It is a truly great book that paints a universe both fascinating to outsiders and immediately familiar to anyone who has ever dwelled there.

Restaurant/hotel people through the decades have shared an unchanging outlook and value system: a world-weary cynicism mixed with flashes of optimism. Keen powers of observation shape the way they speak, hold themselves and even stand in place. Looking out at a group of chefs and waiters sprinkled among 'civilians', even if all are dressed alike, most of us in the life can easily discern who among them are our fellow 'hospitality' workers. There's a look: an injured, ironic, pessimistic-yet-proud and hopeful expression; and a defensive crouch – the posture of a person who knows how bad things can get and who is even now preparing for the worst. And there's a stance, a way that denizens of the service industry hold themselves:

arrogant and forgiving at the same time – a suit of armour that allows us, through defiance or evasion, to face the world.

One of the most comforting things about the 'life' is its seemingly endless continuity. The story 'If You're Not a Fool' could have – were it not for its grand hotel setting – taken place yesterday or a hundred years ago. This ode to thievery and conspiracy could just as well have described daily life in the Gambino Crime Family. Yet it is inarguably and unflinchingly a classic restaurant tale – interchangeable in substance with a million late night anecdotes past and present, swapped over post-shift beers at a million restaurant bars. Herr Otto Brauhaus, of the story of the same name, seems like an old friend, a 'boss' of the old school, the sort of man about whom underlings speculate incessantly; a man alternately loved and feared, pitied and imagined, his every habitual move and tic the subject of interpretation and wonder. Monsieur Victor of the Splendide is the archetypical lifer maitre d' and his story captures precisely the peculiar choreography, reverse snobbery and pecking order of a busy dining room – the strange and terrible powers that allow a lonely, working-class server to lord over captains of industry. 'No Trouble At All' is Bemelmans' version of an urban legend – a classic restaurant anecdote, heard, in assorted versions, over time. Long before reading the story, I had myself heard many variations on the same tale – all told by persons who swore they were there when it happened (or knew someone who had been). I have even heard a similar tale attributed to accounts of Roman feasting. It matters not. It could have happened anywhere, at any time in the history of food service. In Ancient Rome cooks and servers were slaves (albeit pampered ones), and the tale points up the similarities between those who have served at the pleasure of cruel and demanding masters. 'Easy Money' details the horrors of the 'difficult' regular customer and 'The Murderer of the Splendide' is a portrait of a restaurant burn-out on the verge of psychotic breakdown, as well as a very funny description of the kind of speculation, paranoia and superstition that many of us have lived and breathed for much of our careers.

The tone of the book is pitch perfect. In spite of Bemelmans' professed loathing of the business (and his resentment at having to return to it at various times of need), he is decidedly non-judgmental of his fellow workers, saving his wrath mostly for the clientele. It's an accepting point of view, indicative of the love/hate relationship most of us in the life have felt at one time or another – a view of human nature one finds in emergency room staff, professional soldiers and carnival barkers – an almost superstitious certainty that life's ironies will catch up with all of us.

The grand hotels of Bemelmans' time – mammoth spaces filled nightly with the constructed follies of their wealthy clienteles: costumed dervishes, tableaux vivants, temporary lagoons, private dining rooms, permanent residents (all supported by a hidden network of underground labourers like the workers in Fritz Lang's *Metropolis*) – are long gone. Underage piccolos no longer live in the warren of service passageways and sleep under stairs – though early in my career I have surely come across some of them, now advanced in age. The apprentice system has changed somewhat, though one recalls Jean Louis Palladin's comment, not too long ago, when asked why he became a chef, that his parents 'sold [him] into slavery'. But the world of *Hotel Bemelmans* survives immediately familiar to anyone who's ever worked in a large banquet facility, large hotel, multi-unit resort or fine dining restaurant. As a chronicle of days gone by and life in the trenches of the hospitality business, the book is unique, invaluable and unapproachable as the gold standard of the genre.

Hotel Bemelmans serves as both entertainment and as a reminder that behind the glamorous dining room with its crystal and flowers and tuxedoed waiters lies another world of grim, hard, repetitive toil, where the strategies of the human spirit must adapt constantly to survive, where fantasy and ambition and the cold facts are close companions, and where both server and served try their best to achieve their dreams. Ludwig Bemelmans died in 1962, after a remarkable life. But he was formed – however ambivalently he might have felt about them – by his experiences as a waiter; a job where one can look out at the world from a unique perspective, seeing the rich and the powerful, the industrious and the poor, madmen and fantasists behave at their very best and their very worst. *Hotel Bemelmans*, again and again, celebrates the human spirit – the resilience of the hustlers, dreamers, melodramatists and true believers of a life usually out of view. We are very fortunate to have it back for another look.

Welcome to the world of the hotel/restaurant underbelly – old-school style. May it never change.

Anthony Bourdain 2002

1. I Was Born in a Hotel

I WAS born in a hotel in Meran, a small city in Tirol, and I spent the first years of my life in a beer garden. An old maître d'hôtel was my nurse, and the chef himself made up my formula. The beer garden was in Regensburg. Regensburg is a Bavarian city on the banks of the Danube, and it possesses one of the finest Gothic cathedrals. When I was little it had about sixty thousand inhabitants, first among whom was the Duke of Thurn und Taxis. He lived in a castle which it took fifteen minutes to pass; it stood in a park that encircled the city. The Duke retained the Spanish etiquette at his court; his servants wore livery and powdered wigs; he rode about in a gilded coach cradled in saffron leather and drawn by white horses. He supported several jewellers, the city's theatre, a private orchestra, and the race track.

Grandfather's brewery stood on a square facing the Duke's theatre, in the oldest part of the town. His daughter, my mother, was born in Regensburg and was educated at the convent at Alt Oetting. Grandfather loved the city.

My father did not. He called it the cloaca of the world, but with a broader, more Bavarian word, which in Regensburg is used frequently as a term of rough endearment among friends. And so he went to Munich whenever he could escape from

Regensburg; and when he could not, he walked out to the railroad station at least one evening a week. When all the other people went to the breweries, he would walk up and down the station platform until the signal bell announced the approach of the fast train from Paris. This train stopped for three minutes in Regensburg, and in that time my father would lean over the iron barrier and look into the bright windows of the dining-car, over which brass letters spelled out the elegant phrase Compagnie des Wagons-Lits et Express Européens, and under which were a coat of arms and the word Mitropa, in carved wood. There he hung, drinking in the perfume, looking at the furs, at the few fortunate people who were walking up and down and climbing into the carmine-upholstered compartments. He would wait until the red signal lamp at the end of the train had slid down over the narrowing rails and disappeared around a curve on its way to Vienna. When he came back he would complain of Regensburg's houses, its people, its way of life.

He was not altogether wrong, for it was a small provincial town, slow and gossipy. Regensburg went to sleep at nine in the evening, its surrounding country was without much excitement or good scenery, and I disliked it chiefly because I had to attend the Lyceum there and all my professors came to eat in the restaurant of Grandfather's brewery, so that he was always informed that I would not pass the examinations, that I was unruly, impertinent, never serious, always late, and kept bad company.

At the end of my first year at the Lyceum I had to repeat, and when this first year came to its second ending, and it had to be repeated once more, it was decided to send me away to a quiet little academy in Rothenburg, privately managed, for backward boys, where even an idiot could slowly be advanced. But even there I failed again to pass. The Rector, a very thorough and patient man, wrote home and asked to have me taken away.

My mother came to Rothenburg. We sat in the Rector's living-room under an eyeless plaster bust of Pericles. The Rector, in a shabby green coat, felt his way around; almost blind, he looked through spectacles as thick as the bottom of a beer glass, and in the frames of which his eyes swam somewhere outside his face, immense and unreal. After he had said 'Amen' to my future, Mother started to weep, and we left his room.

I said good-bye to my friends. My linen and my stockings and clothes, all neatly marked '51' with the numbers in red on a white tape, were packed by the Rector's wife. We ate at the inn, called the Iron Hat, before we went to the station.

It was a silent trip. I could not find my voice. I wanted to kiss my mother and ask her forgiveness and somehow promise that she should not be sorry, that I would start a new and good life. But at that age one cannot say anything and after a while I played with the long leather strap that hung down from the window of the compartment. Embossed on it was 'Royal Bavarian Railway', and I thought how I would like to take my pocket knife and cut it off. It was such a nice strong leather strap and would be useful for many purposes.

There was a stop in Nürnberg, and a buffet on the station platform. 'You don't deserve this,' said Mother, but she bought me a pair of the lovely little sausages, which are nowhere else better, and a small beer, and then she put her hand on my head and said: 'Es wird schon werden, Ludwig' – 'Everything will come out all right in the end.'

The hope and prayer of every German mother at that time was that her boy would at least finish the six years of Lyceum, which made of him a better-grade soldier when the time came for his military service. He would not be an officer; for that he had to enter the cadet corps. But he was allowed to sleep at home, he did not have to wear the formless baggy uniform issued by the service, the clumsy boots, the cap without a visor. He was marked off, besides having his own well-tailored uniform and a stiff cap with visor, by two little shoulder straps, with a narrow blue and white border. He did not have to stand at attention when an officer passed, hold that position, and follow the officer with his eyes until he had passed. He simply saluted. His term of service was only one year instead of three.

It was a disgrace to be a common soldier, mingling in the barracks with the louts that came from the potato-growing country around Regensburg, commanded to do every kind of stable duty, to shine officers' boots, and to be addressed as 'Gemeiner' – 'common one'. But this awaited me. Mother had said over and over in the train from Rothenburg: 'Disgrace, disgrace, disgrace.'

When we came to Regensburg, to the brewery, I found Grandfather not at all upset. He was happy about not having another 'studied one' in the family wasting money. He felt my arms and saw that I was strong.

In his living-room, in the old house next to the brewery, he outlined a career for me that included one year's apprentice-ship with a butcher, to learn how to judge meat and cut it and make sausages, then a year with a plumber and electrician, and then going into the brewery and starting there the way his own father and grandfather had done and the way he had learned to make beer himself.

Mother held me all the while and said: 'No, Papa, not to the butcher, not to the electrician, and not into the brewery.'

Mother had married my father much against Grandfather's wishes. Father was a Belgian and a painter and he did not own a house; to Grandfather all people who did not own houses were 'Lumpen'. A Lump is a shiftless, lazy, easy-smiling man who has not enough energy even to do evil. Father was also slight of build and careful in dress, and whenever he had come across the square to visit Mother, who was young and very beautiful, Grandfather had said: 'There comes that flycatcher again!' He called my father 'flycatcher' because he walked with such light steps. Not much later, when I was only a few years old, Father fell in love with my French governess. She was dark and elegant, and much happier than Mother. He went away with her, and my parents were divorced.

Attached to the brewery by mortgages were thirty-seven inns, all over the countryside, in which Grandfather's beer was sold. He had two kinds of beer: one a bitter-sweet, thick, black, soupy brew; the other a blond beer, light-bodied, with much snowy foam, and bitter. Every spring Grandfather went on a round of visits to his inns, and my picture of happiness will always be one of him and his hunting wagon:

First the sound of the slim wheels on the gravel in the inner garden; then the deep liquid 'clop clop clop' of the horse's hoofs as the wagon came out of the brewery through the tunnel, over creosote-soaked wooden blocks; and finally the clatter of the hoofs on the cobblestones in front of the house. Grandfather slowly climbing up in front, on to the reed basket seat of the delicate little wagon, almost turning it over on its red wheels as he puts his great weight on its side.

He wore a loose green coat, with buttons cut from antler, a brush on his mountain hat, a whip for decoration in his big hands. He made a sound with his tongue, and the trotter lifted its knees up to its chest, and, weaving back and forth, its neck arched in a coy, young pose, it sailed out. From the back seat waved Grandfather's servant Alois, who always went with him. They stopped and drank and ate in all the inns, and bought calves for the butchery, which was part of the brewery. After years of experience Grandfather could drink thirty-six big stone mugs of beer in one evening. He ate heavy meals besides, hardly any vegetables, only dumplings and potatoes, potatoes and dumplings, and much meat.

In consequence of this diet, Grandfather had several times a year attacks of very painful gout, which in Bavaria is called Zipperl. Much of the time, one or the other of his legs was wrapped in cotton and elephantine bandages. If people came near it, even Mother, he chased them away with his stick, saying: 'Ah, ah, ah' in an ecstasy of pain and widening his eyes as if he saw something very beautiful far away. Then he would rise up in his seat, while his voice changed to a whimpering 'Jesus, Jesus, Jesus.' He said he could feel the change in weather in his toes, through the thick bandages. But he did not stop eating or drinking.

He had a wheel chair at such times, and Alois had to push him on his visits to the other breweries or restaurants in Regensburg. A kind of track was built for this chair in the back yard of the house; it swung over the roof of the shack where the barrels were kept and came down to the ground in a wide serpentine. Then there were little wooden inclines, to make it possible to wheel Grandfather painlessly over the doorsteps, in front and in back of the house, and out into the square.

On the ground floor of the house was a baker, and the stairway and all the rooms in the house smelled of freshly baked bread, nicest on cold winter days. The baker, white of

face and clothes, could see Grandfather being wheeled out, and he would say: 'The Zipperl! Aha! It's got you again, Herr Fischer!' and so said the policeman outside, while he made the streetcar wait, and so did all the other people. Everybody in the city knew Grandfather, and since life was without any other excitement, they had time to say: 'Have you seen Herr Fischer? The Zipperl has him again!' And Grandfather said nothing but 'Jesus, Jesus, God Almighty, ah ah ah, be careful, be careful, Alois! The Zipperl!'

I had a small room in Grandfather's house almost up under the gable of the house. It was most beautiful at night; from my window I could see the whole square at once without turning head or eyes, and when it was dark and the theatre was lit, after the Duke had arrived, his carriages were driven slowly, just to keep the horses warm, around the circle of plants and trees and the small statue which stood in the centre of the square within an iron fence. The rich harness, the liveries of the coachmen and footmen, the lamps, made a magical, lit-up, jewelled merry-go-round.

On the driver's seat of the finest coach, the Duke's, sat a bearded man in pale blue livery, a bearskin cape over his shoulders and a plume on his hat, a hat such as admirals wear, worn sideways with the wide part to the front. I watched this for hours until the play ended, until the circle became a line and the carriages drove under the portico of the small theatre and away to the castle.

In the morning Grandfather had coffee at his window, with a canary bird sitting on the back rest of his chair. There was the smell of cigar smoke, of snuff, of coffee and fresh bread. He dipped four crescent rolls into his coffee and looked out over the square, to observe the people and the business of the city. He had a mirror on the outside of the house so he could see who came to visit us. It was from here that he had always said: 'There comes that flycatcher again.' Around him hung more cages with canaries; he fed them in the morning, and trimmed their claws and changed their diet for them, experimenting how to make them lay more eggs or sing better. He marked the results down in a little book, of which he had two; in the other he kept the business of his brewery. So easy and secure was his life.

On the table in front of him was paper, paste, and a pair of big shears. He made helmets with them, out of stacks of large sheets of durable packing paper, which he bought especially for this purpose. They were simple triangular paper hats, with a bush of blue and white crepe paper stuck on at the end, and they were given away. Any child in Regensburg who came and asked could have one. He made these helmets in great quantities, for the orphanage of Regensburg and the surrounding villages. The children of the orphanage and of the dumb and blind institute waved up whenever they passed the house. So that they could fight properly in two armies, he made, for the children who could see, two kinds of helmets, one with a blue bush and one with red. The blue and white were the Bavarian colours; the red, the French.

This work took up a few hours. Afterward he looked up orders and was very conscientious about filling them, and then, when the rheumatism did not bother him, he took a walk around the park with the brewmaster and listened to his report and told him what to do about the beer.

The brewery also had its own fire department, which always

arrived ahead of the city firemen. It consisted of an old beer wagon, painted red and yellow, fixed up with a bell, hose, ladders, hooks, and buckets. It thundered out of the tunnel of the brewery, pulled by the best horses, the skin of their haunches stretched into folds as they pushed the ground away from under them, sparks raining from under their hoofs as they struck the cobblestones. The wagon had to run around the square twice before it could slow down enough to head into the street that led to the fire.

Next to Mother and myself, Grandfather's greatest trouble was my Uncle Veri; Veri is short for Xavier. He was my favourite uncle; he had the strong dispassionate face of a sportsman; he was so big that the funeral wagon of Regensburg was made to his measure; he was as strong as he was big. When someone had to be thrown out of the brewery, and the men in Regensburg are big and heavy, and can fight, Uncle Veri did it. He would drag the man to the door, go out a little, measure his distance, take a good hold on trousers and coat collar, and thrown the man over the iron fence into the bushes that stood around the small statue.

Uncle Veri loved betting. He once made a wager with a city official that he could make a million dots in eight hours. Two brewery hands had to sharpen pencils, and Uncle Veri stuck them between his fingers, four to each hand. The city official wanted to back out, he said it was cheating, he meant it should be done with one or at most two pencils, but finally he gave in. Uncle Veri hammered with both hands at the sheets of paper, while the waitresses, the brewmaster and his crew, the city official and his friends, all counted dots and crossed them off. It was a typical Regensburg form of amusement, for it could all have been calculated in a few minutes, especially since the city official, who won, of course, happened to be in the Department of Taxation. But meanwhile they drank and ate and sat there and it helped to pass an evening, and at the end everyone was tired and certain that even Uncle Veri could not do it.

But he could lift the stone in the beer garden that had an iron ring hammered into it, and that with one finger. He did that often and for anyone who asked him; the next strongest man in Regensburg needed two hands to do it. To keep in trim, Uncle Veri carried a cast-iron walking stick, and an umbrella with a heavy iron bar down its centre. He pushed the big brewery horses around as if they were flies; and if he saw a brewery man, anywhere in the middle of the city, groan while lifting barrels, Uncle Veri would say to him: 'You make me sick to look at,' especially if it was a man from another brewery, and he would hand him his iron walking stick to hold, and then himself load or unload the wagon, bouncing the heavy barrels on the big leather cushion which is put down to protect the cobblestones. He even slept strongly, sometimes going to bed on Monday night and waking up fresh and rested on Wednesday morning. Everybody had respect for him.

He was bad only with women. All of Grandfather's serious troubles came from that, Grandfather had to pay for the children. When someone looked up from the square, and saw Grandfather busy with stacks of paper hats, and then turned his head and said something to a friend, and both of them smiled, then Grandfather knew that the joke had been told again, that he was busy making paper hats for Uncle Veri's children. Few people, however, laughed up any more, only strangers, because in Regensburg it was an old joke.

Grandfather said that I should start to learn from Uncle Veri how to wash barrels.

Mother cried and said no, she would rather have me dead than be a butcher's apprentice and wash barrels and then be a common soldier and stand at attention while people like the sons of the girls who had gone to the convent in Alt Oetting with her, and who had studied enough to be officers, passed by. Mother's name was Frances, and Grandfather called her Fannerl. 'You're crazy, Fannerl,' he said. Mother took me by the hand and we went out to visit Uncle Wallner.

This uncle was thin, little, and, for Regensburg, a gentleman. He lived in the best, new part of the town, in a villa with a small park. He was a city father, wore a top hat on Sunday and black clothes and gloves and a golden pince-nez – but even with the golden pince-nez he could not see very well. He was very polite to the proper people in Regensburg; he said it was very important to show reverence and respect to important personages. When I walked with him, very slowly because he took little steps, and we met someone he knew and thought worthy, he would swing his hat almost down to the ground and pronounce the name carefully in greeting.

Sometimes when I was with him and we passed one of Grandfather's waitresses on the other side of the street, too far away for Uncle Wallner to recognize her, or the lady who took care of the public washroom at the railway station, or one of the rough girls that Uncle Veri liked, I would get Uncle Wallner's attention and tell him that was the Frau Direktor across the way, or the Frau Inspektor, or the French Consul's wife. Uncle Wallner would stop immediately and turn and whisper the name across the street and sweep his hat through

the air, making a respectful compliment, and he would tell me what a worthy, fine, and gentle lady the washroom woman was. He owned a wholesale grocery business, which was why he was so polite, and after all that was a little fun in this silent city.

Uncle Wallner always advised Mother. He liked to put French phrases into his conversation and speak of a journey he had made to the Paris Exposition in 1889, and to London. 'Mais ça ne va pas, ma chère,' he said to Mother when she told him about the brewery plans. 'A butcher, a plumber, and with Veri as a teacher he would soon turn into a nice ruffian. No, ma chère,' he said, and drummed on the windowpane, and then he sent me out to get him some cigars, so that he could talk alone with Mother.

When I came back, he smiled. He was just showing Mother his new visiting cards; he had become a Herr Kommerzienrat, a Commercial Councillor of the King in Munich, and had had new cards printed with this title on them, and his housekeeper for two days had already been addressing him continually as Herr Kommerzienrat. 'Will the Herr Kommerzienrat have tea now?' she asked, and Uncle said yes. She brought tea and cake, and after this was cleared away, Uncle Wallner drummed on the top of a very beautiful cherrywood table, inlaid with cigar bands under glass. He asked me to sit close to him and Mother and then he started as one does a letter: 'Dear Ludwig,' and he said that I should think about going to Uncle Hans in Tirol, to Father's brother. Uncle Wallner looked very happy when he said that; he added that Uncle Hans was a very wise man, rich and respected and good.

'He is a good man,' Uncle Wallner repeated several times, because up to now I had been told that Uncle Hans was not so good, that Uncle Hans Bemelmans in Tirol was full of 'amerikanische Tricks'.

Uncle Hans Bemelmans, said Uncle Wallner, had many hotels, and hotels are a very fine business. One always has interesting people around, the great of the world; one can travel, see much of life; one eats better than anyone else. In a few years a boy as bright as I was would no doubt be the manager, or even the proprietor, of such a hotel as Uncle Hans had in Tirol. Right there, with Uncle Bemelmans, was the great opportunity. He had not one hotel, he had a chain of them.

There was the Hotel Maximilian in Igls, near Innsbruck, the Grand Hotel des Alpes on the Dolomite Road in San Martino di Castrozza, the Hotel Scholastika on the Achensee, the Hotel Alte Post in Klobenstein, where Uncle Bemelmans had his headquarters, and the Mountain Castle in Meran. In the Mountain Castle even Royalty stopped.

This was wonderful and surprising to me. When Grandfather spoke of Uncle Hans Bemelmans, he called him the 'other Lump', the first Lump being my father, the painter. The 'amerikanische Tricks', Grandfather said, Uncle Hans had learned during several years spent in the United States. The trick which he had brought back from there and which Grandfather told most often was the 'Sanatorium Trick'; it went like this:

For speculative purposes, Uncle Hans had bought a piece of ground in Meran, in Tirol. He found out later that he had made one of his rare mistakes. But overlooking his land was the façade of a very fine private dwelling belonging to a Leipzig builder of funiculars. When he realized he had made a bad buy, Uncle Hans offered his land to this man from Leipzig to enlarge his park, but the man said that his park was big enough. Uncle Hans said nothing and went home. The view from the man's balconies was the best in Meran; it overlooked all the mountains as well as Uncle's ground. So Uncle Hans arrived one day with engineers and measuring-instruments and a workman who stuck red and white poles into the ground, close to the fence of this rich man, who watched all this from his balcony. A few days later more men came and unloaded sand and bricks and started to dig while others unrolled blueprints on a table under a corrugated shed. When the rich man could not stand it any longer, he came to the fence and asked Uncle Hans: 'What's going on here, Herr Bemelmans? What are you doing here?'

Uncle Hans smiled and said: 'I'm building a hotel here, the Grand Hotel Tirol. The kitchen and pantry will be right here where we are standing, and the hotel will be eight stories high and look out on that beautiful panorama.'

'Oh, a hotel!' said the man.

'Well, not exactly a hotel,' said Uncle Hans, 'more a sanatorium.' He took a deep breath. 'The air here,' he said, and hit himself on the chest, 'the air here is very beneficial for certain afflictions,' and he cleared his throat and coughed loudly.

'I see,' said the rich man, and he bought the property a few days later. Now he had to pay much more for it, because there were in addition the charges for bricks and sand and surveying and the shack and the labour. He even paid for having it all taken away again. Uncle Hans took care of that too. He had the sand and bricks delivered to the Mountain Castle, his hotel, where he made a terrace out of them for afternoon dancing and tea.

'That,' Grandfather said, 'was an American trick, well done and complete.'

Uncle Bemelmans, Grandfather said, was in possession of the knowledge of every such device, and that was why he had so many hotels. But though he was rich, Grandfather thought of him as another Lump, chiefly because he was a Bemelmans.

'They,' said Grandfather, 'are washed with every kind of soap and water, and rubbed in with slick oil, and they are therefore hard to catch and slippery.'

Mother came back with Uncle Wallner, but it was hard to change Grandfather's mind, for he too had friends who advised him, three of them, and they had all agreed that the brewery was the right thing for me.

These friends were the Bartel brothers, people to whose wives Uncle Wallner did not raise his hat. One was called 'Cider' Bartel, because he had a cider factory; another was called 'Pitch' Bartel, because he made pitch and creosote blocks and the beer barrels for the brewery; and the third was called 'Dreck' Bartel. This last had a string of evil-smelling wagons with long tubular barrels on them, and a pumping-machine; attached to the last wagon rolled a low cart, in which lay thick, solid, round pieces of hose that fitted together, and out of these an awful juice dripped on to the pavement of the city. One could tell with closed eyes at what house Dreck Bartel and his two sons were pumping clean a cesspool.

Dreck Bartel did not like me very much. I had written a poem about him in the Bavarian dialect, and was caught with it in class, and had to sit 'in arrest' for six hours, and a letter went to Mother about it, and I told Uncle Veri about it, and Uncle Veri knew a tune that went well with it, and in a little while it was known all over the city, and Uncle Veri one night had to throw Dreck Bartel into the park because he became too loud and said he would drown me in a cesspool if he ever caught me.

But finally Mother and Uncle Wallner won.

The old seamstress who worked in the house all year fixing napkins and torn tablecloths took the number '51' off all my linen, clothes, and stockings; and with a new travelling bag Mother took me to the train for Munich, Mittenwald, Innsbruck, Meran.

I was surprised at the first conductor I saw on the Austrian railway and at the stationmaster and switchman, at their manners and dress. I had learned that only the German is reliable and orderly, and here was proof of it. These men were careless, their coat collars open; they played bowls in a shed next to the station while the customs examination took place. It seemed a remote, disorderly, un-German land, beautiful though it was. When the train started, even the signal sounded strange; the sharp policeman's whistle was replaced by a brass trumpet, its sound was the bleat of a young sheep; and the conductor and the train were in no hurry to start.

I crossed the Brenner and came to Bozen, never leaving the window of the train; from Bozen the cogwheel railway goes up the Ritten, to Klobenstein, to Uncle Hans's hotel, the Alte Post. Klobenstein was beautiful; it stood in a ring of distant mountains. The hotel was a lovely, flower-covered, wide, solid mountain house, with thick walls and low ceilings. Uncle Hans and Aunt Marie met me at the station.

From the very beginning Uncle Hans called me 'Lausbub'. Lausbub literally should mean 'lousy boy', but in South Germany and Austria it is almost a tender word and means something like 'rascal'. Uncle Bemelmans was comfortably built, but not fat; he wore a beard like the English King Edward's, but on the little finger of his right hand was an immense solitaire diamond, so big that it looked like circus jewellery.

He had received letters from Uncle Wallner. It was through Uncle Wallner, because he had travelled and was elegant, that all the Fischer-Bemelmans affairs were arranged. Uncle Bemelmans explained at length why I had come and how I was going to be dealt with. He read me long lectures in his little office, a low, warm, panelled room, decorated with many antiques and heated by a painted porcelain oven.

In this office there was a carpet on the floor and I could soon draw from memory all the plants, animals, and symbols in its pattern, because I looked at it for such long stretches while Uncle Hans walked up and down over it, back and forth for hours, his hands folded under the seat of his trousers, and over them hanging the square-cut tails of his cutaway.

In the back of the hotel, along with the iceboxes and the pantries, in a stone-floored room, was an old-fashioned ice machine that pounded away in a steady rhythm. Uncle Hans was always listening to that rhythm. He noticed the moment it became irregular and he would let no one else touch the machine. The instant it changed tempo, he would leave whatever he was doing to fix it. During a lecture he would stop suddenly, reach for his hat, and run to the machine, telling me to wait till he came back. He looked very funny then, because he was in a hurry, and hurry did not go well with the dignity of his face and clothes.

He always quoted America, telling me often that in America

Lausbuben like me sometimes turned out to be very rich men. But in Tirol too, he said, there was bigger opportunity for a Lausbub than for a good boy who did as he was told and would perhaps make a good employee but never be rich.

Here in the hotel I found evidence of a lighter kind of life: the cooking was French, without kraut and heavy dumplings; the conversation had more variety, was not so much of buildings, horses, the Bartels, beer, and the pot de chambre humour of Regensburg. I was disturbed by a sense of disloyalty to my grandfather, because I felt I should not like anything else but his house and his person.

I had brought some drawings and water colours and given them to Aunt Marie. When Uncle Hans saw them and heard Aunt Marie suggest that I study painting, he got very angry. Painters, he said, were hunger candidates, nothing in front and nothing in back of them; besides, if I liked painting, I could always hire an artist, when I became rich by following his teachings. He said I must bury the past and start a new life and be a joy and pride to my poor mother and for God's sake not to become an artist like my father. I would have to start all the way at the bottom of the ladder, he said, like Rockefeller and Edison, and work up from there. There was no reason, he said, why I should not in a few years be a hotelier like himself, or at least manager of a hotel.

Aunt Marie would come into the little office when the lectures lasted too long, and say: 'I think that's enough for today, Hans, let him go.'

The first day, when she showed me the lovely room that overlooked the Dolomites and told me the names of the mountains, and looked at my pictures, she asked me what I

liked most to eat. I told her 'Marillen dumplings', a Viennese dessert of apricots inside a thin coating of dough, cooked in butter, with bread crumbs over them. We had them for supper, and Uncle Hans complained that the Lausbub was being spoiled right from the beginning.

My birthday came soon after my arrival, and Aunt Marie bought me a box of the best water colours and a drawing pad. I had a week of wonderful vacation and was given a horse on which I rode all over the beautiful mountains. Then one day it was decided that from eight in the morning until three in the afternoon I would be an employee and do all the work that was required of me, and for the rest of the time, before and after, and during the night, I would be Uncle's nephew and eat at the family table, and could have the horse.

The mornings in Tirol are the most beautiful time in all the world. I got up at five, saddled my horse, and rode to the sawmill. It stood on a turbulent brook, flanked by high, straight walls of dolomite granite, among tall trees. Near by, under the two tallest and oldest trees, stood a little inn, with a garden, a curved wooden bench, and two round redstone tables. There I stopped at seven every morning and drank a pint of red wine, dipping the hard peasant bread in it. I stayed as long as I could and then rode in a gallop back to the hotel to be on time for duty.

The first time I did this, Aunt Marie was up, and Uncle Hans out on his morning walk. He had said: 'At least he gets un early, the Lausbub; that's something; some of them you can't get out of bed.'

Aunt Marie always looked at me and felt my head and said it must be the change in altitude. 'He has a fever every morning, and look how his eyes shine.' But then they found out about the wine and several other things, and Uncle said that this half-nephew, half-employee arrangement was at an end. He said it would be better to send me to one of the other hotels where Aunt Marie could not help me.

And so I was sent first to the Mountain Castle in Meran, and then in the space of a year I ran through all of Uncle Hans's hotels. Every manager was tried out on me; they all failed and sent me back. The last time was after a very serious offence. Uncle walked up and down again; Aunt Marie cried and said to me while Uncle was with his ice machine: 'Ludwig, Ludwig, what is going to become of you? We love you so much and you are so bad. How will it end? What will become of you?' She embraced me and wiped her tears and mine from our eyes.

When Uncle Hans came back he said there were two places for me to choose between. The first was a correctional institution, a kind of reform school, German, on board a ship, where unruly boys were trained for the merchant marine and disciplined with the ends of ropes soaked in tar.

The second was America.

I decided to go to America.

Uncle Hans was very happy. He said that in the United States they would shear my pelt and clip my horns.

He wrote some letters to hotel people he knew, he gave me much advice, and he said that if I ever became a great hotel man, like Muschenheim or Boldt, I would only become so by looking upon all employees as paid enemies. They are Lumpen, every one of them; there is an exception here and there, but it takes too long to find out and is too risky to take a chance. Then he said: 'Dear Ludwig,' like Uncle Wallner, 'now we'll forget all about what has happened. I'll find out when a boat sails. Now you have a vacation, ride all you want, and we'll all be happy together.' I cried then because I was sorry I was so rotten and always in trouble when they were so kind to me.

Then I went back to Mother, and there it was also difficult, when I saw how she took money for my passage out of envelopes that were marked for other purposes for her own use. We got up early one morning to meet the express to Rotterdam. I was the only passenger from Regensburg on the lonely platform, and Mother said, with her hand on my head, for the second time: 'Everything will come out all right in the end, Ludwig.'

And that is how I left for America.

2. *Monsieur Victor of the Splendide*

MY FIRST job in New York, at the Hotel Astor, did not last long. I filled water bottles and carried out trays with dishes, until I broke too many. So with my uncle's second letter I went to the Hotel McAlpin, where I got a job that lasted a year, at the end of which I spoke passable English, though I was still little better than a bus boy.

Here I wore for breakfast a white suit, yellow shoes, and, suspended in front of me on a thick leather strap, a silver machine, hot and the size of a baby's coffin. For three hours every morning I walked around the men's café, with the heavy silver coffin hanging before me. It contained in a lower compartment two heated bricks, and above on a wire net an assortment of hot cross buns, muffins, biscuits, croissants, and every other kind of rolls, soft and hard.

This work ceased at half-past ten, and then I sat for half an hour on the red tile floor in the grill room and polished an elaborate fence of stout brass pipes which kept apart the waiters rushing in and those rushing out.

In the evening my hands were as cold as my stomach was warm in the morning, for at dinner, in another white suit and with white gloves and white shoes, I walked around the main dining room with a silver tray. On the tray rested a thick layer of ice, and bedded on the ice, frosted with coldness, were silver butterchips. I exchanged full butterchips for empty ones.

When this job eventually came to an end, I looked in my trunk for another letter. The last one was to Mr. Otto Brauhaus, manager of the Hotel Splendide.

The Splendide, from the outside, was a plain building, but its interior was like that of a great private house. It completely lacked the anonymous feeling of the usual hotel, in which one might fall asleep in the lobby, be carried to another hotel, wake up, and never know it was another.

A page in silken breeches, a livery as rich as that of the Duke of Thurn und Taxis and of the same blue, showed me to the office. Under a sign that read: 'Don't worry, it won't last, nothing does', sat Mr. Otto Brauhaus, worrying. He spoke to me in German, wrote something on a little card, and then gave it and the letter from Uncle Hans to the page.

The page took me to the dining room of the hotel, to a thin, foreign-looking man who looked like a high-placed Jesuit. His face in a frame of closely shaven violet beard-stubble, he spoke with controlled, eloquent motions of his head and long thin hands. He never looked at me but kept his eyes downcast as if hearing a confession. His altogether appropriate name was Serafini. He was from Siena and was the assistant headwaiter of the Hotel Splendide. To me he looked like St. Francis in a tail coat.

In a hôtel de grand luxe, such as the Splendide, which is a European island in New York, there is no headwaiter, no captain, no waiter. Everything is much more elegant. The manager of the hotel is le patron; and the head man in the restaurant, more important in such a hotel than the manager, or even the chef, is simply 'Monsieur Grégoire', 'Monsieur Théodore', 'Monsieur Victor', or whatever his first name is, and no matter what his nationality. His lieutenants, the captains, are called maître d'hôtel; and under them the waiters are not garçons (that is more the term for a café waiter), but chefs de rang, because each one has for his station a rank of several tables. The chef de rang never leaves his tables or the dining room; he has a young man who runs out to the kitchen for him, and this quick young waiter is a commis de rang. Even the bus boys are called débarrasseurs.

Mr. Serafini said very considerately that there was no position for me at the Splendide, since all the employees in the dining room were obliged to speak French. When I told him I spoke French, he changed the conversation to that language and then asked me to wait.

I waited in the high, oval dining room for a long time, happily observing the well-designed saltcellars and pepper mills, the fine clean pattern on the plates, the stucco ceiling, and the carpets. Waiters came to set up the room, and they were distinguished-looking men, of better appearance than the guests in the other hotels I had worked in, carefully dressed, quick, capable. Most of them, however, wore spats and pretty shirts. I waited until these had gone and an orchestra arrived and tuned its instruments. Finally, the headwaiter-in-chief, that is, Monsieur Victor, appeared.

Serafini looked down at my hands and whispered to me to come. He placed Mr. Brauhaus's card and Uncle Hans's letter before Monsieur Victor. On Uncle Hans's letterhead were not only the names but also the pictures of every one of his hotels, and Monsieur Serafini said in French: 'A young man of good family, he is recommended by the patron.'

Without looking at me longer than was necessary to see that I was there, Monsieur Victor said: 'Engage him, put him to work as a commis, see what he can do.'

Monsieur Victor was one of the best in his difficult trade. He knew wine and food, he had a perfect memory for names and faces; he also knew who was in Society, who was almost in Society, and, what is most important, who was not. With such facts in his head, he guarded the interests of the hotel and of his own pocket.

During luncheon and dinner Monsieur Victor stands at the head of the wide stairs that lead from the Jade Lounge up into the restaurant. He usually leans on his desk, a maître d'hôtel's desk, with eight drawers, seven of them neatly marked from the top down for the days of the week: Lundi, Mardi, Mercredi, Jeudi, Vendredi, Samedi, Dimanche. The eighth drawer is for special parties and reservations far ahead, and in the top part of the desk, under a lid that lifts up, are reservation lists and place cards and signs marked 'Reserved'.

Monsieur Victor has a secretary in a tight hole-in-the-wall office, and his first assistant, Monsieur Serafini, takes people from his hand and, following Victor's instructions pilots them to the table whose number is whispered to him in French. At that table a chef de rang takes their order.

On a balcony overhanging Victor's desk is a small orchestra, the leader of which is a very good Hungarian violinist. He plays an eternally unchanging repertoire of dinner music and, like Victor, he looks out over the Jade Lounge as the guests arrive. While Victor is chiefly concerned with the social position of the arrivals and, first of all, when they are still distant, looks at their faces, the Hungarian violinist fastens his eyes on the women's legs and turns round to look at the rest of them only as they pass by him into the restaurant. Thus a person entering at the far side of the Jade Lounge is watched advancing to the stairs by many eyes: by all the guests who sit in the Jade Lounge and on the balcony, by Victor and his assistants, who stand to the right of him, by the violinist, and also by all the other musicians. They never have to read their notes; they have played these same pieces of hotel music so often that they have become part of the dining room, like the tables, the chairs, and the salt and pepper shakers.

Victor's assistant holds a list of reservations in his hand. The best tables are for Society; close by them sit celebrities, actresses, publishers. In a wider circle are the people who are photographed much and appear in the rotogravure sections, who are found at the Atlantic Beach Club, in Miami, and occasionally murdered or mixed up in fashionable messes; also

Italian aristocracy, young men who give morning concerts or dancing lessons, and movie stars. Beyond these come the tables of the untouchables. Victor's salary from the hotel is not large, only $350 a month, plus his food, a dressing room, linen, and a valet; but his income in a good year is about $40,000.

Society contributes little of that, and they treat him badly, but no matter when they arrive and in what mood or unexpected numbers, he will bow deeply, address them loudly by name, so that all the other waiting guests may be properly impressed, and seat them immediately. He is very careful not to address one of their women by her last year's name. Their complaints are immediately attended to, and when they leave they are again bowed out with a compliment that would cost other people at least twenty dollars. All that because, without them, the restaurant is through, and would be closed in a short while.

But other guests, too, may receive good tables, after they have stuck a little folded bill into Monsieur Victor's hand. When he is not certain from experience of the size of the bill, he always hears an imaginary telephone bell ringing and rushes into his office. Attached to the wall at the level of his hand is a mirror; in it Victor can see whether there is five or ten dollars printed on the corner of the bill, and, around Christmas time, whether it is twenty, fifty, or a hundred. During the five hasty steps that take him back to the door, he has performed a lightning-quick calculation, an exercise in the nice adjustment of many factors: the available table, the time of the day, the day of the week, and the amount of the bank note. The assistant hears a softly pronounced table number, and the guests are led to a table. If they are delighted or make faces, the little mirror in the office knows why.

But such people have no hope whatever if they don't pay. They will join the outermost circle who fill out the noisy, draughty corners, sit close to service tables, and are squeezed against mirrors and the edges of the balcony stairs – women in bad copies of the latest fashion, from mousy little couturières with French names written on the windows of their side street shops; Westchester housewives in grey squirrel coats and galoshes on rainy days. They order an œuf Bénédict and a glass of milk before going to a matinee. There are, besides, a lot of innocent people who just walked in off the street, thinking that this was a restaurant. A description of Victor's behaviour to them may well serve as a manual for his trade.

Entering the Jade Lounge they are far away from him and below him, which is to their disadvantage. They have to cross the wide hall and climb up the stairs, and there they are met by the music, by Victor, and by his moping assistants, one of them with the seating diagram and the large list of reservations in his hand.

As these intruders stand in front of him, Victor looks them over with a slow deliberate inventory of shoes, trousers, hands. He stops at the neckties: the face he has seen below, when it came in through the door at the end of the Jade Lounge. Victor has his heels together; he stands straight, then leans forward a little and turns his head in a listening gesture. The guest in front of him is by now ill at ease and wishes he had not come; he is a plain, well-dressed, and respectable-looking person.

'Your name?' asks Victor. The man now has his hand to his tie, at which Victor has been looking all the while.

Victor repeats the name to his assistant, lisping it slowly.

The assistant looks at the list and finds no such name.

'You have no reservation?' says Victor now, with the tone in which he might say: 'Where did you steal that watch?'

'Reservation?' says the man.

'Yes, reservation,' answers Victor. He turns to his assistant and says: 'Il n'a pas de réservation.'

'Oh!' says the assistant, regretting this on behalf of Victor. Victor, who has never once looked at the wife of the man though she has been standing beside her husband all this while, says, if he likes the look of the man, in French and to his fingernails: 'Find him a table somewhere.' If he doesn't like him, then suddenly and with finality he looks at the man's face and tells him: 'Sorry, I have no table for you,' turns on his heel, and walks into the dining room, to bow and smile left and right to the good guests at the first tables.

Sometimes people will baulk at this treatment; a brave and corpulent businessman will try to shake off Victor. An invisible wrestling match starts, the man pushing back the lapels of his coat, putting his hands in all of his pockets and taking them out again, looking into the faces of bystanders for support, and pointing at empty tables inside the room. In such cases Victor takes the list of reservations from his assistant, drums on the edge of it with the end of his golden pencil, and looks past the man's ear into faraway space.

The man usually says: 'I called up this morning at nine o'clock. I was there when my secretary made the call. It was a few minutes past nine, she asked for a table for two at one-fifteen; now it's ten minutes after one and you say you haven't got a table. Look at your list there, and see if you haven't got the name, Stanley Cohan, C-O'—

'I've told you, Mr Cohan, that I have no reservation in your name,' says Victor.

'I called up this morning,' the man starts again.

'Yes, I know, Mr Cohan, I have a very careless secretary.'

Victor leaves him and takes someone else personally into the room, or just turns again to smile and nod at seated guests. The assistants fight out the rest.

This sometimes ends in a man running after Victor with a threat of a punch in the nose, or, in case of Westerners, with an offer to buy the whole hotel just to fire Victor.

There is also the address to the wife: 'Come on, Vi, let's get out of here, let's go some other place. You know there are places in this town where they know how to take care of people. Why, I wouldn't eat here if they paid me. Come on.'

The orchestra plays a selection from *Naughty Marietta*, and they climb down the stairs and are gone.

Monsieur Victor and his assistants look after them without anger, with the detachment of a bullfighter who has done his routine work and waits until the horses have dragged the animal out, ready to start on the next. With folded arms they look at the chandelier, then into the room, tapping the tempo of the music with their pencils. In a few seconds it starts all over again.

Occasionally Victor meets his match, a man who will not be thrown out, one who is quite capable of taking Victor by the collar of his coat, shaking him, or pushing him out of the way. Victor is very sensitive in feeling out such people; they are seated.

The technique – looking at the tie and shoes and not the face, the voice, the faraway look – all this Victor has taken over from his most important clients, from Society.

3. The Animal Waiter

THE DAY was one of the rare ones when Mespoulets and I had a guest at our tables. Most of the time I mugged into a large mirror in back of me. Mespoulets stood next to me and shook his head. Mespoulets was a chef de rang and I was his commis. Our station was on the low rear balcony of the main dining room.

Mespoulets had a passion for his language. 'Your accent is good,' he said, 'your grammar very bad. I shall try to improve your French.' He had plenty of time to teach me.

'When I say "Le chien est utile," there is one proposition.

When I say "Je crois que le chien est utile," there are two. When I say "Je crois que le chien est utile quand il garde la maison," how many propositions are there?'

'Three.'

'Very good.'

Mespoulets nodded gravely in approval. At that moment Monsieur Victor walked through our section of tables, and the other waiters near by stopped talking to one another, straightened a tablecloth here, moved a chair there, arranged their side towels smoothly over their arms, tugged at their jackets, and pulled their bow ties. Only Mespoulets was indifferent. He walked slowly toward the pantry, past Monsieur Victor, holding my arm. I walked with him and he continued the instruction.

"'L'abeille fait du miel." The verb "fait" in this sentence in itself is insufficient. It does not say what the bee does, therefore we round out the idea by adding the words "du miel". These words are called "un complément". The sentence "L'abeille fait du miel" contains then what?'

'It contains one verb, one subject, and one complement.'

'Very good, excellent. Now run down and get the Camembert, the salade escarole, the hard water crackers, and the demitasse for Mr. Frank Munsey on Table Eighty-Six.'

Our tables – Nos. 81, 82, and 86 – were in a noisy, draughty corner of the balcony. They stood facing the stairs from the dining room and were between two doors. One door led to the pantry and was hung on whining hinges. On wet days it sounded like an angry cat and it was continually kicked by the boots of waiters rushing in and out with trays in their hands. The other door led to a linen closet.

The waiters and bus boys squeezed by our tables, carrying trays. The ones with the trays full of food carried them high over their heads; the ones with dirty dishes carried them low, extended in front. They frequently bumped into each other and there would be a crash of silver, glasses, and china, and cream trickling over the edges of the trays in thin streams. Whenever this happened, Monsieur Victor raced to our section, followed by his captains, to direct the cleaning up of the mess and pacify the guests. It was a common sight to see people standing in our section, napkins in hand, complaining and brushing themselves off and waving their arms angrily in the air.

Monsieur Victor used our tables as a kind of penal colony to which he sent guests who were notorious cranks, people who had forgotten to tip him over a long period of time and needed a reminder, undesirables who looked out of place in better sections of the dining room, and guests who were known to linger for hours over an order of hors d'œuvres and a glass of

milk while well-paying guests had to stand at the door waiting for a table.

Mespoulets was the ideal man for Monsieur Victor's purposes. He complemented Monsieur Victor's plan of punishment. He was probably the worst waiter in the world and I had become his commis after I fell down the stairs into the main part of the dining room with eight pheasants à la Souvaroff. When I was sent to him to take up my duties as his assistant, he introduced himself by saying, 'My name is easy to remember. Just think of "my chickens" – "mes poulets" – Mespoulets.'

Rarely did any guest who was seated at one of our tables leave the hotel with a desire to come back again. If there was any broken glass around the dining room, it was always in our spinach. The occupants of Tables Nos. 81, 82, and 86 shifted in their chairs, stared at the pantry doors, looked around and made signs of distress at other waiters and captains while they waited for their food. When the food finally came, it was cold and was often not what had been ordered. While Mespoulets explained what the unordered food was, telling in detail how it was made and what the ingredients were, and offered hollow excuses, he dribbled mayonnaise, soup, or mint sauce over the guests, upset the coffee and sometimes even managed to break a plate or two. I helped him as best I could.

At the end of a meal, Mespoulets usually presented the guest with somebody else's check, or it turned out that he had neglected to adjust the difference in price between what the guest had ordered and what he had got. By then the guest just held out his hand and cried, 'Never mind, never mind, give it to me, just give it to me! I'll pay just to get out of here! Give it to me, for God's sake!' Then the guests would pay and go. He would stop on the way out at the maître d'hôtel's desk and show Monsieur Victor and his captains the spots on his clothes, bang on the desk, and swear he would never come back again. Monsieur Victor and his captains would listen, make faces of compassion, say 'Oh!' and 'Ah!' and look darkly toward us across the room and promise that we would be fired the same day. But the next day we would still be there.

In the hours between meals, while the other waiters were occupied filling salt and pepper shakers, oil and vinegar bottles, and mustard pots, and counting the dirty linen and dusting the chairs, Mespoulets would walk to a table near the entrance, right next to Monsieur Victor's own desk, overlooking the lounge of the hotel. There he adjusted a special reading lamp which he had demanded and obtained from the management, spread a piece of billiard cloth over the table, and arranged on top of this a large blotter and a small one, an inkstand, and half a dozen penholders. Then he drew up a chair and seated himself. He had a large assortment of fine copper pen points of various sizes, and he sharpened them on a piece of sandpaper. He would select the pen point and the holder he wanted and began to make circles in the air. Then, drawing toward him a gilt-edged place card or a crested one, on which menus were written, he would go to work. When he had finished, he arranged the cards all over the table to let them dry, and sat there at ease, only a step or two from Monsieur Victor's desk, in a sector invaded by other waiters only when they were to be called down or to be discharged, waiters who came with nervous hands and frightened eyes to face Monsieur Victor. Mespoulets's special talent guaranteed him his job and set him apart from the ordinary waiters. He was further distinguished by the fact that he was permitted to wear glasses, a privilege denied all other waiters no matter how nearsighted or astigmatic.

It was said of Mespoulets variously that he was the father, the uncle, or the brother of Monsieur Victor. It was also said of him that he had once been the director of a lycée in Paris. The truth was that he had never known Monsieur Victor in Europe, and I do not think there was any secret between them, only an understanding, a sympathy of some kind. I learned that he had once been a tutor to a family in which there was a very beautiful daughter and that this was something he did not like to talk about. He loved animals almost as dearly as he loved the French language. He had taken it upon himself to watch over the fish which were in an aquarium in the outer lobby of the hotel, he fed the pigeons in the courtyard, and he extended his interest to the birds and beasts and crustaceans that came alive to the kitchen. He begged the cooks to deal quickly, as painlessly as could be, with lobsters and terrapins. If a guest brought a dog to our section, Mespoulets was mostly under the table with the dog.

At mealtimes, while we waited for the few guests who came our way, Mespoulets sat out in the linen closet on a small box where he could keep an eye on our tables through the partly open door. He leaned comfortably against a pile of tablecloths and napkins. At his side was an ancient *Grammaire Française*, and while his hands were folded in his lap, the palms up, the thumbs cruising over them in small, silent circles, he made me repeat exercises, simple, compact, and easy to remember. He knew them all by heart and soon I did, too. He made me go over and over them until my pronunciation was right. All of them

were about animals. There were: 'The Sage Salmon', 'The Cat and the Old Woman', 'The Society of Beavers', 'The Bear in the Swiss Mountains', 'The Intelligence of the Partridge', 'The Lion of Florence', and 'The Bird in the Cage'.

We started with 'The Sage Salmon' in January that year and were at the end of 'The Bear in the Swiss Mountains' when the summer garden opened in May. At that season business fell off for dinner, and all during the summer we were busy only at luncheon. Mespoulets had time to go home in the afternoons and he suggested that I continue studying there.

He lived in the house of a relative on West Twenty-Fourth Street. On the sidewalk in front of the house next door stood a large wooden horse, painted red, the sign of a saddlemaker. Across the street was a place where horses were auctioned off, and up the block was an Italian poultry market with a picture of a chicken painted on its front. Hens and roosters crowded the market every morning.

Mespoulets occupied a room and bath on the second floor rear. The room was papered green and over an old couch hung a print of Van Gogh's *Bridge at Arles*, which was not a common picture then. There were bookshelves, a desk covered with papers, and over the desk a large bird cage hanging from the ceiling.

In this cage, shaded with a piece of the hotel's billiard cloth, lived a miserable old canary. It was bald-headed, its eyes were like peppercorns, its feet were no longer able to cling to the roost, and it sat in the sand, in a corner, looking like a withered chrysanthemum that had been thrown away. On summer afternoons, near the bird, we studied 'The Intelligence of the Partridge' and 'The Lion of Florence'.

Late in August, on a chilly day that seemed like Fall, Mespoulets and I began 'The Bird in the Cage'. The lesson was:

L'Oiseau en Cage

Voilà sur ma fenêtre un oiseau qui vient visiter le mien. Il a peur, il s'en va, et le pauvre prisonnier s'attriste, s'agite comme pour s'échapper. Je ferais comme lui, si j'étais à sa place, et cependant je le retiens. Vais-je lui ouvrir? Il irait voler, chanter, faire son nid; il serait heureux; mais je ne l'aurais plus, et je l'aime, et je veux l'avoir. Je le garde. Pauvre petit, tu seras toujours prisonnier; je jouis de toi aux dépens de ta liberté, je te plains, et je te garde. Voilà comme le plaisir l'emporte sur la justice.

I translated for him: 'There's a bird at my window, come to visit mine. . . . The poor prisoner is sad. . . . I would feel as he does, if I were in his place, yet I keep him. . . . Poor prisoner, I enjoy you at the cost of your liberty . . . pleasure before justice.'

Mespoulets looked up at the bird and said to me, 'Find some adjective to use with "fenêtre", "oiseau", "liberté", "plaisir" and "justice",' and while I searched for them in our dictionary, he went to a shelf and took from it a cigar box. There was one cigar in it. He took this out, wiped off the box with his handkerchief, and then went to a drawer and got a large penknife, which he opened. He felt the blade. Then he went to the cage, took the bird out, laid it on the closed cigar box, and quickly cut off its head. One claw opened slowly and the bird and its head lay still.

Mespoulets washed his hands, rolled the box, the bird, and the knife into a newspaper, put it under his arm, and took his hat from a stand. We went out and walked up Eighth Avenue. At Thirty-Fourth Street he stopped at a trash can and put his bundle into it. 'I don't think he wanted to live any more,' he said.

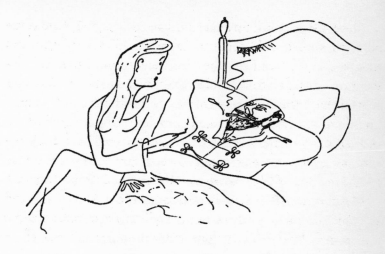

4. Grapes for
Monsieur Cape

THE MAÎTRE d'hôtel who was in charge of the bad balcony, and of us, was called 'Beau Maxime' because he was very ugly; he was also called 'Useless'. Maxime was a bankrupt hotelkeeper from Paris. His ugliness was decorative; he had arthritis, and could hardly see out over the two cocoa-coloured hammocks of wrinkles that hung under his smeary eyes. He had his station on the dining room balcony where he could walk up and down with his cane and his beard and see himself reflected in the mirror.

He was a great trouble to the chefs de rang, the commis, and the kitchen because he took the guests' orders down wrong, forgot things, dictated orders upside down; his hand was too shaky to write, he held the menu up against his face and read it through a monocle which he held in his hand.

When guests had eaten, smoked, and talked, and there was still no sign of a tip for him, a kind of hysteria would come over Beau Maxime. He became part of the table then. With heavy breath, he moved glasses about, took away a sugar bowl, dusted off a few bread crumbs with the edge of his menu. Then he would leave for a while, but not for long, and the chicanery would start all over again. Again he moved the glasses back to where they were before; his eyelids twitched as he looked at the people; he brought a clean napkin to cover up a little coffee stain, took away a vacant chair. If still nothing had happened, he bent to the guest's ear and asked if everything had been all right.

He mumbled as the guests started to leave, and watched them in the mirror and outside of it with a kind of despair in his face and hands, as if in a minute it would be too late to keep something terrible from happening. He kept behind them, pulled out their chairs, and bowed, and if again nothing happened, then he played his last card. He hung his stick on the banister, the service table, or over the back of a chair, and ran after them. He had a glove in his pocket, which he kept for just such purposes; he pulled this glove out and, in the centre of the Jade Lounge, asked if they had forgotten it. Sometimes this worked; they would say no, but give him his dollar, and then he climbed back to the restaurant and up to his balcony.

He ate unbelievable amounts of food. The maîtres d'hôtel had luncheon and dinner before the guests, a very bad arrangement. They should be fed afterward; a man who has just filled himself cannot recommend things well, he is asleep on his feet and makes unpleasant noises. But they did also eat afterward.

On the stations where the chefs and commis had their service tables, which contained extra plates, silver, napkins, vinegar, oil, ketchup bottles, and mustard pots, there were also electric heaters. On these heaters the commis put all the food that was left over after his chef had served the guests. After the guests had left, the commis took the food down to the employees' dining room, where the chef de rang and his commis, sitting across from each other, shared it. With these meals they usually had a bottle of wine, and since the portions were liberal, and the food excellent, and too much of everything was ordered, the men ate very well and of the best, that is all of them did except the chefs and commis on Beau Maxime's station.

For after each serving he visited all the service tables on his station, of which there were three, and carefully lifted the covers of the casseroles, stirred around in them with a fork, fished out wings of capons, little tender foie gras dumplings, pieces of truffle, cocks' combs. Then he sent a commis for soup plates and, while the poor chef and the commis stared at him, he filled one of the plates with the very best of their leftovers. He grunted while he did this, his eyes shone and almost fell into the pots. For his second soup plate he would take a lobster claw, tilt the casserole to get the fine sauce for it, add some rice. In the third plate might go a little curry. When he had enough, one of the commis whom he had robbed, a pale little French boy, had to take the plates upstairs to the captain's dining room. (On the stairway, when no one could see him, the commis carefully spat into all three plates.) Beau Maxime followed, a long French bread under his arm as if it were an umbrella.

Up there, he ate slowly, then moved his chair over to the window. From this third-floor window one could see over the curtains and into the fitting-room of a corsetière on the second floor of the building across the street, where, in the afternoon, fat women undressed to try on corsets. Beau Maxime took off his shoes and put his feet on a pile of used napkins that were put there to be counted later. He watched the scene for an hour and then fell asleep. A bus boy cleared away the dishes and reset the table for the dinner of the maîtres d'hôtel, which was served at five-thirty. Maxime woke up in time for that, put on his shoes, and turned around, to eat.

*

He was the worst, this Beau Maxime, but all maîtres d'hôtel love to eat. They lean over sideboards, behind high screens, to stuff something quickly away. They are especially fond of little fried things which they can pick up from hot dishes as the commis bring them up from the kitchen, such easily disposed-of things as whitebait, oyster crabs, fried scallops, frogs' legs, and fried potatoes. They have learned to eat so that their cheeks and jaws do not move; they can eat in the middle of the dining room and no one know it.

One of the maîtres d'hôtel in the Splendide, a very good-looking one, had a front tooth missing, it was being repaired. At one very busy luncheon he took a green olive from a tray behind the screen on one of his service tables. Just then he was called to a table; the publisher Frank Munsey wanted to order the rest of his luncheon while he waited for his soup to cool. Mr. Munsey looked over the card that was handed him and decided on some tête de veau en tortue. As the maître d'hôtel repeated this, with its many T's, the olive pit shot out through the hole in his teeth and landed in Mr. Munsey's soup.

Fortunately the publisher was bent over talking to someone at the next table and saw nothing. The maître d'hôtel nervously asked if he could not take the soup back and get something hotter, but Mr. Munsey, a very much feared guest, said he had been waiting for it to cool, it was just about right now.

But there is a way out of such difficulties, a technique of upset and confusion, often employed in dangerous situations with hard clients. The maître d'hôtel first instructs the chef de rang and the commis; there is a small quick meeting – then excitement, noise, shouting, a waving in the face of bills of fare, some pushing, and one, two, three, the soup is gone. All this happens while the maître d'hôtel is a few tables away, so that the client can call him to complain. He comes, is surprised, and calls the waiter names: 'Specimen of an idiot, where is the soup of Monsieur Munsey?' 'Ah, pardon – I thought—' 'You should not think, stupid one! Ah, Monsieur Munsey, pardon, pardon.' The soup is back on the table after the commis, behind the screen, has fished the olive pit out with his fingers. For the rest of the meal the guest has perfect service, and when he leaves, the maître d'hôtel says once more: 'So sorry about the soup,' and for this he gets sometimes one, two, or five dollars, but never from Mr. Munsey.

But then, this maître d'hôtel was luckier than the one who had his station on the balcony diagonally across from Maxime's. He was a restless, hoppy Frenchman whose body was forever bending into the shape of compliments. He walked mostly backward, like a crab, pulling customers from the door to his station. When he had nothing else to do, he made little pirouettes, looked at himself in a corner of the mirror, quickly, birdlike in gesture, tugged at his sleeves, pushed a handkerchief into his cuff. Old guests whom he knew from the Paris Splendide he greeted with both arms up in the air, wiggling to the door with dancing paces, with smiles of joy on his face. He had been in America only three weeks when I met him.

He had a trick of showing the anatomy of the kitchen on his own body. With his palm held flat as the blade of a carving knife, he traced the shape of a breast of guinea hen from under his arm to the lapel of his dress coat and down to his ribs. Lifting his leg up to the level of the table, he showed on it the cut of meat that was used for an ossi bughi à la milanaise. When speaking of fish, he again used his palm, laying it flat if the talk was of sole, and with the other hand he cut fillets therefrom. He made a good deal of money, for many people love this theatre.

One did not. She was the wife of a steel man, who was also a judge. She was old and ugly; her dresses were like the robes of a stout priest, they fell flat from a plateau of flesh under her chin and covered a tub filled with fat. Stomach, legs, and breasts were pressed together in this volume so one could not see where they began and ended. Out of the shoulders came two arms, red and thick, coarse-skinned, with common hands. The feet were in tight shoes.

From her hat there usually hung a veil; when the veil was lifted, it revealed a face that had the texture of an old pocket-book; on its worn-out corners rested the ends of a mouth that was closed to with a snap. Grey, carmine, and purple veins covered her face, and patches of its skin would jump as does the skin on the flanks of horses when flies come near them. Her ears were thick bunches on one disorderly shape that included face, neck, and shoulders.

She had to stop for breath at every step when she came up the short, decorative stairway of the restaurant. She would stop to hold on to the banister, to groan and take hold of herself, and she would look around as if for help, as if angry, yet not what the word helpless means.

Behind her, bald-headed and quiet, walked the Steel Judge, mostly in light grey clothes and with a face that was old, Japanese, and cigar-coloured. Madame always referred to him as 'The Judge'.

Large compliments went to them from the man who opened the door of their car on the sidewalk, from Monsieur Victor on the stairway, from all the maîtres d'hôtel, the chefs de rang, the commis, the musicians, from the last coatroom girl. For they were very liberal, and gave a small fortune away at Christmas time.

Madame also brought with her on every visit her own butler. He carried her own wine cooler and at large parties arrived with a second man to supplement his supply of the champagne she liked. The judge and his wife were invited to the very best parties, but no matter at whose table she sat, Madame insisted on her own champagne.

She laughed with the sound of a wild bird, a screech that filled the large oval dining room with its 'kwaaa, kaaa, kwaaaaa', and she laughed most in the company of her friends, two women who were always with her when she came alone – one who was equally fearful and dressed with the same costly despair, the wife of some streetcar magnate; and the second intimate, a woman with traces of gentility, a face that once must have been nice, who could not see, squinted, and had an Italian villa in Long Island, but a political husband with a red nose. They called themselves, when speaking of anything they would do together, 'We Girls'.

These three arrived one day when the only free table good enough, at which they could be seated immediately and without trouble, was on the edge of the balcony, in front of the mirror, on the station of the hoppy Frenchman. He bowed and scraped, danced and pirouetted, and pulled out their chairs. They sat down, and Madame complained, as she often did, about the fact that the menu was printed in French.

'What is,' she asked the maître d'hôtel, 'what is an escalope de veau à l'ancienne?'

He lifted his leg and with a flat hand showed her from what part of the animal the cutlet came. That was easy, but veau was difficult. He thought about the problem for a minute with many grimaces, and then smiled. He bent down, made a cute figure, and put his face close to the hat to say that he did not know the américain word for veau, but that he would try to explain.

'You have a son, Madame?'

'No,' she said.

'Well, we assume you have a son, Madame.'

'So what?'

'You, Madame, are vache, your son is veau. Escalope de veau is a cutlet of son of cow.'

She laughed her terrible laugh again, called for Monsieur Victor, and said: 'Fire that son of a bitch.'

Everyone in the hotel was saying: 'Monsieur Cape is coming, Monsieur Cape is coming from England.' There was much cleaning up and shining and everybody seemed to be afraid of Monsieur Cape. For Monsieur Cape was the president of our company. His offices were in London, and from there he always went on his rounds first to Paris where the company had another big hotel, then across to Rio de Janeiro and Havana, where the company also had restaurants, and finally to the Splendide.

Serafini told me that from Thursday on I would be on duty every morning at seven, with clean collar, brushed hair, shined shoes, and fingernails in shape, to serve Monsieur Cape's breakfast; and that, he added, was 'a great honour'.

At last the great man arrived, was received with much bowing and scraping, and was installed in our most palatial accommodations. It was a completely isolated duplex home with its own salon, dining room, staircase, and back service entrance. Up the latter, every morning, I brought breakfast to him and his niece. For he had brought a very beautiful niece with him, a girl with blue eyes and ash-blonde hair. He had many nieces, the chambermaid told me; this was the fifth one, and always a different one came with him from England, and the maid closed one eye when she said that.

In bed Mr. Cape was very small, and not much bigger when he got up. He had a red face with a small beard at the bottom, which made it look like a radish upside down. He talked very

little and walked back and forth, playing with the keys in his pocket and looking at the floor, like Uncle Hans. One of the first things he did whenever he came from England was to go to the coatroom of the restaurant, where there was a beautiful Irish girl, take her arm, go behind a sea-green drapery with her, and there whisper a joke into her ear. Unlike the nieces, it was always the same joke.

For his breakfast I had to go down into the kitchen and first of all order a basket of fruit from an old Frenchman in charge of them. The fruit was kept in the innermost and coldest refrigerator of a series of three, one inside the other. I gave the old Frenchman a slip on which I had written: 'Un Panier de Fruit', and under this, underscored with two thick lines: 'Pour Monsieur Cape'.

It always took a lot of time. The old man searched for the keys, unlocked each refrigerator in turn, skewered the slip on a long bent needle that hung over his desk, and said to himself several times: 'Un panier de fruit, pour Monsieur Cape.' When we were inside he rearranged the fruit in the basket several times to get the right Fruit Basket feeling.

When all was built up to his satisfaction, he placed a bunch of grapes on top, a big beautiful Belgian hothouse bunch with fat grapes that were so closely pressed together that some of them had square sides. These grapes came six bunches to a box, in a bed of ground cork and soft tissue paper. Then, in the open spaces around the grapes, the old Frenchman put a few more figs and plums, and finally he straightened out and said: 'Voilà, mon petit, un panier de fruit pour Monsieur Cape.'

I carried the basket of fruit carefully upstairs. In the warm air outside of the icebox a film of water in tiny beads set on all the fruit; the plums were the most beautiful that way. Fruit should always be served so, from out of the cold.

On my first trip up, I also took with me a finger bowl, a pair of silver shears for the grapes, and the linen. Then I went down again, by the private staircase, through the reception room of the apartment, out of the door to the hotel corridor, down with the service elevator, across the pantry, and down into the kitchen. On the second trip up, I brought the orange juice for the niece, the porridge, and the tea. For everything I had to write slips with 'POUR MONSIEUR CAPE' underlined.

After I had carried all this upstairs, I sat in the salon and waited until Monsieur Cape rang. The little alcohol flames burned under the silver kettle – he made his own tea – and under the porridge, which stood in a dish of hot water. For the toast I had to run down a third time while Monsieur Cape ate his fruit. It was a job nobody liked.

It took a long time for him to wake up. I started with the basket of fruit at seven-thirty and busied myself with this breakfast until about nine-thirty, because, while I was there, no one could call me away for any other duty. On the desk in the salon were the accounts of the hotel. I read them every morning; much was in red ink; it did not seem to be a very profitable hotel. Uncle Hans's hotels were much better paying. After I had read the accounts and the English funny papers, there was nothing to do.

I started on the first day to eat a few of the grapes on the Belgian hothouse bunch. The bunch got to look bad on one side, so I turned it around. But still Monsieur Cape did not ring, and I ate more on the good side. Then the bunch was altogether bad-looking; it was impossible to serve it to anyone and so I finished it and put some figs in its place. From then on I ate a bunch of grapes every morning.

Soon after I had eaten the grapes, a door would open and I would hear a little swish of nightgown and soft steps. That was the niece going to her own bedroom. Then another door would open and close and soon the little bell would ring and Monsieur Cape got his breakfast. The niece would come in and say 'Good morning' to me and to the uncle, and then she would sit on the side of the bed and help him prepare his tea. When I bent over, I could smell her hair and see that she was very young and firm and beautiful.

When I took the dishes down and brought the basket back to the icebox, it was about nine-thirty and the first chef was in his office, through the window of which he could see me pass and hand the basket back to the old man.

The first chef was, of course, also a Frenchman, but he was tall and, unlike most cooks and most Frenchmen, very quiet and self-controlled. One had to stand close to him to hear what he said, for he never raised his voice, not even in the greatest luncheon rush, when dishes clattered and the cooks were red in the face and excited and everybody ran and shouted. He was very saving for the hotel and he knew the contents of all his iceboxes. He also knew about the fruit and the basket for Mr. Cape and, of course, about the grapes.

When I came back with the basket, he always stepped to the door and looked at it, and said quietly: 'They are costly, these grapes of Belgium.' I wrote out a slip then, for 'Une grappe de raisin de Belgique', and for whatever other fruit had been used up, and the old man took it in exchange for the slip I had given him before for the whole basket. The first slip was torn up, and the slip for the grapes was collected by the accounting department with all the others and billed, but of course the president of the company had everything free and never received a bill.

All this went along very nicely for weeks. In the morning I served Monsieur Cape and in the evening worked in the roof garden, overlooking the city from the thirty-second floor. There was a foyer on it with little tables and a large buffet that was made of tin containers filled with ice and with a little fountain in its centre.

About six o'clock I had to be up there and help arrange cold dishes on the ice: large salmons in parsley and lemons, glacéd pheasants, poussins in aspic, cold bœuf à la mode, galantines of capon, hors d'œuvres, saucissons d'Arles, sauce verte, mayonnaise, beautifully decorated salads, strawberry tarts with whipped cream, compotes – many fine, good things. The first chef supervised all this and watched out that nothing disappeared.

On a very hot evening Monsieur Cape and his niece came and waited for their dinner guests in the chairs in front of the buffet. In a little while Monsieur Cape was walking back and forth, with his hands in his pockets playing with his keys. The chef had not seen Monsieur Cape since his arrival and he bowed and smiled. The guests were arriving now and engaging Monsieur Cape in conversation as they walked away from the buffet, and I thought everything was going to turn out all right. But the chef walked in front of them, and Monsieur Cape shook hands with him and introduced him to his guests. The air became thick, and though the chef spoke so quietly, I could hear him say: 'Monsieur Cape loves the Belgian hothouse grapes I send up every morning, yes?'

'What Belgian hothouse grapes?' asked Monsieur Cape.

I did not hear any more because I went out quickly with some plates.

The chef sent for me, he held my arm so tight it hurt, and he said quietly: 'Sacré voleur! It is shameful, such a young man of good family as you are! You will never be allowed to serve Monsieur Cape again.'

5. Herr Otto Brauhaus

THE SPLENDIDE had four hundred rooms, a great number for a luxurious hotel. Hotels larger than this became like railroad stations, eating and sleeping institutions. They have to take in anyone who comes along. The staff changes too frequently to give perfect service, to become acquainted with the guests. In the bigger hotels, the manager is usually a financial person, a onetime accountant who leaves actual contact with the guests to a platoon of day and night assistants, a kind of floorwalker with a small desk in the middle of the lobby and no authority except to say good morning and good night, a man whose business it is to shake hands and watch the bellboys and be in charge in case of fire.

In a hotel like the Splendide, however, it must be assumed, for the purposes of good management, that every guest is a distinguished and elegant person who, of course, has a great deal of money. The prices are high and must be high; the cost of provisions is probably the smallest item. The charges are for marble columns, uniforms, thick carpets, fine linen, thin glasses, many servants, and a good orchestra. And the management of such a hotel is a difficult, delicate business. It produces in most cases a type of man whose face is like a towel on which everyone has wiped both hands, a smooth, smiling, bowing man, in ever freshly pressed clothes, a flower in his lapel, précieux and well fed.

Rarely does one find in America a hotel manager who has survived the winds of complaint, the climate of worry, and the floods of people, and of whom one can still say that, besides being short or tall, thin or fat, he has this or that kind of a personality. Such a one, a real person, honest, always himself with a unique character, was Otto Brauhaus, manager of the Hotel Splendide.

Otto Brauhaus was an immense stout man; he had to bend down to pass under the tall doorways of his hotel. Big as his feet, which gave him much trouble, telegraphing their sorrows to his ever-worried face, was his heart. For despite his conception of himself as a stern executive, and strict disciplinarian, he could not conceal his kindness. He liked to laugh with guests and employees alike, and the result was that his countenance was the scene of an unending emotional conflict.

He was a German, from the soft-speaking Palatinate. For all his years in America, he had somehow never been able to improve his accent. Too genuine a person to learn the affected English of Monsieur Victor, who was a fellow countryman, Brauhaus spoke a thick dialect that sometimes sounded like a vaudeville comedian trying for effect. He was, in any case, inarticulate, and hated to talk. Two expressions recurred in his speech like commas; without them he seemed hardly able to speak: 'Cheeses Greisd!' and 'Gotdemn it!'

His friends were all solid men like himself. Most of them seemed to be brewers, and they would have occasional dinners together, small beer-fests, up in the top-floor suite. There they drank enormous quantities of beer and ate canvasback ducks with wild rice. They held little speeches afterward and ate again at midnight. They spoke mostly about how proud they were of being brewers. Almost weeping with sentiment and pounding on the table with his fist, one of them would always get up and say: 'My father was a brewer. So was my grandfather, and his father was a brewer before him. I feel beer flowing in my veins.'

Then Herr Brauhaus usually summed up their feelings by rising to say: 'My friends, we are all here together around this table because we are friends. I am demn glad to see all my friends here.' They would all nod and applaud and drink again.

But things had not been going too well with Brauhaus's friends, these elderly men who ate and drank too well. In one week Mr. Brauhaus went to two funerals. He came back very gloomy from the second, saying: 'Gotdemn it, Cheeses Greisd, every time I see a friend of mine, he's dead.'

Beautiful was it also when he described his art gallery. Of the Rubens sketch he owned, he often said: 'If something happens to me, Anna still has the Rubens,' and of his primitives he said: 'Sometimes when I'm alone, I look at them, and they look at me, so brimidif, like this,' and he would look sideways out of his face, just like his primitives.

He was not given to false conceptions of personal dignity, though he insisted on his hotel's being treated with proper respect. Once when he had hung up outside his office, one hour after he had bought it, a beautiful expensive heavy coat lined with mink, and it was stolen, Mr. Brauhaus ran out into the luncheon crowd which filled the lobby and howled: 'Where is my furgoat, Cheeses Greisd!' But it was gone and never came back.

On the other hand, one day when Mr. Brauhaus happened to be walking through the Jade Lounge he saw an elderly lady sitting there alone at a small glass-top table, on which were tea and crumpets. She was knitting. Turning to me he said: 'What do they think this is? Go over there and tell that woman to stop knitting.' He pronounced the 'k' in the last word. 'Tell her that this is a first-class hotel and we don't want any knitting here in our Jade Lounges.' He disappeared into his office.

I was a little afraid to follow orders, for the elderly lady was severely dressed and looked quite capable of taking care of herself. I therefore passed the patron's instructions on to Monsieur Serafini, who looked at the lady, went 'Tsk, tsk, tsk' with his tongue, and called a waiter. Fortunately, before the waiter could reach her, the old lady packed her knitting into an immense bag and smiled up at a tall man who had come in the door. She was his mother and he was the new British Ambassador.

*

Brauhaus's goodness of heart, his reliance on the decency of his people, his unwillingness to face them when they had caused trouble, meant that he was always being taken advantage of by the smooth, tricky, much-travelled people who were his employees. 'Why doesn't everybody do his duty, why do I have to bawl them out all the time?' he pleaded with them.

But when someone went too far, then Otto Brauhaus exploded. His big face turned red, his voice keeled over, he yelled and threatened murder. The culprit's head somewhere on a level with Brauhaus's watch chain, the storm and thunder of the big man's wrath would tower and sweep over him. Brauhaus's fists would be raised up at the ceiling, pounding the air; the crystals on the chandelier would dance at the sound of his voice: 'I'll drown you oud, I'll kill you, gotdemn it, Cheeses Greisd, ged oud of here!'

Fifteen minutes later, he enters his office and finds waiting for him the man he has been shouting at. Brauhaus looks miserable, stares at the floor like a little boy. He puts his hand on the man's shoulder and squeezes out a few embarrassed sentences. First he says: 'Ah, ah – ah,' then comes a small prayer: 'You know I am a very pusy man. I have a lot of worries. I get excited and then I say things I don't mean. You have been here a long time with me, and I know you work very hard, and that you are a nice feller.' Finally a few more 'Ah – ah – ah's', and then he turns away. To any man with a spark of decency, all this hurts; almost there are tears in one's eyes, and one's loyalty to Otto Brauhaus is sewn doubly strong with the big stitches of affection.

Since he could not fire anyone, someone else had to get rid of the altogether impossible people, and then an elaborated guard had to be thrown around Brauhaus to keep the discharged employees from reaching him in person or by telephone. Once a man got by this guard, all the firing was for nothing.

One night it was announced that Mr. Brauhaus was leaving on his vacation. Such information seeps through the hotel immediately, as in a prison. The trunks were sent on ahead, and late that night Mr. Brauhaus took a cab to the station. But he missed his train, and, since the hotel was not far from the station, he decided to walk back. With his little Tirolese hat, his heavy cane, and his dachshund, which he took with him on trips, he came marching into his hotel. Outside he found no carriage man, no doorman, inside no one to turn the revolving door, no night clerk, also no bellboy and no elevator man. The lobby was quite deserted; only from the cashier's cage came happy voices and much laughter.

Mr. Brauhaus stormed back there and exploded: 'What is diss? Gotdemn it! Cheeses Greisd! You have a birdtay zelepration here?'

They made themselves scarce and rushed for their posts. Only the bottles of beer were left, as the revolving door was turned, without guests in it, the elevator starter slipped on his gloves, and the night clerk vaulted behind the counter and began to write. 'You are fired, all fired, everyone here is fired, gotdemn it!' screamed Herr Brauhaus. 'Everyone here is fired, you hear, raus, everyone, you and you and you.' He growled on: 'Lumpenpack, Tagediebe, Schweinebande!' He had never heard or seen anything like this.

The men very slowly started to leave. 'No, not now, come back, tomorrow you are fired,' Brauhaus shouted at them.

He was so angry he could not think of going to sleep, and as always on the occasions when he was upset, he walked all the way around the hotel and back to the main entrance. There the doorman got hold of him. With sad eyes, he intercepted Mr. Brauhaus, mumbled something about the twelve years he had been with the hotel, that only tonight, for the first time, had he failed in his duty, that he had a sick child and a little house in Flatbush and that his life would be ruined.

'All right,' said Brauhaus. 'You stay, John. All the others, gotdemn it, are fired.'

But there was no one to protect him that night. Inside he heard the same story, with changes as to the particular family

misfortune and the location of the little houses. They had all been with the Splendide since the hotel was built; the bellboy had grey hair and was fifty-six years old. Mr. Brauhaus walked out again and around the block. When he came back, he called them all together. He delivered them what was for him a long lecture on discipline, banging the floor with his stick, while the dachshund smelled the doorman's pants.

'I am a zdrikt disziblinarian,' he said. They would all have to work together; this hotel was not a gotdemn joke, Cheeses Greisd. It was hard enough to manage it when everyone did his duty, gotdemn it. 'And now get back to work.'

A late guest arrived. He was swung through the door, saluted, wished a good night, expressed up to his room with a morning paper and a passkey in the hands of the grey-haired bellboy. No guest had ever been so well and quickly served. 'That's good, that's how it should be all the time,' said Otto Brauhaus. 'Why isn't it like this all the time?' Then he went to bed.

6. Mr Sigsag goes to sea

THE GRILL Room of the Splendide was also under the charge of a man named Victor, but whereas Victor of the restaurant was corpulent, Victor of the Grill was thin. Fat Victor was German, but thin Victor was Hungarian, and therefore more elegant. They hated each other, never spoke, and thin Victor undoubtedly engaged me because it would annoy the restaurant's Monsieur Victor.

Thin Victor was never arrogant to his guests; the bad ones he would keep waiting with promises, and then hide them behind pillars. He had a sense of humour, but also theatrical attacks of temper. When something went wrong, he would wring his hands in front of the guests and call the waiters 'criminals'; he would stamp his feet at an omelet that was not fluffy enough, but he was good to work for; unlike the other Monsieur Victor, who fired someone every day, he discharged no one if he could possibly help it.

All the maîtres d'hôtel and all the chefs de rang in front looked down upon the staff of the Grill Room. These men were shorter and fatter, as the room was also lower and the columns at its sides thicker and shorter. The waiters here were mostly Italians, with a few Armenians and Bohemians and a Greek. They spoke bad French and waited on a lower class of people. Pushed away to one side of the Grill Room, which was always full, was a three-piece orchestra whose only function was to drown out the noise of the service, the clatter of dishes, glasses, and silver.

The great Society went in front; back here came musical comedy stars, and millionaires in search of a quiet corner behind a pillar, where they could not be seen while they squeezed the hands of their young women. Here came film presidents, who ate in a hurry and chattered and haggled over the table with knives or forks in their hands; stockbrokers, owners of fur businesses, people who ran fast, risky under-takings and spent money freely.

I became acquainted with a little Bohemian waiter stationed way in the back of this room. His name was Wladimir Slezack, but since no one could pronounce it, it had gradually become Mr. Sigsag. He was the smallest man in the restaurant, and because he worked very hard and was very fast on his feet he was a favourite of thin Victor.

Every waiter in a hotel has a 'side job'. A side job is extra work, other than serving, that he must perform before or after meals; most of it done in the morning. One man is in charge of filling and collecting all the salt and pepper and paprika shakers and seeing that they are kept clean. Others must get the clean linen from the linen room every morning and check it at night;

others collect the dirty linen. Another has to keep the stock of sauces and pickles, make the French and Russian salad dressing, keep clean the oil and vinegar bottles and the mustard pots. This side job is called the 'drugstore', and it was assigned to Mr. Sigsag.

Mr. Sigsag lived in a little room on the East Side, where he read the works, in many volumes bound in limp green leather with gold stamping, of a man who called himself the 'Sage of East Aurora'. These concerned trips to the homes of great men, but the biggest book was one entitled *Elbert Hubbard's Scrapbook* (that was the name of the Sage). With these books and included in their total price had come candlesticks, jars of honey, maple sugar candies, and other souvenirs, all in the one package with the volumes. When I visited him he was expecting some new volumes from East Aurora, this time with book ends included to hold his little library together.

Mr. Sigsag studied these books earnestly and drew the lessons from them that he should. They filled him with respect for a life of work and success. He was also a student by correspondence of the La Salle University and had subscribed to several courses, but he told me that what was most important in life was not knowledge, or hard work, but the right connections, also the ability to 'sell' oneself, to call guests by their correct names and to remember their faces.

From his library, now lying one volume on top of another, he took a book of which he was very fond, a waiter's bible. After his working hours at the Bristol in Vienna, he had attended a school which the hoteliers of Vienna maintained for the training of new waiters. He graduated from it with high honours. A diploma, a coloured lithograph, decorated like a menu with pheasants, geese, wine bottles, and grapes, surrounded his name printed in the centre. It was signed by the dean of the school and the president of the Society of Hoteliers, Restaurateurs, Cafetiers, and Innkeepers of Vienna and by the city's burgomaster, and hung in a frame over Mr. Sigsag's desk. So well had he been liked at the school, that the maître d'hôtel principal had had him pose for the photographs that illustrated the manual of the waiter's art, which was learnedly entitled: *Ein Leitfaden der Servierkunde mit besonderer Berücksichtigung der Küchenwesens* ('An Introduction to the Science of Serving, with Special Reference to Culinary Matters').

The photographs showed Mr. Sigsag, a little waiter in a tail coat, standing in the proper positions for receiving a guest and for recommending dishes from the menu, and also standing incorrectly while doing this. They showed him handing a newspaper to a guest, carrying a tray, lighting a diner's cigar, and demonstrating how to carry the sidetowel, as well as various ways of how not to carry it. There was a list of books at the end of the book, for further study, among them the *Almanach de Gotha* and various cook books, and there were colour charts of sleeve stripes and collar stars showing the various grades of army and naval officers. One whole chapter was given over to the art of folding napkins into the shapes of swans, windmills, boats, and fans.

Mr. Sigsag spent his free time puttering on a secondhand motorboat which he kept up near Dyckman Street; he asked me to visit him there sometimes. Two weeks from the day I first visited him, he told me that thin Victor was giving a party at a small place outside the city, along the ocean, in Bath Beach. Several of the maîtres d'hôtel, the head cashier Madame

Dombasle, and even the room clerk were invited to it, and so was he, Sigsag, because of his motorboat, in which he was to take Madame Dombasle and her two beautiful daughters out there. After the luncheon he would take all the guests for a little fishing trip, and Monsieur Victor would pay for the oil and gasoline. A little more work had to be done on the boat and Mr. Sigsag invited me to help him and to come along to the party.

He seemed to have influence. He got days off, with mysterious ease, to work on the boat. These were lovely days. Arriving at Dyckman Street by subway, he put on old pants and undershirt and washed and scraped the little boat as it stood high and dry on the land. Mr. Sigsag talked of the importance of having friends and of working hard, and also of Madame Dombasle's two beautiful daughters.

It took him several months to scrape and burn the old paint off his small ship, and, on account of the belly of the boat, he had much trouble getting the red paint that is used at the bottom to end evenly where it meets the white. I helped him on my free day and when we were through we went to a little lunchwagon where we got wonderful ham and eggs and some beer to take back with us to the boat. Then we lit a lamp, and if one did not look at the big electric powerhouse across the river, this was a scene of peace. The niceness of people could be seen here in their desire to flee from the city; all about us were other little grounded boats, on which men had laboured after working hours, quiet, simple men with pipes and old clothes and without much money. The decks of their boats, high above the land and surrounded by grass, looked amusing; on them their wives sat and cooked on little oil burners or gasoline stoves. The boats were of comical design: impossible cabins were built on decks much too small for them and had to be broken up, with half a cabin in the stern and another piece of it stuck on in the bow. On some of them were little roof gardens with flower boxes, hammocks, easy chairs, and even bird cages. They made up a little city of green, yellow, and blue houses that could swim away. It had none of that impersonal elegance or mass ugliness of manufactured things; everyone had done something with his own hands for his own pleasure. It was all so happy and sad and, above all, good; even the ground was nice, covered with coils of rope, old dinghies, rusted anchors, and green and red lanterns.

As the lights grew stronger in the little portholes and were reflected on the sides of the boats next to them, and the gramophones started to play, and the smell of food came out of imitation funnels, we stopped work and sat in the cabin while Mr. Sigsag told me of his youth.

Wladimir Slezack, the eleventh son of a Bohemian blacksmith, was born in a village two hours out of Przemysl. When he was old enough, though still a child, his father paid to have him apprenticed as piccolo at the great Hotel King Wenzeslaus in

Przemysl. Here he served part of his apprenticeship and then went on to Vienna, where, his recommendations being of the best, he got a job in a small hotel.

The child piccolo is an institution in all European restaurants. His head barely reaches above the table; his ears are red and stand out, because everybody pulls them. And when he is a man, he will still pull his head quickly to one side if anyone close to him suddenly moves, because he always did that to soften the blows that rained on him from the proprietor down to the last chambermaid; they hit him mostly out of habit.

For the rest the boy learned to wash glasses, to fold newspapers into the bamboo holders and hang them on the wall, to learn the grade of an officer by the stars on his collar, to bow, to chase flies from the tables without upsetting the glasses, to carry water and coffee without spilling, and to know the fifty-one varieties of coffee that are served in Viennese restaurants, starting with the mélange, which is a pale mixture of coffee and cream served in a glass with whipped cream on top, down to the capuchin, which is a tiny demitasse of black coffee served with nothing but two pieces of sugar on a little silver saucer.

He studied how to make up and write the bill of fare, let the awnings up and down over the sidewalk in the summer, and scatter ashes out on the ice on winter mornings. He also cleaned ashtrays and matchstands, and one could still see his right thumb bent sideways from polishing two hundred of these every day; they were made of a light-coloured, very sensitive brass, and the cigarettes burned deep stains into them that were hard to get out.

The boys started to work at six in the morning; they ate

standing up, and got to bed at eleven at night. A free day was not provided for, since on Sundays and holidays the restaurant was busier than on other days serving happy people. The piccolos slept in the restaurant, and Wladi, who was the smallest of them, slept in a kitchen drawer under the pastrycook's noodle board, where it was warm. The others had to sleep in the dining room on cold benches under which their dirty pillows and covers were stowed away in a drawer during the day.

Little Wladi was fortunate not only in his sleeping quarters, in which he was at least warm, but also in his parentage. So many of the other boys were the chance sons of a chambermaid and a transient guest or waiter, or at best a soldier loved on a bench when the trees were in bloom and all was beautiful on the Prater.

A restaurant in the morning, before it is aired and swept, and the guests enter, is an unhappy place. The stale smells of tobacco smoke, of empty beer and wine glasses, and of spilled food and coffee stay on and hang about the draperies and furniture. It is no place for a growing child; this life eventually draws on the faces of these little boys two lines from their nostrils to the corners of their young lips and it makes them pale and brings out the thin veins at their temples. They get to look tired and highbred; in later years this pallor and nervousness will give them just the right touch of grand hotel elegance they will need for their parts. The boys also learn to repeat the smut they hear from the guests, and to smoke, and to drink themselves to sleep.

Nevertheless, the piccolo was looked upon with envy by the apprentices of plumbers and cobblers; they had the red ears, too, but not enough to eat, and no cigarettes, no drinks, no tips. The

piccolo could at least save money. It was the custom in Austria for guests to leave three separate tips. The biggest was for the Zahlkellner, the captain to whom one paid the bill and who had taken the order; the next was for the Speisenträger or Saalkellner, the ordinary waiter who actually served one; and the third, a little stack of coppers, was for the piccolo. These three tips had to be left in clearly defined heaps and far enough apart from one another; for the restaurant law was that all the coins that the first waiter could get within the reach of his outstretched thumb and index finger was his. That is why, in old Viennese restaurants, the three tips were always left very far apart from one another, almost on the edges of the small marble tables.

Despite the big hands of the headwaiters, the piccolo was often able to earn and put aside a good sum of money; he had little chance to spend it. His dress coat, a child's garment, he had made by a cheap tailor, or bought it secondhand from another piccolo; his trousers could be dark blue or grey, for in the bad light of the restaurants no one could see below the levels of the tables; finally, there was a waistcoat. Under the latter the piccolo need not wear a shirt; a celluloid plastron, like a bosom cut out of an evening shirt, was attached by a button to his celluloid collar, and a tie held the arrangement together. Save for his shoes and socks, the dickey, and cuffs, which were stuck in his coat sleeves, the piccolo stood naked in his trousers and frock coat. His hair was plastered down with brilliantine, and kept in order with a greasy comb that he carried in his waistcoat pocket.

He knew all about love and women, and had never played. He looked most unhappy when in the spring he brought ice cream out to the restaurant garden for some well-dressed child with its father and mother, who smiled at him when the music played and the large-grained sand was hard to walk on. And when one sees somewhere in a cheap restaurant, say in a beer hall in Coney Island, one of those old waiters who are known as 'hashers' leaning on a chair, with ugly, lightless eyes and a dead face that is filled with misery and meanness, one is seeing that little boy grown old, with flat crippled feet, on which he has dragged almost to the end of his useless life his dead childhood.

But little Wladimir was made of stronger material, he survived, he went to school, he saved his money and paid his father back what had been spent to make him a piccolo, and he went to France and England and finally to America. Now he had a job as chef de rang in the best hotel in New York, in the Grill Room of the Splendide, and the maître d'hôtel was his friend. When looked at from Przemysl, this was as great and brave a success as any recorded in the high tales Mr. Sigsag read in the honey and candlestick books of Elbert Hubbard.

After he had ended his story, Mr. Sigsag looked in his little account book; he had set aside a certain sum for entertainment, another for the launching of the boat, for a uniform and the beer, but we also needed some food to serve on the trip. He promised to show me something tomorrow: how to get a little food without paying for it.

The next day, after all the guests had left and the lights were turned out in the Grill Room and the cashier had added up her bills, closed the books, and gone away with the money, Mr. Sigsag led me to the little tiled closet where he prepared his salad dressings. He kept all his sauces, the mayonnaise, and the mustards in an icebox which had a small door, about three feet high and four wide, at the height of his head; he had to stand on a box to reach into it. This mustard closet was built into a huge refrigerator that opened out on the kitchen and had its back to the Grill Room, and it hung like a cage some feet above the level of the kitchen.

Mr. Sigsag made sure no one was around and then started to take everything out of the small icebox. He placed on a table the bottles of chili sauce, A-One sauce, sauce Escoffier, walnut and tarragon sauce, all the vinegar bottles, the chutneys, and the twenty-five French and twenty-five English mustard pots which were in daily use. Then he lifted out the grating on which the bottles had stood, and now I could see the big kitchen icebox filled with cheeses, tubs of rolled butter in ice water, and salads. He brought over a chair and asked me to hold his legs while he reached for a cheese.

'Shh,' said Mr. Sigsag, and I looked around once more; there was no one outside. He climbed in and reached down, but he was too short to reach the cheeses. I held his knees, then his ankles, and then his shoes; then I had his shoes in my hands and Mr. Sigsag was down with his face in some Camembert. Also there was a noise. I closed the icebox door. It was the night watchman; he looked in and I polished away at some bottles. The man sat down, lit a pipe, and started to talk; it was a long time before he left again on his rounds.

In the meantime, Mr. Sigsag had been trying to get up; kneeling and standing and sliding and then sitting down again in all kinds of cheese. He first handed out a Pont l'Evêque, hard and solid. 'There will be trouble anyway,' he said, 'we might as well take it along.' Then he gave me his cold hands, but for some time I could not lift him out. They were smeared with cheese and slipped out of mine. I gave him a napkin, with which he cleaned his face and hands, and finally I could pull him out, his sleeves and trousers full of cheese. He took a shower downstairs, changed his trousers, but he still smelled.

The next morning, Sunday, I met him very early at the boat, which was in the water now, looking new and beautiful. The sun had just risen and shone warmly on the planks. We put the beer on board, and the cheese, also knives and paper napkins, and then we dressed in the uniforms, scattered around cushions, bought oil and gasoline, and started off, past the electric light plant, and out into the Hudson, under the railroad bridge at Spuyten Duyvil.

The trouble started at about One Hundred and Sixty-Eighth Street – pop, then pop and poppoppop and the motor stopped. The boat started to rock and turn around with the incoming tide.

Mr. Sigsag took a big piece of the motor out of the heavy cylinder; he did this by undoing two screws. The motor was a primitive engine called a 'Make and Break' motor that functioned without sparkplugs. Mr. Sigsag sandpapered the two small points on the piece he had taken out, he poured a mixture which he called 'dynamite' out of a little can into the hollow, then replaced the part and screwed it tight. The motor almost flew out of the boat and tiny lightning flashes shot out all over the loose parts. This happened three more times before we reached the Battery, and Mr. Sigsag's uniform was soiled with finger marks.

'There they are,' said Mr. Sigsag and pointed to three women who were strolling up and down to the left of the Aquarium. Madame Dombasle and her two daughters were very French-looking and sweet in their airy batiste gowns that reached to the floor. Madame carried a fragile parasol and the young girls wore large satin sashes and bows around their waists and openwork gloves up to their elbows. We tooted the whistle three times and they waved their arms and the parasol.

The entrance to the little harbour at the Battery is hard to negotiate; there are strong currents and only a small opening between high sea walls. We almost made it, were swept away, and then turned and tried again; finally, by keeping the boat, which was almost as wide as it was long, away from the wall on one side with a hook and on the other with Mr. Sigsag's feet, we made the calm square of water that was filled with driftwood and a broken life preserver. Madame was helped on board, which was not easy, for she was stout and giggled and did not jump when Mr. Sigsag said 'jump.' She almost got one foot between the pier and the boat. The daughters, tall, lovely, dark, and young, were easier.

Madame admired the boat, the uniforms, le petit comman-dant. 'How many tons has your little liner?' she asked. Mr. Sigsag took them to the roof of the cabin from which they could enjoy the best view of the harbour; there they sat on cushions, under the parasol, and smiled back, a little afraid, jumping when we tooted the horn as a signal that we were off.

I steered the boat while Mr. Sigsag sat in front and explained New York to the ladies, who, having landed in Boston, had not seen much of it – the beautiful bridges, the Statue of Liberty, the ferryboats, the tall buildings. There is a powerful current here; the tide comes in through the Narrows, and it is besides a very much disturbed area of water. There is much driftwood that may get into the propeller, and ocean liners go in and out, fire and police boats, private yachts, the great Staten Island ferryboats making high waves, railroad tugs with strings of cars on long barges. Waves come in from all directions, so that one cannot bother to cut them at the proper angles, and the little boat was tossed high and to all sides.

I noticed that after half an hour we had not reached the latitude of Governor's Island; in another half-hour the prison on that island moved slowly past and ten minutes later the motor coughed and stopped. Mr. Sigsag was just serving beer and cheese sandwiches. While Madame Dombasle and her daughters rose up and down in front, Mr. Sigsag disappeared inside to fix the motor. We lost much distance and were back again near the prison and close to the island; then came a ferryboat and the ladies were wetted to the knees. They shrieked but they were afraid to move, and looked around just as Mr. Sigsag came out of the cabin. The smell of oil and beer and the rocking had made him sick and he bent over the side of

the boat. When I saw that, I also got sick. The boat turned again. Mr. Sigsag got up, took a deep breath, smiled at the ladies, and then went in to his motor again.

Then the ladies got sick and held on to one another. In the low cabin were two benches: Mr. Sigsag put the cushions on them and slowly pulled Madame Dombasle back on the narrow gangway, knocking her head as they went in. When she had lain down, Mr. Sigsag offered her some beer, but she whimpered: 'No, please, no.' The daughters got sicker and the younger one was taken down and laid on the other bench with her long slim legs folded back. The bottles rolled over the cabin top and jumped into the bay.

We crossed over away from the main current and made better speed along the Staten Island shoreline. Mr. Sigsag felt better and cracked jokes, but in the cabin the ladies were sick again, and seasick women are not attractive. One of the daughters came out for air, her dress wet and ruined; she sat up bravely and leaned into the wind and brushed her black hair from her cheeks where it was stuck in spittle. We forged slowly ahead, and it is a wonderful thing that a boat goes on even when everybody on board is feeling terrible.

We turned past the point at Fort Wadsworth and went to the left and finally came to Bath Beach, where we tooted the horn again. Thin Victor and his wife, the maîtres d'hôtel, and Mr. Fassi, the chief clerk, were at the docks to meet us. They all looked strange without their dress coats and stiff shirts, wearing instead gay suits with belts at the back and straw hats with coloured bands; but when we arrived there was as much scraping and bowing as at the hotel. The colour came back into our ladies' faces; they retired to a room and came down again in good order, with hardly a trace of damage in their clothes and hair. Frenchwomen know how to repair themselves very quickly after a disaster. The trip was soon forgotten and even laughed over.

Built of wood, with whitewashed stone urns around it, in which were planted palms, the old hotel gave one somehow a feeling of vacation and freedom. It stood near the shore in a large garden with children's swings in it. The Hungarian chief bus boy had decorated a corner of the dining room, which was panelled with long strips of dark-varnished wood and contained a piano. There were flowers on the table, and one of the Splendide cooks had been brought out to prepare a very good meal. There was a printed menu and good wines: cigars and cigarettes were handed around; and the maîtres d'hôtel sat about in accented comfort, their legs spread wide apart, smoking with a careless air, and saying with face, hands, and feet: 'We are gentlemen today.' Also they summoned the old

waiter by calling 'Psst,' something they themselves detested when the guests in the Splendide did it, but here it meant: 'See how thoroughly we can be guests.'

Madame Dombasle and her beautiful daughters were toasted; then the younger one, Céleste, sat down at the piano and played. The instrument needed tuning, many of the strings rattled in rust, and it sounded as if one were hearing an echo, but she played several salon pieces, 'Ouvre tes yeux bleus, ma mignonne', and 'Si j'avais des ailes'. Then there was conversation, everyone sat down, and Monsieur Victor spoke.

As an old colonel would explain delicate tactical problems to his subalterns, so he went over many phases of his career. The talk covered the Continent; it was of glorious dinners, of places and people, of Monte Carlo and Ostende, of the Carlton in London, of encounters with difficult guests of the highest position, of Prince Bibesco, the Kaiser, and other trying cases, and of old King Leopold. Victor told of the time when His Majesty, Alfonso of Spain, came to the Carlton Grill, and there was only one table left, reserved for Marie Tempest, the actress, who came in just as the King did. It was a breathless moment. 'I don't know how I did it, it came to me from somewhere, the inspiration,' said Victor, but he solved the terrible dilemma – simply with the phrase, 'The great king, the great actress,' and he sat them both down at the same table. A whispered 'Ah' went around our table, accompanied by French, Italian, Hungarian, and German gestures of appreciation of so brilliant a performance.

Thin Victor shrugged his shoulders at these expressions of grateful admiration from his maîtres d'hôtel and went on to the problems confronting him now, reviewing matters that had gone badly or very well. The maîtres d'hôtel furnished details, agreed or disputed as to dates or the number of people that had been at a certain table on a certain day or the dishes they had ordered. It slowed up the story-telling, but it brought them closer together. Their eyes hung on Victor's lips.

Next to me, all the way at the end of the table, sat Mr. Sigsag, and when I sometimes asked him a question, he said: 'Shh!' very angrily, and listened intently to the head of the table, and laughed at the jokes, and looked dark at serious passages. He let no detail escape him.

Only one man remained aloof. This was Fassi, the room clerk, who had observed a certain distance all evening long. He sat at the right of Victor; smoking his cigar and gazing at the ash, he carried to this table the disdain of the front office for restaurant and kitchen help. Only when Victor told what Mr. Joseph Widener had ordered for dinner yesterday did Fassi stir and say: 'Ah, yes, yes, yes, Joseph Widener,' leaving the Mr. off, 'Joseph Widener, I spoke to him only yesterday, no, Thursday, wasn't it?' and he made it clear therewith that, while Victor took the orders of Mr. Widener, he, Fassi, spoke to the great man about the weather, about horses, and about the general things men talk about.

There was dancing afterward, and the room clerk danced with one of the daughters, Victor with the other, and Mr. Sigsag with the mother.

The report of the party and its great success was all over the hotel the next day. Madame Dombasle was at her chair, at the head of the cashiers' desk, and told the ladies of her experience on board ship. 'I was certain that my end had come,' she said, and looked at the stucco ceiling of the restaurant. 'Guess how many glasses of Tokay I drank last night at Monsieur Victor's party – you saw me there, didn't you?' said the Hungarian chief bus boy, so that everyone could hear it. The maîtres d'hôtel showed a little more respect for me. As for Mr. Sigsag, he was soon a maître d'hôtel, and we never heard anything about the cheese.

7. Life Class

I SPOKE passable English, but America was still foreign to me, the great distances and high buildings seemed to hide everything from my understanding. Life in Regensburg had been clear: Grandfather made and sold beer; people sold him hops, malt, barrels, and calves, and ate in his restaurant; his employees lived in a house that was as good as his and ate the same food and had the same security and the same pleasures, except perhaps for the hunting wagon and the trotter; they sniffed the same kind of snuff and everybody drank the same beer, the best that could be brewed. Up in Uncle Hans's hotel it was a little more difficult, but I still could see everything come and go, and follow it.

I spoke of this to Mr. Sigsag, and he said it was all very simple; all I had to do was to read the books, for example, *A Message to Garcia*, the trips to the homes of great men, and everything would at once be clear, the secret of success being Application, Hard Work, and Loyalty. I read the books, and Mr. Sigsag and I had some unpleasant words about them.

I looked at the people whom these books praised, as they lived and ate in the Splendide. I said that Mr. Hubbard was the literary maître d'hôtel who bowed people in and out of his books; the book ends, candlesticks, and maple sugar candy made it all the more obvious. Also, the soft leather bindings, the type, and even the candlesticks were junky and in bad taste.

'Who are you to say such things?' cried Mr. Sigsag, very angry and looking at me with perturbation and suspicion.

We had been sitting on his docked boat when we had this argument, and suddenly I stepped off without a word to Mr. Sigsag, and I walked around the Dyckman Street neighbourhood worrying over his question.

A few days later, I went to an art shop on Fifth Avenue, belonging to the Bavarian firm of Hanfstaengl, to have framed a painting I had done, out of homesickness, of grandfather's brewery at night, with the Duke's carriages in the square and Uncle Veri throwing Dreck Bartel into the little park. The bearded old clerk looked from the painting to me and said: 'This is the Arnulf Square in Regensburg. Who did it?' When I told him it was mine, he asked me to bring all my other work. 'I think you should study,' he said. 'If you'd like, I'll send you to Thaddeus. If he thinks you have talent, he'll take you in his school.'

It seemed like the answer to Mr. Sigsag's question. Thaddeus looked over my work, thought I would not be wasting my time to study painting, and asked me how much I could afford to pay. I was putting aside five dollars a week, and that was what Thaddeus charged me.

Like all German artists, Thaddeus was primarily a thorough draughtsman; he worked with prismatic clarity, with hair-breadth precision, hardly if ever erasing a line. If, as happened very seldom, a line went wrong, he threw the board away and started over again. His eye and hand were one with the line of his model; he worked fast, and his finished pictures, done in pastel, tempera, or black and white, were of such workmanship that they seemed to come out of a printing press rather than from an easel.

His studio was a high room, about the size of the Splendide's small ballroom, and on a balcony, reached by a stairway, were his living quarters, three little rooms – a bedroom, a library, and a Bavarian peasant living room. From the ceiling of the studio to the floor hung heavy magenta curtains; there was a fireplace, a screen for the model to dress, a model stand, easels, shelves for the students' materials, and an oven.

A Negro cleaned up and a motherly little woman kept house for Thaddeus, answered his telephone, and complained of his morals and his language. Occasionally she threw down whatever she had in her hand and left him. She understood, said this Frau Hammer, that a big healthy man like Thaddeus could not live like a saint, but to drag in, every night, a different one of these cats was too much for her. As additional provocation Thaddeus would, while she washed the windows of the studio, or wrapped paintings for an exhibition, draw large obscene pictures of female anatomy in violent red, and, just before she could say anything, he would add a little stem, draw petals around it, and make a magnificent flower, an orchid, a strange jungle growth, or even a butterfly out of it. Often he would afterward hang the sheet up in the studio and when his young students stopped in front of it and exclaimed: 'Oh, look at the beautiful flower!' he would grin at Frau Hammer, and the old woman would say: 'You Schwein, you devil, I don't know why I stand for it,' but she would sit down and sew on his buttons and darn his socks and look at him lovingly.

Most of the girl students were in love with Thaddeus. He was tall and broad-shouldered, had white hair, a magnificent godly head, and pale eyes. They held his hand and looked meltingly and intimately at him, while he kissed their hands and petted them and took them out to a little German restaurant where he bought them plum tarts, Apfelstrudel, and coffee. He was always very honest with the announcement of his intentions, long before that became the general fashion. He would disappear with one of them to his little peasant room, but not for long, only to kiss her, to hold her head between his hands, to gaze into her eyes; and the door was left open, for it was only a preliminary invitation. There were at times ruffled feelings, little studio jealousies, that this or that one had more of him than another; but he managed to keep his little herd of tender young kine generally happy. Again one saw him in a restaurant or a theatre with someone from outside, whom we had never seen before, someone fascinating, young, and always beautiful. He had a good life.

The work was serious. The students arrived at nine, searched

in their compartments for their materials, and pulled their easels out from behind a curtain, where they had been put away by the coloured man, because in the afternoon Thaddeus worked on portraits, murals, and various commissions. After the easels were in place, there was the general noise of charcoal scraping and then the model took the stand.

The model was in most cases one of that hard-working and unexciting group of girls who wander from studio to studio, badly paid and often half frozen. It is difficult work, for the poses have to be held a long time; a watch lies on the edge of the model stand and one of the students keeps time. These girls are seldom beautiful; sometimes one with a negligible face has a full rounded body, while a lovely head is often spoiled by badly formed arms, legs, or breasts. Sometimes everything is almost right and there is one glaring, disturbing fault that upsets one; and of course feet are always bad, with callouses, overriding toes, blue-grey nails.

To Thaddeus, and to the students, these girls were simply studies in anatomy, but sometimes, as in the case of the Danish opera singer who showed up one day for drawing lessons, there would be a more human approach.

There was something of the baby and its wardrobe in the design of this person and his clothes. Everything about him was airy, light as a soufflé, fluffy, and warm. His hat was a Viennese plush, grass green; his ties had wallpaper patterns in the colours of cork and coffee; his suits and topcoats, always new and neatly pressed, were of pastel shades. He wore rings on his fingers, an Indian print handkerchief neatly tucked in his breast pocket, spats, a lightweight Malacca cane. On the street his hat seemed to float in a straight line through the air while he ran under it with his body and stomach hanging forward and his legs making hurried little steps a little too late to catch up.

His voice was high and unreal, as if it were in a long hollow corridor; he always sounded his 'Mimimimimimi' while washing his hands and putting his clothes away, the coat over a hanger and hook, the hat lifted with both hands so it would not lose shape, the cane leaned against the wall; then he would look at hat, coat, and cane, arrange his hair with a little silver folding comb, clear his throat, and be ready to draw.

The first day he watched the others unfolding their easels, tacking on the paper, and scraping the charcoal. Then he did all this himself, as if he had been here a long time. He hummed most of the time, and during rest periods looked at his work with much satisfaction, walking away from it with his hands in his pocket and hanging a few ladders of notes here and there on the air, infrequent trumpetlike blasts of melody – 'Meheheheheh, baba boobo mehmeh.' After that he cleared his throat again, into a second handkerchief which he carried in his inner coat pocket, and went back to work.

The second day Thaddeus wanted to show him how to divide his paper and measure correctly, but the singer took both his hands and led him away from the easel. 'Lieber Meister,' he said, 'dear Master, I don't know what to make of it, how to explain it to myself, this talent, which I have never suspected in myself. Singing, that is hard. Years, bitter years of study and discipline, but this, why' – his voice rose and he whipped up on his toes – 'it's play, fun, effortless amusement, pure and simple. I can't explain it, but that's how it is.' Thaddeus walked up the stairs into his bedroom to laugh.

The art of the singer consisted of coming close to the model, walking around her, and taking her in with his clear baby-blue eyes. He stepped back when he was done with that and picked out the angle from which he wanted to draw her; that was always from the front, a little to the right. To this place he moved his easel. Then he stepped back again, closed one eye, and started to draw the outline of one breast, the lower half-circle; then the other breast, the second half-circle; then he sharpened his charcoal again. It was usually time for the first rest for the model.

When she took the stand again, he checked the measurements; then he walked close to the girl and inspected her bosom as a doctor would, stepped back to measure again, and finally, having found the right position, drew the nipples and aureoles carefully into the centre of the two half-circles. The drawing now looked like the lower halves of two targets, except that the line was wobbly, thin here, thick there.

In the third session, he shaded the two half-globes with a smudge-stick and his finger, and this kept him busy for two sessions, which included also a little rubbing out of impossible highlights with soft gum. That done, he blew fixative on his work and rolled it up, to take it home with him. After washing himself very thoroughly while singing 'Mehmeh,' he carefully buttoned his overcoat, smoothed out the silken muffler, held his hat up with both hands, stepped under it, and left.

Thaddeus finally drove him away. One Monday morning the opera singer arrived to find on the model stand an Indian brave in full war regalia. He took one look at the model and left, not to return till the next Monday, since he knew models were hired by the week. But the next Monday we had posing for us a Russian wrestler in a tigerskin. This time the singer showed some annoyance as he left for another week. But the third Monday brought him to the end of his patience. Thaddeus had really gone too far: We had on the model stand a young German posing in a Lohengrin costume, in fact in one of the important roles played by our singer at the opera. Thaddeus was watching out of the window up on the balcony and the students were biting their knuckles behind their drawing boards when the singer ran up the stairs, shouting that he was sick of it. Was this an art school or what? He was leaving and would never come back again!

LIFE CLASS

*

Another student was Clarita, as she insisted that we call her, very rich and, though under the strong lights she looked a little tired, still handsome and desirable. Beautifully dressed, with well-taken-care-of hair and hands, she arrived in a loose mink coat which she wore like a bathrobe, dragging it after her, throwing it around, and sitting on it. She had a little chauffeur in tight breeches, a visored cap, and black puttees, who drove her about in a black and silver Rolls Royce town car.

Clarita was very friendly and jovial. She would look at the work of all the pupils and laugh with them, but she did not work from the general model. She had a corner of the studio to herself, shut off by a large screen. But before she retired to her work behind it, she would stand before the tall mirror, throwing her head back and loosening her ginger hair with widespread fingers. Then while she told about last night's party, she slipped off her bracelets, lit a cigarette; stepped into a pair of Mexican huarachos, and put on a pair of white overalls of which her chauffeur brought a newly washed stack every Monday.

When she finished a painting – she worked only in oils – she would whistle for her chauffeur and drove off with him, sitting beside him in front, for a shopping tour of Greenwich Village. She bought brass candlesticks, thick, old, leather-bound books, ceramics, hammered copper bowls, sometimes flowers, loose or in a pot, an antique children's rocking horse, old maps, sometimes fish, a lobster, odd bottles, a petroleum lamp, and old frames. From one such trip she came back with a truck that carried a window frame, a length of fire escape, a carpenter, and a load of bricks. She helped to carry in the bricks, a cigarette dangling from her lower lip as she bent over them, and she had them built around her window frame, with the fire escape fastened against the outside and a pot of flowers standing on the inside. The chauffeur had to lean out of the window and pose as a tired working man and in the rest periods she sent him out for yellow and red electric bulbs so that she could get the right light for a setting sun.

She worked hard, holding her brush at the very tip, standing off from the scenery to measure it with squinting eyes. It usually took her three days to finish a painting; then another picture was immediately set up. She gave away most of the properties, but the paintings disappeared as soon as they were dry. She never asked anyone for an opinion, not even Thaddeus. She came here simply for the atmosphere of the studio.

'And what does she do with the pictures?' I asked Thaddeus. 'She sells them,' he whispered with awe. 'To magazines.'

Whenever a student brought in a reproduction of one of her paintings, Thaddeus would cover up his eyes and shout: 'Take it out, out with this Schweinerei.'

Clarita's husband was on the Board of Directors of several corporations, among them that of the publication which printed Clarita's pictures in four-colour offset lithography.

Thaddeus was a splendid teacher. Many of his students were poor and paid him no money, but he was equally attentive to all of them. He would go rapidly from pupil to pupil, explaining constructions, pointing out a wrong line, sketching large graphic models of nose, lips, ears, to help them understand. He never made fun of a student no matter how bad the drawing. To a man in front of a sheet of paper containing a scribbly design of a broken stick with five fingers on the end of it, he would say slowly: 'Look, it's an arm; its bones are here and there, here they meet; here is muscle; here are veins and ligaments; this is soft shoulder; here is a joint – you can lift a rock with it and throw it, you can scratch your back with it, push the hair back from your forehead, lean on it, you can talk with it and with the fingers on the end of it. Think about all that, and try again.' If, after all the trying, nothing came of it, and the pupil was not a beautiful girl, Thaddeus told him quietly and definitely to go and try no more, that it was hopeless.

My happiest moment every morning was when I came here from the hotel. I felt as if I had come on a little vacation to the mountains. Thaddeus spoke my language, he understood me and offered me a refuge from the hotel. Here was freedom and integrity and good work. All my troubles would leave me on the ride down to the studio. But also this work was making my other life, the life of the Splendide, tolerable, for I was learning to see.

For in the hotel too there is design; not in its elegant rooms, not in the fashionable people, but in the shoes of Otto Brauhaus, in such guests as the wife of the Steel Judge, in our frightened old waiters, in the hands of cooks – fat fingers sliding around the inside of pots buttering them, sitting together on a carrot and slowly feeding it to the chopping knife. There is colour in the copper casseroles and in the back of Kalakobé, the Senegalese Negro who scrubs them in a white-tiled scullery.

All this I was learning to see for the first time as I spent my mornings in the studio, and that is all I did there. For I never drew a line in that art class. I couldn't. I saw my picture clearly, simply; I saw it finished with my line and with my colours; but the moment I started to draw, a paralysis overcame me; the fear of doing it wrong made a knot of me inside.

Thaddeus understood this; he had looked at all my work before I came to his school; he knew my problem, and he said: 'Just sit and look, drink it up and don't worry. It will form itself. It is finished inside of you. I can't help you much, nobody can. The colours, the design, the line, are all of your own, you yourself must get them out.'

This was a bitter pleasure, a fragile, glasslike feeling. The urge to give something form would run down to my elbows or my wrists and get stuck there the moment my hand tried to work. But sometimes in the middle of the night, or at a moment when I was not thinking of effort, as when I waited for an elevator in the hotel and was scribbling something simple on the wall – a chair, a table, a shoe, a face – then it was suddenly there, right and good. I needed no one to tell me that it was so. But down in the studio I would be frozen again. Though I watched the model for three hours every morning and could draw her from memory, I was never able to break the spell.

8. The Brave Commis

IN THE locker room next to mine in the waiters' dressing room hung the clothes of Robert, a young French commis who worked in fat Monsieur Victor's restaurant. This young man had a dream; for every waiter, like every prisoner, has a dream. With the older ones it is about a chicken farm, or becoming rich through an invention, or various small businesses, or a return home to a little house and peace; with relatively few is it a hotel or a restaurant – of this they say: 'Sale métier, filthy profession.' But the young ones have more daring dreams: becoming an aviator, a detective, a movie actor, an orchestra leader, or a dancer; and because the French champion prize fighter is visiting America, this young blonde commis de rang is going to lead a very healthy life and become a boxer.

He has the boxer's picture pasted up on the inside of his locker door; he does not eat stews and dishes that are made with sauces; when he comes down with his chef to the employees' dining room, he brings that man's food, but runs up again for plain vegetables, cheese, and a cutlet for himself; he drinks no wine and empties a quart of milk into himself at every meal. He arrives at the hotel in a trot, his fists at the sides of his chest; he has come all the way down Fifth Avenue this way after a short run through the park. In the locker room he makes a few boxing motions – l'uppercut, le knockout – dancing and twisting his head and then with a loud: 'Ah, brr, bhuff,' and: 'ça, c'est bon,' he takes a cold shower. He has immaculate linen, fine muscles, and he brings his chest out of the shower as if it were a glass case full of jewels. He takes a shower after all meals, rubs himself down afterward, and then sits in his undershirt in the employees' barbershop, reading books on boxing and arguing with Frank, the American engineer, about who knocked out whom, when, and where.

Up in the restaurant he looks fine, first because he is tall and handsome, secondly because he stands straight and the mess jacket and the long apron look good on him, and thirdly because he is always clean. Victor likes him because he is always smiling and is as quick as lightning. He takes the stairs up from and down to the kitchen – thirty iron steps, of which every other man complains – as if they were built for him to train on. He makes the run up in two seconds flat, pushing four steps at a time from under him and flying past the heavily loaded older men so that he almost upsets their trays. They stop and curse him, but he laughs back over his shoulder, takes a stack of hot plates out of the heater, and worms his way to his station through the crowded dining room with an elegant twist. To reward him, when the visiting French champion comes to the restaurant with his friends, he is seated at the young commis's station and gets service such as no one else receives.

Victor has also promised the young man a future: he will make him a chef de rang at the next opportunity, then in a little while maître d'hôtel. Men so engaging, so fine-looking, who, moreover, know their business well and are quick-thinking and intelligent, are few. And he is a Frenchman, and so does not underestimate the value of such a future and the advice of Victor. He is, besides, very sober in his estimate of the boxing profession. He will try it while he keeps one foot in the Splendide. If all goes well, if he should be another champion, fine. For lesser rewards, no. Meanwhile he will have had fun, and acquired a well-trained body, which is a good possession, especially since most maîtres d'hôtel and managers are fat, bald, pale, and flatfooted. For one so youthful he shows much good sense in his planning.

He asked me once to go to the Young Men's Christian Association with him. This institution seemed to me far from a benevolent undertaking. The commis had a miserable cell for a room and paid well for it; the walls were covered with invitations to various pleasures and benefits to mind and body, always with the prices clearly marked. The quarters were crammed and so were the pools and gymnasiums. The walls needed painting and the runners were shaggy and worn. The guests were nice clean-cut earnest boys who wished to get ahead, but the atmosphere of the place, I thought, was commercial, unhospitable, and false.

The commis introduced me to the gym instructors with the casualness of an old habitué, and for my benefit he put on a little boxing show with one of them and with a ball suspended from a parquet board, which to me, who understood little, seemed very good. When it was time to get back to the hotel to set the tables for dinner, he took another shower and we arrived at the Splendide in a hurry. I was out of wind and perspiring but he took his shoulders out of his narrow athletic undershirt and asked me in loud French to tell those others what I had seen this afternoon in the way of 'le boxe'.

The brave commis did finally become a chef de rang with a good station, being jumped over the heads of several older men. He made very good money, but more of it went into boxing, and he became stronger and stronger. Because he was such a good, swift, smiling waiter, he received some of the most difficult guests, and one day during a rush he had to serve a man who was generally feared, for he had had many men dismissed. Mr. Mistbeck, a blanket manufacturer, lived in the hotel. He should never have been allowed in the hotel at all, but he had millions. He was on some kind of diet, and everything had to be cooked for him without salt or sugar; a long list of how his food was to be prepared hung down in the kitchen. Also he had his own wines and his own mustard; he mixed his own salads; and all this, in the middle of a rush, was always difficult. The cooks cursed; there was sometimes delay.

Mr. Mistbeck then became abusive. He knocked on his glass, shouted: 'Hey,' or 'Hey, you,' said: 'Tsk, tchk, tchk,' or 'Psst', and pulled his waiter by the apron or the napkin at luncheon or by the tail coat at dinner. His wife, a little frowsy, scared, but kindly woman, would try to calm him. That only made him madder; he spoke so loud that the people at the tables around him looked up in surprise; his face turned red and blue, and a vein on his forehead stood out; he moved the silver and glasses, bunched the napkin into a ball, pounded on the table, and sometimes got up and walked to the door, his napkin in his hand, to complain to Victor.

His complaints always started: 'I have been coming here for the last five years, and, goddamn it, these idiots don't know yet what I want, you charge enough in this lousy dump!' Or it would go: 'Listen, you' – he held the waiter while he said that – 'listen, you old fool, one of these days I'll buy this goddamn joint and fire every one of you swine and get some people that know how to wait on table; now get going!' With that he would push the man loose. During these embarrassing moments, his poor wife would turn red and look down on her plate and behave as if she were not there. When the waiter was gone, Mr. Mistbeck would continue to shout at her, as if she too had kept him waiting or brought him something he did not like.

One of the dreadful things about the hotel business is that it offers no defence against such people. The old waiters who have families just mumble: 'Yes, sir. No, sir. Right away, sir. I'm sorry, sir.' They insult the guest outside the room, on the stairway down to the kitchen; that is why one sees these poor fellows talking so much to themselves – they are delivering a long repartee and threatening to throw out some imaginary customer and telling him what they think of him. Sometimes an incident will rankle for days afterward, and they will continued to mumble tremblingly at a pillar, chair, or through a window out into the street. One can tell from their faces what they are saying, and it usually comes to an end with the swish of a napkin or the quick folding of arms. It is also then that they don't see an upraised hand or hear a call.

Mr. Mistbeck sat at the station of the new waiter, the former brave commis. He was for some reason even unusually abusive, nothing suited him, and finally he pushed back his chair, threw away his napkin, and, getting up, took hold of the young man's lapels to deliver his usual speech. Now the brave commis could not stand being touched; his hands leaped up in fists. In a second, Mr. Mistbeck had l'uppercut, and le knockout, and had fallen into his chair with his arms hanging down, his face on his fork, and his toupee on the floor.

That ended the Splendide career of the brave commis for some time. Downstairs he was congratulated by all the waiters; in the barbershop he had to show Frank the engineer just how he had done it; and Victor gave him a good recommendation. 'When this blows over,' said Monsieur Victor, 'you come back here.' It blew over soon; in one month the employees celebrated the demise of Monsieur Frank Munsey and of Mr. Mistbeck, who died of apoplexy.

9. No Trouble at all

ON THE occasion of Mr. Brauhaus's birthday, in the inner, intimate circle of the Elite Headwaiters' Association, or at an outing such as the excursion of the maîtres d'hôtel to Bath

Beach – on such parties, when a sufficiently large and important audience was available, the thin Monsieur Victor sooner or later found someone who asked him to tell the story of the world's greatest maître d'hôtel.

He prepared the scene for this piece by describing the fabulous Cocofinger Palace Hotel, in which this great maître d'hôtel functioned, as an institution so vast that the potagier used a motorboat to put the noodles into the soup. The story itself went like this:

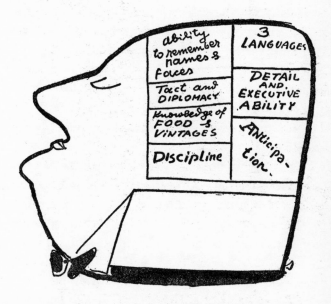

The world is full of maîtres d'hôtel, many of whom are able, well-informed men. But only one in a hundred thousand is blessed with that rarest, most priceless of qualities so generously evident in Gabriel, the Maître d'hôtel of the Cocofinger Palace Hotel in New York.

We see this peculiar talent in the profile above, behind the ear, under 'Detail and Executive Ability'. It is the faculty of 'Anticipation', an astral clairvoyance with which to sense catastrophe anywhere in the wide realm of his authority. Not only to feel it ahead, but to prepare for it, and minimize the effect thereof.

One more look at the graph and it is evident to anyone why, with such talents, Gabriel has come up, up, up, from the position of third piccolo at the humble Red Ox Tavern in Obergurgl, through the pantries and over the red carpets of Madame Sacher's, the Negresco, Shepheard's, the Meurice, Claridges's, up to the golden doors of the restaurant of the hotel of hotels – the Cocofinger Palace in New York.

Gabriel smokes Dimitrinos, he has twenty dozen shirts, he thinks in French, his hats come from London, and both Noel Coward and Cole Porter have asked him who builds his faultless tail coats.

To his many subordinates, he speaks through his assistant, one Hector de Malherbes. Between the Maître and Malherbes is perfect, wordless understanding. Never were Gabriel's great talents and the mute felicity of Malherbes more clearly demonstrated than on the night and day of February the twenty-fifth, 1937.

On that Thursday at three-fifteen in the afternoon, when the last luncheon guests had left, Gabriel leaned on his desk with its seven drawers, one for each day of the week, and nodded gently to Malherbes. Malherbes bent down to the drawer Jeudi – because it was Thursday – and took from it a salmon-coloured folder with a sulphur label on which was written: 'Birthday Party, February 25, 1937, Mrs. George Washington Kelly.'

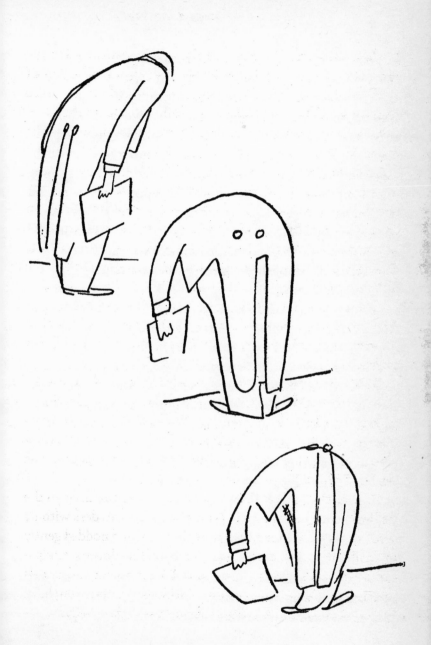

Gabriel carried the folder up to his room. Malherbes bowed and left. In his room Gabriel took off the faultless tail coat which was rounded from much bowing, hung it up, sat on his bed, and carefully unfolded the bills that five-, ten-, and one-dollar patrons had pressed into his hand. He added them up and entered into a little crimson book: 'February 25, Déjeuner, $56.' Then he took off his boots, leaned back into the pillows, stretched his toes in the sheer black Sulka silk socks, and opened the salmon-coloured folder.

Madame George Washington Kelly was a very difficult and exacting client. The Italian waiters called her 'bestia', the French 'canaille', and the Germans 'die alte Sau'. She had a desperate countenance, partly concealed by a veil; behind this her face shone the colour of indigo. Her skin had the texture of volcanic rock seen from the air with dirty snow swept into the crevices.

She dressed with complete immunity to fashion, except for the Beaux Arts Ball. On the night of that elaborate affaire she had come with her friend, the 'Spirit of the Midnight Sun', and together they had engaged the rooms and made the preliminary plans for his birthday party, of which Malherbes had said to Monsieur Gabriel in sotto voce French, 'It is not a birthday party – it is a centennial celebration.' Gabriel had stared him into silence.

After many more visits and consultations with architects, stage designers, and florists, Madame had decided to build at the end of the ballroom a replica of her Miami retreat, 'O Sole Mio', in its original noble dimensions. This was to be set among hibiscus, poinciana, and orange trees in bloom, surrounded by forty three-foot royal palm trees and fronted by wide terraces.

Cutting through the centre of the room, from the terrace on the north to a magnificent flight of stairs on the south, ran the lagoon, filled with real water, and in this water was to float the genuine gondola which Mr. George Washington Kelly had brought as a souvenir from Venice and taken all the way to Miami. The stairs on the north end rose to a balcony; from there, a birthday cake was to be carried down, placed on the gondola, and rowed across to Sole Mio, where Mrs. Kelly's own negroes would bring it to her table to be cut.

The gondola was in Miami, also the royal palms, also the four white-haired negroes, brothers named Morandus. The Fire Department had sent a captain to study the position of the hydrants and windows, to connect a pumping truck, and to fill the lagoon, which it was estimated would take fourteen hours.

To do all this properly, the complete entertaining facilities of the Cocofinger Palace Hotel had been rented for a week ahead of the party and a week following it, to clear away the debris. Mr. George Washington Kelly was many times a millionaire.

Since Monday of the first week, the Cocofinger Palace had been filled with draughts from open doors and windows, with tall ladders and empty smilax crates. Careless carpenters, careless stagehands, and careless plumbers and florists ruined the peace and the carpets of the hotel with hammering, riveting, and soldering together the two-hundred-foot tank that was to serve as the lagoon. Following on the heels of the plumbers came the painters, who painted the sides of the lagoon emerald green and put a pattern of underwater scenery on its bottom. An eminent artist from Coral Gables supervised this.

The menu for this party was dictated by Madame herself,

without benefit of Gabriel's advice. It was in the tradition of her entertainments and composed itself – at twenty dollars a cover for four hundred guests – of the following: Caviar aux blinis, bortsch, homard Sole Mio, faisan Miami, purée de marrons, pommes soufflées, salade Georges et Marthe, bombe Washington, café.

For the one thousand five hundred additional guests for supper, she had chosen an equally unfortunate repast. This, at ten dollars a cover, consisted of velouté Marthe aux croûtons, poussin en cocotte Washington, nouilles polonaise, petits pois parisienne, bombe Sole Mio aux fraises cardinal, gâteau Georges, café.

Breakfast was to be served from four o'clock, at two dollars and fifty cents a person. Provision was also made for eighty

musicians' suppers, suppers for chauffeurs, maids, the secretaries at the door, and the announcer and the detectives, at one dollar a person.

Cocktails were to be served during the reception: a fantastic violent drink of Madame's own invention, named 'High Diddle', the most secret formula for which Madame fortunately gave to no one. Closely guarded, her trusty servants – the Morandi – were to mix this, bringing most of the ingredients themselves from Florida.

After Gabriel had read the papers thoroughly and made several notes, he rose, looked into the mirror, and took a loose smoking jacket from his closet. He slipped on a pair of white gloves and walked below. Malherbes was waiting for him. It was six o'clock.

Gabriel nodded, and his assistant followed him with a silver pencil and a morocco portfolio.

They walked through the kitchen, where the cooks fished red lobster out of steaming casseroles and chopped them in half. From there they went to the cellar; here, men broke open cases of Cordon Rouge 1921 and put them away in tubs. From here, they walked up to the ballroom proper. The tables, seating eight guests each, were set to the left and right of the lagoon. Sole Mio was finished, and on the lower terraces in front of it – as indicated on the plan – was the crescent-shaped table, facing the room. Here, Monsieur and Madame George Washington Kelly and their son George Washington Kelly, Jr., as well as their most intimate friends, would sit.

Two painters were busy pouring and stirring fifty gallons of turquoise ink into the lagoon, to give it the precise colour of the waters around Miami. The Coral Gables artist had left with

them a sample of that shade on a piece of water-colour paper, and from time to time they compared this and then added more ink. Up on the balcony of Sole Mio, two electricians were focusing spotlights across the room, up to a magenta curtain on the other side.

From the street could be heard the 'poooommmph, puuuuuumph, poomph' of the Fire Department pumping-truck which filled the lagoon with water.

Gabriel, walking into the hall, saw the last of twenty royal palms – in tubs, with their leaves carefully bandaged – being carried upstairs, and below from the street appeared the neck of the Venetian gondola.

The great Maître nodded to Malherbes. Malherbes ran down to the door and told the men: 'Watch out for the paint, you.' Later on, in the office, he made certain that a gondolier had been engaged. Yes, he had. He was to report at the ballroom in costume, with a knowledge of how to row the gondola and the ability to sing 'O Sole Mio'.

Gabriel went to his room, lit a cigarette, and rested in his bath for half an hour. Then he dressed.

As on every evening, so now, he received the dinner guests of the hotel at the door of the restaurant

Madame George Washington Kelly's party over in the ballroom was in the able hands of his third assistant, Monsieur Rudi, a withered onetime stableboy of Prince Esterházy's.

At regular intervals a courier crossed from the ballroom and whispered to Malherbes, 'The guests are arriving.' Then again, 'The cocktails are being passed.' After this, 'The guests are entering the ballroom.' Then, 'Madame George Washington Kelly is very pleased,' and on to 'The guests are sitting down,' and 'The soup is being served.' These bulletins were translated into French by Malherbes and whispered on to Gabriel, who nodded.

Dinner was almost over in the restaurant when Gabriel went into a little side room where, on a table behind a screen, a plain meal was prepared for him. It consisted of some cold pheasant cut from the bones, field salad with lemon dressing, and a plain compote of black cherries cooked without sugar. In ice under the table was his favourite wine, an elegant, slim bottle of Steinberger Kabinett, Preussische Staatsdomäne, 1921.

In the middle of the meal, before he had touched the great wine, Gabriel rose abruptly and quickly walked across the restaurant. Malherbes, who had eaten out in the second little room off the restaurant, swallowed quickly and followed him. Almost running, they crossed the entrance hall of the ballroom and went up the staircase, to the third palm.

Gabriel suddenly stopped there, and beside him, as always, stopped Hector de Malherbes. The dessert had just been served, the remnants of the bombe Washington were being carried from the room by the waiters, and, as set forth in the sheet of instructions, the lights were lowered.

Two heralds sounded the *Aïda* theme as a command to silence and attention.

The heavy magenta curtains sailed back, and high above the audience appeared the birthday cake. It was magnificent, of generous proportions and truly beautiful, the masterpiece of Brillat Bonafou, chef pâtissier of the Cocofinger Palace Hotel, twice the winner of the Médaille d'Or de la Société Culinaire de Paris, Founder and President of the Institut des Chefs Pâtissiers de France. In weeks of patient, sensitive, loving labour he had built a monument of sugar, tier upon tier, ten feet high, of raisin and almond cake. It was of classic simplicity, yet covered with innumerable ornaments that depicted scenes from a happy sporting life. Up and down the cake dozens of cherubim were busy carrying ribbons; these – Bordeaux and emerald – represented the racing colours of the G.W.K. stables.

But the most wonderful part of the wonderful cake was its top. There, complete in all details, stood a miniature replica of O Sole Mio, correct as to palms, orange trees, the lagoon, the gondola. Under the portico, an inch high, smiling, hand in hand, stood Monsieur and Madame George Washington Kelly: Madame with a bouquet of roses, Monsieur with his ever-present cigar, an Hoyo de Monterrey, at the end of which was a microscopic tuft of cotton. That was, however, not all. Over the miniature Sole Mio hovered a brace of doves. In their beaks, most artfully held, were electric wires, so arranged that flashing on and off they spelled first 'George' and then 'Martha', 'George' in Bordeaux, and 'Martha' in emerald green. Five lady midgets, dressed as the Quintuplets, carried the cake downstairs in the light of the amber spotlights.

An Hawaiian orchestra played 'Happy Birthday to You, Happy Birthday to You'. Everyone sang, and all eyes were moist.

The gondolier started to punt down the lagoon to receive the cake.

At that moment, with all eyes upon them, one of the Quintuplets, Yvonne, stepped on an olive pit, and turned her ankle. The cake trembled, swayed, and fell into the lagoon, taking the midgets with it. 'Fsssss-hsss', went the electric wires.

But where is Gabriel?

He stood under the royal palm and nodded quietly to

Malherbes. Malherbes lifted one finger and look-up at the man with the spotlight.

The amber light left the lagoon and raced up the stairs. Out came the trumpeters again and sounded the *Aïda* theme, the curtain swung open once more, again the Hawaiians played 'Happy Birthday to You, Happy Birthday to You'.

As if the last dreadful minutes had never been on the

watches of this world, there appeared to the unbelieving eyes of Monsieur and Madame George Washington Kelly and their guests and friends – THE CAKE again, unharmed, made with equal devotion, again the work of Brillat Bonafou, identically perfect and complete, with the scenes of the happy life, the cherubim, cigar and smoke, lagoon and gondola, and the lights in the dove-beaks flashing on and off, 'George' in Bordeaux and 'Martha' in emerald green; the new cake was carried on the shoulders of a new set of Quintuplets.

The miserable first set of midgets swam to the shore of the lagoon, scrambled out, and tried to leave the ballroom in the shade of the tables.

Gabriel hissed 'Imbéciles!' to Malherbes. Malherbes hissed 'Imbéciles!' down to the wet midgets.

The new cake was rowed across, besung, carried to the table, cut, and served. Not until then did the great maître d'hôtel leave the protecting shadow of the royal palm. Now he walked quietly, unseen, to his room; for, in spite of possessing every talent, and, besides, the gift of 'Anticipation', Monsieur Gabriel was a very modest man.

10. Easy Money

OCCASIONALLY, AFTER his regular hours in the Grill, Mr. Sigsag worked in the banquet department, and took charge of small dinner parties on one of the upper floors of the Splendide. In a private dining room large enough for a horseshoe table, covers for sixty people could be laid; with the aid of folding doors, it could be made small enough to accommodate a group of four in intimate comfort. This suite had its own serving pantry and its own complete kitchen. A chef, his assistants, scullery help, and a pantryman had to be there for even the simplest dinners. The staff which served there – the maître d'hôtel, the captains, the bartenders, the footmen – were chosen for their tact and good presence and because they were able to work all night long and be as awake at five in the morning as they had been at nine the night before.

The suite was frequently used for gay dinners and for instantaneous courtships. It was also engaged for the discussion of serious affairs. Men important in business or with positions of responsibility in Washington met here, and in the course of an evening a violent change often came on them. They arrived with dignity and they looked important and like the photographs of them published in newspapers, but in the late hours they became Joe or Stewy or Lucius. Sometimes they fell on their faces and sang into the carpet. Leaders of the nation, savants, and unhappy millionaires suffered fits of laughter, babbled nonsense, and spilled ashes and wine down their shirt fronts. Some of them became ill. Others swam in a happy haze and loved all the world.

On such a party, a drunken financier would throw one arm about a senator and hang the other arm around a judge's neck. Then the three would fall back on to a soft sofa. The financier would shout, 'Waiter! Hey, waiter – pencil and paper! Oh, where is that goddamned waiter?'

A waiter was nearly always right there, and he carried a pencil and a pad. On this pad he usually wrote his orders and, to facilitate service, he made a duplicate with a sheet of carbon paper, which he kept for himself in case of dispute. When a guest asked for a piece of paper, the waiter handed him his pad. But first he moved the carbon, ordinarily under the first sheet of paper, a few sheets back and tucked it well out of sight. When the guest had written his note and had torn it off, the waiter took back his pad and went behind a screen or out into the pantry to see what the guest had written. The morality of this did not bother the waiters. The tender plant that is morality does not thrive in a grand hotel and withers altogether in its private rooms. The information that they read was frequently of no value to them, but once in a while it turned out to be very profitable. The waiters were always hopeful. Sometimes, by means of the carbon paper in his pad, a waiter had access to information for which bankers and statesmen would have licked boots, and had it long before tense young men in Wall Street were rushing around with it.

If the party lasted long enough, it was not necessary to bother with the carbon paper in the pad. While certain of the guests were starting to make trouble and breaking things, there was always at least one who backed the maître d'hôtel, a favourite waiter, or the wine steward against the bar and said, 'Ambrose, I am going to make you rich!' Then he stood away and tried to bring the man's face in focus. 'Now, listen, Ambrose,' he said, and both his hands came down on Ambrose's shoulders, like two hammers. Ambrose's knees gave way and he was pinned against the bar. While he was down, he tried to pick up his benefactor's cigar before it burned a hole in the rug. When he came up, the guest hung his weight on him and said, 'Ambrose, I told you I was going to make you rich, didn't I? Well, I will,' and hammered him again. Ambrose came up for the second time, and then, slowly, thoroughly, as if for an idiot, it was explained to him what stock to buy and when to sell.

In this fashion, working as an assistant maître d'hôtel in the banquet department, I became rich several times. It was not unusual, after a small dinner, for one of the waiters to make a thousand dollars or a bus boy five hundred.

Information got in this way was closely guarded. The serving staff of the private dining room were used to making money, and they were not eager to share their privileges with the rank and file of the hotel staff. Only to von Kyling, the head of the banquet department, and to one or two close friends were they likely to impart what they knew. Nevertheless, such information occasionally leaked out. When a guest left one of these parties, the maître d'hôtel or a waiter would see him down the corridor, push the elevator button, and wait at a respectful distance. After the guest had entered the lift and laid his hat and cane on the seat, he sometimes came out again, told the elevator boy to wait, and for the tenth time repeated some piece of information to his friend. The elevator boy strained his ears, and next day the information was all over the hotel.

The Wall Street fever hit the banqueting department hardest. The waiters who work for banquets are more bohemian than regular waiters. They dislike steady employment and they are migratory workers. They are in Palm Beach and Havana after the New York season; they work in a club and play the horses in Saratoga during August; with the opening of the Metropolitan they are back in New York. They start and stop work at irregular hours and make irregular money. During the market boom it was hard to keep them working. But all the employees played the market, whether they had inside information or not. The conservative element – cooks, chambermaids, valets de chambre – invested chiefly in shares of Cities Service. Even Monsieur Victor caught the fever.

Once a week, on Thursday, a peculiar thin man, a Mr. Tannenbaum, came to the main dining room for luncheon wearing a dark, high-buttoned suit and cotton gloves, which he did not take off until he sat down. Monsieur Victor reserved the same table for him, week after week. He was immediately given a stack of napkins and a second table was put close by. On this second table the waiter put several alcohol burners and lighted them.

After Mr. Tannenbaum had tucked his gloves in his pocket, he took a napkin, opened it, and began to polish the silver on his table. He drew the cloth between the prongs of his fork, pulling it this way and that; then, with grimaces, he rubbed the knives and the spoons. Next, he wiped his water glass and the tumbler for his milk and looked through them, holding them up against the lighted chandelier. Last, he shined the plates. When all this was done he covered the glass with one napkin, the silver and the plates with another, and turned his attention to ordering.

The waiter whose misfortune it was to serve Mr. Tannenbaum was the old, meek, unexcitable Italian, Giuseppe. He was always at his station half an hour before mealtime and always there until the last guest had gone. He never forgot anything, never broke a thing, spoke to few people, and left the room only for a quick glance at the market quotations in the afternoon papers. Of all the waiters in the restaurant, Giuseppe was the only one capable of looking after Mr. Tannenbaum.

Mr. Tannenbaum lived on a strict diet of cereals, boiled rice,

celery, stewed fruits, and milk. His food was brought steaming to the side table and put over the alcohol flames before it was allowed to cool. His butter was brought in a special covered dish, his gluten bread wrapped in two napkins. All the time he was eating he watched for flies. His meals were almost a religious ceremony. Lights burned, silver shone, vessels were covered and uncovered or moved from one side of the table to the other. The ceremonial of the washing of the hands took place before he ate his compote of stewed fruit. Silent prayers were said by Giuseppe lest something go wrong and he be discharged. To this atmosphere of Te Deum and fetish, the ascetic countenance of Mr. Tannenbaum was entirely appropriate. It was the face of a man a few days drowned, his hair the colour of ashes.

At the end of the meal he added up the bill and frequently disputed prices; they were always adjusted in his favour. From the inside pocket of his coat he drew a fresh pair of white cotton gloves. When he had put them on he carefully arranged the coins he had received in change and gave Giuseppe the smallest possible tip. He never gave anything to the captain or to Monsieur Victor. Nevertheless, Monsieur Victor watched over him as over a sick horse. He hovered about Mr. Tannenbaum's table from the moment he was seated until he left the restaurant. The reason for his solicitude over this aseptic guest was that Mr. Tannenbaum had charge of investing the funds of a great university and of several large charitable organizations, as well as the fortunes of a few people who were almost God.

Monsieur Victor played the market on the information from the private parties; but occasionally, when Wall Street seemed too wild, he took a cab down to the financial district and was admitted to Mr. Tannenbaum's office. So sage was the advice he received there that in the late fall of 1929, when we read of a great many of our guests jumping out of windows and a great many others were beginning to talk to themselves in the street, Monsieur Victor rubbed his hands together with joy, was debonair with his guests and employees, and thought of building himself a villa on the Riviera.

Giuseppe, though, never received a word of advice from Mr. Tannenbaum, the most difficult of all his guests. Giuseppe owned a little house somewhere in Queens – one of a thousand exactly alike. In that house lived his Italian mother, his wife, and his two sons. Giuseppe had sent both boys to college, one to study architecture, the other medicine. Now that they were through school the old waiter felt his worst troubles were over, and he wanted to invest his earnings.

One of his guests, an official of the National City Bank, advised him to buy all the stock of that bank he could carry. Giuseppe did, and made money on it. A steel man who lunched at one of his tables told him to sell his National City Bank stock and buy U. S. Steel. He made more in that stock. His third piece of advice came from a woman who had persuaded her husband to employ Giuseppe's architect son. She told Giuseppe to invest in Postum the profits he had made in National City Bank and in U. S. Steel. Giuseppe followed her advice and it worked out quite well.

Naturally, the stockmarket interfered with the service of the Hotel Splendide. Waiters stood in line trying to get at a

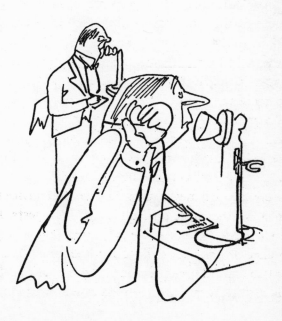

telephone to call their brokers. In the restaurant they collected in groups, where they discussed trends, exchanged market tips and advice, and shouted quotations at one another. They calculated profits on the backs of menus and they disappeared for long stretches of time, during which they sat in some out-of-the-way corner of the hotel, dreaming and planning what to do with their profits. Whenever the market was bullish, they became wild-eyed and nervous. A few hundred dollars to the good, they whistled in the pantry and ran up and down the stairs that led to the kitchen. At such times complaints from the guests increased tenfold. When someone asked a waiter why he had to wait so long for a slice of lemon for his fish, the waiter was quite likely to answer that he did not carry sliced lemons in his pockets, that he had to get them from the kitchen, and that he had only two legs and two arms.

One lovely day in June 1929, Giuseppe picked up a newspaper one of his guests had left behind and in the middle of luncheon went out to look at the financial page. He did some mental calculation and he saw that he was a free man with enough money to last him as long as he lived. When he came back he walked straight to Monsieur Victor, who was standing in the centre of the dining room. First Giuseppe took off his apron, threw it on the floor, and stepped on it. Then he made a loud speech in which he told Monsieur Victor what he thought of him. After that he spat on the carpet in front of Monsieur Victor's shoes, pushed an assistant maître d'hôtel aside, and walked out.

Monsieur Victor was so upset that he had to remain in his office the rest of the afternoon. He seemed inches shorter than usual. One eye stared out into the foyer. Toward evening he told his secretary to make sure that all the maîtres d'hôtel in New York were informed of this disgraceful affair, so that if Giuseppe ever came to them looking for work, he would be dealt with properly. The next day Monsieur Victor paid a visit to Mr. Tannenbaum. When he returned he said, 'Giuseppe will be back again – on his knees and crying for a job.'

He was right. In November Giuseppe came back, properly bent and broken, and as he stood before Monsieur Victor in the maître d'hôtel's office, he let the rim of his hat run through his hands. Monsieur Victor looked at him from his necktie down to his shoes, omitting the face entirely. When Giuseppe was asked to explain his scandalous behaviour, he made helpless gestures with one hand, dropped his hat, and picked it up. Eventually he squeezed out an apology that was almost inaudible. Monsieur Victor had to say to him several times, 'Speak louder, I can't hear what you're saying.' And after Giuseppe had finished, Monsieur Victor turned his head away and said, 'Mumbling won't help.'

Giuseppe went out into the pantry when the interview was over and suffered a crying spell. The waiters talked to him on their way to and from the dining room and later in the afternoon one of them went home with him.

Monsieur Victor let Giuseppe wait a week. Then because Giuseppe had been with the hotel for a very long time, because he was a very good waiter, and because Mr. Tannenbaum and the Dreyspools were asking for him and complaining about the man who had been put in his place, Monsieur Victor forgave him. He dictated an order against gambling, and, as he eventually took Robert back, so Giuseppe was on his old station again.

11. If You're Not a Fool

MR. SIGSAG took me to the motorboat show to show me a new cruiser, a powerful forty-foot boat that he had ordered. We climbed aboard and sat in the cabin; Mr. Sigsag could afford all this, because he had been promoted to the position of assistant to the manager of the banquet department.

'If you're not a fool,' Mr. Sigsag said, 'you'll come with me and be my assistant.' I told him that I had enough money to go and study painting in Paris for a few years. 'Never mind art,' he said, 'a few years of work and then you can study, go to Paris, Rome, and be independent.' He painted a picture of the Good Life to be found in hotels, just like Uncle Wallner's picture years ago in

Regensburg; and, like Uncle Hans, he also talked about art as if it were an affliction.

He explained how he had come by his new and different position as assistant to the manager of the banquet department of the Splendide. The manager, Joachim von Kyling, had watched Sigsag in the Grill and had asked for him; it was just what the Sage of East Aurora had always said would be the reward of Loyalty, Application, and Hard Work. Mr. Sigsag had been there a year now and was eager to share his luck with me. 'It's a gold mine,' he said. 'If you're not a fool, you'll come in with us.'

And so I became Mr. Sigsag's 'associate' in the banquet department of the Hotel Splendide and was known as 'Monsieur Louis'.

The most difficult part of the hotel business is the proper management of its banquet department. A restaurant is a song compared with it. A restaurant is unchanging, its chairs and tables stay in place, its function is to serve two or three meals a day, to a clientele that varies in numbers only little – with the days of the week, with rain and sunshine, summer and winter. The guests do not expect the impossible; they make allowances, and it is easy to adjust complaints.

But a banquet department is an ever-changing business. There are state dinners, weddings, concerts, anniversaries, coming-out parties, receptions – every kind of large and small celebration of an important day or event, and the givers of such parties invest much money in them. They have looked forward to the day of it, sometimes for years; they will remember it for the rest of their lives; look at photographs, old menus, programmes of it; talk, write, and think of it. It is therefore very important that absolutely nothing goes wrong. If the last and least-important guest is offended by an employee, thinks he is being neglected, or finds a piece of china or a splinter of bone in his soup, then the entire party is ruined. The host will forget all that has been good about it and mention only the bad.

Yet there are a thousand things to go wrong. Rooms have to be thrown together into suites and their arrangements set up and taken down with the speed of a circus performance. Employees have to be engaged in changing formations and numbers; one must know their abilities, their faults, their trustworthiness. Silver, linen, china, music, food, flowers have to be ordered, and during Prohibition wines and liquor had to be provided. The business of dealing with bootleggers, musicians, society women, and French chefs demands tact, sureness, and mostly patience.

All this work requires eight hours a day of solid thinking, and as yet only the preparations have been made. Then comes the conduct of the parties themselves, the actual work of bringing into existence what has been contracted for. And these two kinds of work overlap: while menus are being written and contracts signed in the office for future parties, the music is starting to play and a party is demanding close supervision. The work starts at nine in the morning, and ends sometimes at three or six the next morning. Mr. Sigsag is as pale again as he was as a piccolo. Monsieur Wladimir has not one unoccupied second in the day's long stretch. In his short sleep he twitches and dreams of parties, his lips move, he calls the names of waiters and guests, in joy or in anguish. He wakes up with a jump from the couch, where he has lain down for an hour in the afternoon, he has dreamt that the bower fell on the bride, that the ballroom was on fire, or that we had only one waiter for two thousand people.

The staff contained an old German bartender, Pommer, his two assistant bartenders, then twenty first chefs de rang who could be made maîtres d'hôtel, a secretary, and about thirty more good waiters. After those came an army of extra waiters, transients who worked in all the hotels and were engaged according to the needs of the party. Their number sometimes went up to three hundred.

The cleaning of the ballroom and its service rooms was the work of three housemen, who were also reinforced by extra labour. The head houseman was a quiet Italian, next after him was a Swede, and then came a German. There was besides a troop of sweepers and cleaners, little men, all of them Portuguese, whom Sigsag referred to as the 'Gnomes', only he pronounced it 'Genomies'. They really were like the little people who live under the roots of trees. They were always together, and always carrying something – a rug, platforms, palms, furniture – and, altogether in character, they ate in a low storeroom under the stairs in one of the ballrooms, and when they worked very late, they slept there on rugs. The Genomies spoke only Portuguese, and their leader translated everything to them out of English, which he understood only after he was shown everything with plans and drawings. The Genomies were also used for carrying wine, and breaking open the cases of champagne and whisky.

Prohibition had taken from hotels the most remunerative part of their business. The bars and wine cellars had to be cleared, and the immense foot-thick doors of the refrigerators, when opened, showed empty storerooms. All that fell into the hands of the banquet department. The hotel was reasonably safe from police interference. The services of the city's most reputable bootleggers were at our command; their trucks rolled up to our door without any pretence at camouflage; and cases plainly marked Champagne and Whisky were delivered in broad daylight. The policeman leaned on the ballroom door and watched them being carried in; for this immunity not a penny of graft was ever asked; it meant only a few drinks for the police after the parties were over, and a bottle or two at Christmas.

The business was a gold mine, as Sigsag had said. The profits on wine and liquor were of course high; we paid no rent; and the best people in America were our customers. There was no overhead; refrigerators, light, office expense, telephone, glasses, ice and waiters were paid for by the hotel; and a thick golden stream of profit ran into what von Kyling called 'the General Welfare'. This was the total sum of money which came together from profits in champagnes, from salaries, extra compensation for the long night hours, the generous sums the guests left after the party was over, the commissions on flowers, on music, on a number of lesser things. This then was divided, the largest part to von Kyling, the next largest to Mr. Sigsag, and the smallest third to myself. And along with the profits from the immense turnover of champagne – a hundred cases sometimes being used in some single party – there were of course liberal tips on how to treble that profit on the stock market.

Von Kyling came from Hamburg, but he never talked of his youth, except to mention that once he had done something very foolish. He had served his apprenticeship in Brussels and had worked in Paris and London. He had been manager of a restaurant on a large German steamer when it was interned in

New York, and since that restaurant belonged to the Splendide company, they offered him the post of banquet manager at their New York hotel. He knew his business thoroughly and had an excellent mind. Nothing ever happened while he was in charge that was not foreseen, provided for, or in time straightened out. Brauhaus left him strictly alone, for interference in so intricate a department would have been disastrous and, besides, under von Kyling's able management the banquet department was the only branch of the Splendide that made money. It made, in fact, tremendous sums.

Von Kyling had inborn good manners; he was at ease with the most important guests of the hotel and attended to the arrangements for their parties in person. He bowed little, had a good voice, spoke excellent French. He kept between him and the guests a protective distance without resorting to the tricks of puffy self-importance and preciousness employed by the maîtres d'hôtel in the restaurant to defend their persons. His face showed great kindness and humour but he would sometimes punish a subordinate for a mistake by falling into a moody silence and not speaking to him for two weeks. He was strict, but fair and honest.

In the centre of all the madness that went on all about him day and night, von Kyling walked steadily and had no temptations to live high. He kept his head in all emergencies and always remained an orderly citizen. He bought all his personal effects in the mass, watching the papers for sales and buying five pairs of shoes at once. He wore a dreadful kind of knitted underwear, a union suit that covered him from ankles to wrists, with a door in the back, because at a fire sale he had got two dozen of them for thirty-five cents apiece. He bought hats that way, too, and evening shirts in shops along Seventh Avenue that were about to close up. His plain suits were made by a little side-street Bohemian tailor. He loved the theatre, but he always sat in the top balcony seats and looked at the show through opera glasses that had been left in our lost and found department.

He never played the market. Once when we received a very good tip from the head of a large banking establishment, he bought fifty shares of Postum outright and locked them away. The day after, as he walked through the lobby, he heard a waiter telephone to his broker a selling order for five hundred shares of American Can. Wide-eyed, von Kyling took hold of the man by the coat and said: 'You are telling your broker to sell five hundred shares of American Can? Have you that much money?'

'Margin,' said the waiter. 'We all play the market. I made eight hundred dollars last month.'

'Who is "we all"?'

'All the waiters, the cooks, the pantrymen, the doormen—'

'You all play the market?'

'Yes, even the bus boys.'

Mr. von Kyling took his cheap hat and ran to his bank and sold his fifty shares of Postum.

Mr. Sigsag had his yacht, in a year I had a Lincoln, but Mr. von Kyling had a motorcycle with a side car. With this vehicle and dressed in a pair of breeches and a leather coat which he had bought at an Army and Navy store, he rode about the countryside. 'You sleep best on a small pillow,' he said.

He had his life clearly mapped out. He hated the hotel, the guests, and he had contempt for most of the employees, 'bowing, scraping, everybody's servants'. When the large coming-out parties kept him up late, and he was very tired and therefore friendly, he would lean over the balcony railing, and wave his arm over the room full of society eating their supper below him, and say to me: 'One more year, my boy, and then they all can scratch my back. One spoon, one fork, one plate, one glass, no guests, no visitors, no entertaining.' And after that he would go into his office and look through his farm catalogues. He counted almost the days when he would be out of it. He wanted a small place in the country, a little car, the furniture from his parents' home in Germany sent over, and to live simply and alone.

Von Kyling studied over the plans, looked up dates, and checked everything. Without him, Sigsag in his eagerness would have had two or more parties booked in the same room on the same evening, and only one orchestra on another night to play for three dances. To keep a clear head, von Kyling went home early in the evenings. Mr. Sigsag attended to the parties and, after I had learned the problems, I took charge of the staff.

Sigsag's attitude toward von Kyling was somewhat like that of a European son to an austere father, or an assistant priest who was helping his superior celebrate a service, or an interne watching a master surgeon operate – a mixture of respect, devotion, and friendship. He worried about von Kyling's health, about his business, about his having enough sleep or time for his daily walks. Every morning he made a small compliment from the hip at von Kyling's arrival, showed him his report, went over the correspondence with him, made several small suggestions, personally ordered von Kyling's breakfast, and, when it came, mixed cream and coffee, put the sugar into the cup, even stirred it sometimes, and lit his cigarette.

On the top floor of the hotel, next to the small private dining rooms, was an icebox. It was as big as a room and used in the summer for the service of garden guests. In the winter this was the banquet department's 'private' icebox. When at our big buffet suppers or wedding receptions there would show up something especially good to eat or drink, we would have it sent up there. We could, of course, at any time order anything we wanted from the kitchen, but it was nicer to have our own icebox; and when sometimes we all three accidentally met inside it, for we all had keys, nothing was said, though von Kyling (who was very fond of good wines and cold things, his only luxuries) would always wipe his mouth and leave, saying: 'Somebody should be in the office.'

When he saw something on the buffet he very much liked, he would say quietly to Sigsag: 'See if you can rescue that Westphalian ham, those trout in aspic, before it's too late.' That meant before it was too far gone, and such suggestions were law to Mr. Sigsag. The ham would disappear as soon as the music started to play and the people began crowding around the buffet. Mr. Sigsag would then run up to the office to report that everything was in order – in the icebox. Von Kyling would go upstairs, open a bottle of the best wine, cut himself a slice of pumpernickel, and have what he called a 'snack'.

There were always on the icebox shelves the most costly delicatessen: game pâtés, cold sturgeon, little Swedish fresh-water lobsters, and many ten-pound tins of Grosrybest caviar, the kind with the big smeary grey eggs. On the tiled floor were bottles of wine, of the best of those that had been rescued from parties, not routine wines or California bottles, but European vintages which our best guests had had imported themselves and stored in our cellars far in advance of their parties. Among Sigsag's constant worries was seeing to it that the icebox was always full.

One day at a coming-out party, before the service started, von Kyling went to the cellar to check the wine. Von Kyling had a bottle opened to taste it. It was a superb vintage champagne, and he said to Sigsag in confidence: 'I wish you could rescue a few bottles of this. This is the best champagne I ever tasted.' And von Kyling knew wines and was not given to speaking in large terms.

Now it happened to be a week before Von Kyling's birthday, as of course Mr. Sigsag knew, and these parties were usually supplied with twice the amount of wine really needed. So as Mr. Sigsag supervised the Genomies while they brought up the cases (marked with the name of the owner) early in the evening to be iced, he thought out a brilliant system of economy that would do honour to Mr. von Kyling's birthday.

At the coming-out suppers the tables of the host and his friends were always very close together, and next to them was the debutante's table. Mr. Sigsag took the staff list away from me, and directed the arrangements himself. At the host's tables Mr. Sigsag spaced the wine waiters close together, all good men and one to every eight guests. They were ordered to all but wash the tables with champagne, to keep the glasses filled to the brim. 'Remember,' he commanded, 'keep them filled up,' and they obeyed instructions so well that the host had to call Sigsag over and complain: 'For God's sake, stop these men from pouring the champagne like that. It's awful. Tell them to fill the glasses only half full. It looks terrible. Stop that man there. Look at him.'

Adjoining the tables of the host and his close friends was a second region, a ring of tables which the host could observe if he turned his head. At these the wine was served with somewhat less speed, but still generously, so that when a toast was called for, those in the second region could raise glasses that were filled to within two fingers of the brim.

On the balconies, in the smaller rooms, and down in the Jade Lounge, was a third sphere, where sat the young people. At these tables Mr. Sigsag had furnished smaller glasses, whose lesser size, however, would seem to the host the effect of perspective. Here on the outskirts of the party, the wine waiters were few and far apart. They had immense stations, one for an entire balcony. They ran around with empty bottles and shouted: 'Tout de suite,' 'Coming,' 'Coming,' 'Right back,' 'Un moment.' And they did come back – after a while and with one bottle. The kids shouted: 'Hey, hey – let's have some—' but the waiters were gone again. The youngsters had each received one half-full glass of champagne by the time supper came to an end and the dancing started again.

All this while Mr. Sigsag had been 'rescuing' champagne, and the Genomies had been taking it up a back stairs to the private icebox. Then Mr. Sigsag took von Kyling up there, opened the door with a proud smile, and showed him forty cases of champagne, besides three of Scotch and two of rye.

Von Kyling said: 'Are you mad?' He held Sigsag by the arm. 'I said rescue a few bottles!'

'Well, I thought, because . . .' Sigsag began, but von Kyling called the Genomies and stood there until the last case was taken down again.

Sigsag staggered around, crying and begging; he reached

after each case as it was carried out, and tried to bargain for twenty, for ten, for five, for at least one. 'For you, Mr. von Kyling, because it's your birthday.'

'We'll all be in jail on my birthday on your account,' said von Kyling.

Sigsag held his head. He started all over again; nobody would miss them; the host had plenty more, besides millions to buy all the wine he wanted; there were anyway twenty more cases downstairs to give back. Von Kyling was deaf. He made his worst face, the kind that usually lasted two weeks.

When the party was over, the host, as usual, asked for von

Kyling and said: 'Mr. von Kyling, everything was lovely. We had a charming time and everybody has complimented us. I don't suppose there is any champagne left?'

Von Kyling, also as usual, said: 'Just a moment, I haven't the final figures yet, but my assistant has. I'll get him for you in a minute, excuse me.'

Sigsag was waiting behind a palm. He approached them in the way he met all guests: little strings inside seemed to pull him into an abject, reverent pose; his stomach was drawn in, his head at a devout angle, the eyes humble. 'We have,' he stated, holding up the back of a menu, 'sixty cases still unpacked and six loose bottles of champagne, six cases of Scotch, four of rye, and about twenty loose bottles, besides some liqueurs.'

'What!' said the host. He had never before got back anything anywhere. We were obviously more honest than other houses. He called his wife. 'Listen to this, Consuelo. They have a cellar full of champagne left and, besides, here, read this.' He handed her the card.

Mr. Sigsag stood to one side, smiling and bowing.

'Impossible,' said the host. 'It's impossible, Mr. Sigsag. Why, I've never heard of anything like it. The way you've been pouring it out, too! I think it's wonderful. Look here, Mr. Sigsag, now you keep a few cases for yourself, and one for Mr. von Kyling, and of course keep the open bottles, and open a case for the men. I'll send for the rest tomorrow.'

He already had a cheque written out for service, but he asked for ink and wrote out a bigger one. Then he put his arm on Sigsag's shoulder and said: 'Now you go and buy yourself this stock tomorrow' – he wrote it down on the menu – 'buy all you can. I'll let you know when to sell it.'

If You're Not a Fool

There was much profit in this advice, enough to buy a freight car full of champagne. Besides, for his birthday, Mr. von Kyling had three cases and six bottles of very good champagne.

In the early morning hours, after one such rescue, when Mr. Sigsag had again done well for the General Welfare and the happy guests had departed, he walked tiredly up to the ballroom. There he turned and looked around. When he saw no one was watching him, he leaned back and yawned and then forward and rid himself of gas. Then, he saw two night cleaners carrying a rug – one in front, the other in back. They carried the rug like a huge snake between them. Each had an end of the rolled-up carpet on his shoulder. There was nothing unusual about this. The rug was a very expensive, golden-hued, Chinese prayer rug of which Mr. Brauhaus said whenever he saw it, 'Watch out for that Gotdemn roock. If anything happens to that roock, I'll kill you.' The night cleaners were carrying the rug very carefully but Mr. Sigsag became suspicious because the rug sagged in the centre.

'Put that rug down,' said Mr. Sigsag, and the night cleaners put the rug down.

'Unroll it,' said Mr. Sigsag.

They slowly unrolled it, and inside it appeared the top of an anniversary cake, a loaf of French bread, and a soggy napkin in which half a dozen broiled suprêmes of capon, Virginia ham, and mushrooms were mixed and tied up. There were, besides this, two quarts of Veuve Clicquot.

Mr. Sigsag put his hands on his hips. 'It is shocking,' he said to the night cleaners darkly, 'and disappointing – that people who are employed here for years and whom I thought I could trust, turn out to be common thieves. I don't mind if you help yourself to a drink or an open bottle – but to pilfer the guests' champagne. That is something else. Take these two bottles and bring them to the office. I shall decide what to do about you in the morning. This stealing has to be stopped once and for all!'

One of the night cleaners had a very small mouth. He picked up the bottles and said in sour tones, 'Monsieur, I don't think that we are the only crooks in this hotel.'

'What?' said Monsieur Sigsag to the night cleaner. He took the bottles away from him and carried them to the office himself and locked them up.

12. Coming Out

THE LARGEST, the most elaborate parties given in a fashionable hotel are the debuts. They brought prestige to the Splendide, and in all the newspapers were published long accounts of the decorations, the menu, and the number and names of the guests. Pictures of the debutante appeared in the fashionable magazines, and her debut at the Splendide was announced months ahead of, and described many times after, the party. The captions always read: 'Miss So-and-So, who is coming out on December twelfth at the Splendide', and, for a year after: 'Miss So-and-So, who came out on December twelfth at the Splendide.'

Such a party is very costly, and only people with a great deal of money can afford it. There is a standard for food, decoration, and music below which one cannot go, and the staff needed consists of about two hundred and fifty to three hundred men. The guests are in the neighbourhood of two thousand.

There are, during a winter, twenty or thirty coming-out parties, and at the end of them all, our men are half-dead; even the girls who attend them look worn out. A succession of parties, each lasting from seven-thirty in the evening until four or five in the morning, and requiring an additional two hours to get things cleared, leave about three hours' sleep for everybody. The housemen and the Genomies sleep on rolled-up carpets and on the felt covers of the large tables, covering themselves with used tablecloths and making pillows of old napkins. So do many of the late waiters. After they wake up, it takes an hour for them to come out of their stupor. They have to drink to keep going. Hardest of all works Mr. Sigsag.

Von Kyling gets home a little earlier than the others: one man must keep a clear head to supervise, to see that no fatal mistakes in booking are made. He has a hard time these days restraining Mr. Sigsag, who is always taking on additional parties. On the Sunday on which we might have rested he has booked a little wedding of forty people on the first floor and a dance of the Brooklyn Consumptive Relief League for the afternoon. 'It pays the overhead,' he says. Also the moment there is a room free, as for instance, after a coming-out dinner has been served in the Orchid Salon, he books it for the same night for a dance by a Hungarian society. It is then not only a strain to clear the room in half an hour of tables, carpets, silver, china, and to force draughts into it, to get the smoke out, but we must also calm down the Hungarian lady in charge of the dance who has arrived in the middle of the coming-out dinner and who will never believe that at the time at which the room will be hers, it will be clean, fresh, and properly arranged. During the rest of the evening it will also be hard to keep the Hungarians from running upstairs and trying to get into, or hanging on the edges of, the other party. But no matter how von Kyling cries, there is nothing to be done with Sigsag; he continues to throw everything out of gear, and even to bring in morning concerts or lectures on busy days.

The most brilliant parties are managed by a very highborn, virtuous lady of ruined fortunes who runs a 'social service' and blue-pencils the invitation lists for her clients. She receives a percentage from the hotel and a fee from the host and she comes several times before the party, bringing her hostess with her. Her general colour scheme is that of a dairy – cream-coloured dresses, lacy and negligee-like; yellowish-white hair; the ancient face powdered flat white; pale blue tile-coloured eyes; a butter-hued fan. Her voice is a précieux alto that stabs through the ears up to the back of the head. To von Kyling she speaks with a perpetual umlaut: 'Good Uevenueng, von Kuehlueng.' There is about her a cloud of perfume of a bitter musky scent, affected by many old ladies, and around her neck is tied a black velvet ribbon. When she calls during the day, she is dressed in a trotteur, and wears a hat with a thousand cloth violets, a Queen Mary toque.

This lady also engages the announcer and a stern man with white gloves who stands next to the secretary at the door, beside a little green-covered table on which lie two pads and pencils. The people without invitations are turned back here. We also have to supply men at all the doors, at the elevators, at every possible entrance and exit, but some of the young men get in anyway. It is this secretary from the 'social service' bureau who, after all the doors and rooms have been staffed, distributes the place cards on the dinner tables in the Orchid Salon. She has also removed the donors' cards from the hundred baskets of exquisite flowers hung around on the wall and has written on the backs of them the kind of flowers they came with so that the proper personal thanks may be sent.

The rooms engaged for a typical coming-out party – at a very high rental – include the entire public facilities of the hotel: the Orchid Salon for a dinner for the closer circle of friends, up to perhaps two hundred and fifty; the ballroom for the reception of the guests and for the dancing; the restaurant, the Jade Lounge, and the adjoining rooms for supper; and a little top-floor suite, connected with the ballroom by a high-speed elevator (usually employed for the bringing up of linen, ice, and glasses, but now with its scratches covered by a silken curtain), to which the host may take his elderly guests and where, at the best parties, a Budapest string orchestra plays, card tables are laid out, champagne and supper are served, and, if possible, the young people are kept out.

The rooms are rented for three days: one in which to build them up, another to finish them and have the party, and the third to tear them down again. For when the arrangements are made by an energetic hostess, she will often arrive with a squadron of orchestra leaders, architects, florists, and stage designers, and think nothing of asking us to move a wall or break down a few doors for such entertainments. Carpenters and plumbers hammer, florists run around. There is confusion and draughts through the house up to within three minutes of the party, and while the last painter and florist are being pushed out at the back, the first guests are coming through the front.

The hostesses try to outdo one another in decorations. For one party the suite will be clothed in soft silks and have not one sprig of greenery; for the next it will become a Southern plantation with old white-haired coloured retainers in livery imported from Georgia. For the third party it will be transformed into a replica of an Italian villa. Many ideas are beautiful, more are mad, and some are laughable, as, for example, the interior of a tropical cabaret in the south of France, which one woman in despair imported, complete with primitive murals, bamboo tables and chairs, artificial banana trees, monkeys, and an elephant-hide bar.

There were décors all in white, all in silver, all in gold. The famous palms of the late King Leopold of Belgium, every leaf carefully bandaged, were once brought in from Long Island, carried up the stairs by twenty men, and put into a Florida mise-en-scène, while forty florists worked for a day to wire oranges and blossoms into boxed trees.

In the restaurant the dinner for the ordinary hotel guests is still being served, while outside, in the pantries, a regiment of waiters is busy polishing glasses and silver and preparing everything so that it can be rushed at a moment's notice on to the tables of the coming-out supper. It is in the pantries too that the florists finish the centrepieces, and a half-hour after the last restaurant guest has left, the room has been ventilated, the tables completely set up anew, and rearranged according to the seating plan specified, together with the Jade Lounge and adjoining rooms – ready to serve the two thousand for supper. And in between all this, there is hardly time to change and put on a clean shirt.

The menus for the family dinners downstairs have usually been well selected and not too heavy, but the supper is and always will be a problem. The dancers are young and hungry, and therefore need something fairly substantial; but they want to get back to the dance floor as soon as possible, and therefore the meal must be brief. Hence the monotony of the menu: the eternal consommé, the small breast of guinea hen on Virginia ham with mushrooms, the small plain salad, and the dessert.

Coming Out

There are hostesses who have tried to be original at supper and recklessly substituted such things as Boston baked beans or corned beef hash. These only make the room smelly; such dishes belong in a tiled restaurant, in the daytime. However, supper is really not important, neither are the decorations; all that matters is the music and the dance floor, proper temperature in the ballroom, and the liquor. No one cares about the food except a few old people who have never forgotten their wonderful dinners of ten years ago. A ham sandwich would make the youngsters just as happy.

As for the liquor, it is under lock and key in the pantries, and the cases of champagne are broken open and iced under the watchful eyes of Pommer, the old German bartender, who directs the seeming confusion with sure, fast commands.

For the big parties there were usually three orchestras, of about sixty men each and of the best; a favourite one was frequently brought in from Washington. There was always a fight among the bands for the best side of the ballroom, and they also fought us for space. To satisfy them we would have had to give them half the ballroom and leave no space for dancing. We therefore always first built their platforms flat against the walls and so steep that the musicians seemed almost to be sitting on top of one another. Then when they tearfully begged us for just a little more room, we would let them out a few inches and make them happy. The bands always tried to outplay one another, waging a musical warfare that would grow fiercer with the night, and at the end of the party the men would be so excited that it would be hard to stop them.

These orchestras are efficient machines; their rhythms pound like the pistons of a precise engine while angry brasses yell the melody and violins sing a soft embroidery above them. There is a discipline and order here that is rare even in symphonic orchestras, a clean, mathematical rightness of musical ornament that is partly in the composition of the pieces but is mostly in the playing of them. I think it gives a clearer portrait of the 'American' than anything else. It 'clicks', it washes away all tiredness, it makes laughable any worry, it is a form of liberation. One cannot be in the centre of this magnificent machine and be upset about anything except the fear that the drummer may drop his stick. In one of the best bands there was a drummer who made such naked faces as he crouched over his instruments, who was so completely given over to his playing, that one was embarrassed to watch the revelation of the savage animal let loose.

The conductor of this orchestra was untiring. He had a cheap face, with something of the ape in it, and an overfriendly smile. Also he wore the typical musician's overcoat, a paunchy bathrobe of material such as Teddy bears are made of, held together by a wide sash with no buckle, tied around him; a derby went with this costume. This man had worked his way to the top; the young people insisted on him, and a party was considered dead if he was not there. He pounded the podium with his feet like a madman, smashing the rhythms through its planks and almost breaking them. He worked his men angrily, but no one could get out of an orchestra the sure, high sensuous playing he did. Many of his musicians were from the Philharmonic, and I never could understand how, after one of these sessions, they could be any good at another tempo. They earned a great deal of money, and deserved it, for they worked very hard and enjoyed their work. They all spent freely and most of them wore overcoats like their leader's and owned wire-haired terriers and smoked big cigars. They liked to speak of their wives and mothers and of their homes on Mosholu Parkway, or the Grand Concourse, or Myrtle Avenue, or the numbered avenues of Astoria, or in some apartment house with a magnificent name in Jackson Heights. Their leader was said to be a millionaire.

He was disliked by his men, and more so by our waiters, because he would never quit. At half-past three, and again at half-past four, he would play quiet pieces, and just at the point when the hostess had had to decide whether to keep him another hour, he would stamp out his wild favourites, shouting at his men: 'Don't die on me, boys, don't die on me.' During the soft pieces he had let some of his best musicians go out for a drink and a rest; at ten minutes to the hour they were back giving all they had in them. The party had meanwhile thinned, and there was more room to dance in, and now no one would go home. He always brought three shirts, collars, and ties with him, and we gave him a room to change in. He never drank or smoked; he played; and at the end of every hour the manoeuvre was repeated, if possible until six or seven. At three o'clock we served breakfast, but a 'good party' was one in which the guests went home in the daylight.

The supper was usually served at one. A half-hour before that, Frank the engineer came up to prepare the opening of the doors of the restaurant, the two wings of which were each forty feet high and twenty-five feet wide and folded back like a screen of immensely tall glass panels. When the supper march was played – sometimes thrillingly by a Highland troupe of tall, handsome bagpipers with leopard-skin aprons under their big drums – the dancers streamed down and overran the suites of rooms that had thus been thrown together. During the supper another orchestra played in the dining rooms while the dance musicians ate a supper, as good as the guests', down in the Grill Room. At the same time the chauffeurs and the maids who came as chaperones and who waited from eight in the evening, when their young charges came to dinner, until four or five the next morning, in the lobby or in some draughty entrance hall, with a French or German book, received sandwiches and coffee.

Upstairs the piano keys were being washed. They would be covered with a grey smear from the pianist's pounding, this sweaty soup reaching back between the black keys, and the board at the end of the keys was scratched from the scraping down of fingernails. A waiter walked around to look for forgotten fans, pocketbooks, gloves, and heels – a job I often assigned to old Gustl because among his other weaknesses he confessed to one for ladies' heels, which he liked to feel in his pocket. The housemen swept the carpets and the floor, and the engineers drew out the smoke and pumped in cold air, but not too much because the cold air would run along the carpets of the ballroom balcony, and from there it poured down two wide circular stairways and into the dining room, where the candles flickered and the curtain, if closed, swung up into the room. All this had to be remembered and done right, down to the detail of one supper that had to be served to the social secretary in her corner, with a glass of wine and a smile. Mr. Sigsag took care of that; he appreciated the worth of servants, butlers, and secretaries, to the point of sending a certain one a little birthday box of flowers with the compliments of the hotel on every thirteenth of June.

Standing on the bridge of the balcony and looking down, one could see a scene of unmatched elegance. First there was the brilliant arrangement of the rooms, in three descending levels – ballroom, restaurant, Jade Lounge – with wide spaces between them; even the service facilities were well-nigh perfect, for the architect had consulted the chef and the maître d'hôtel as to the placing of doors, kitchens, elevators, stairways, and pantries. The interiors, too, were not merely in good taste but also intelligently planned. The restaurant, oval in shape and large enough to seat four hundred people, yet had all the happy intimacy of design of that most beautiful of all rooms, the little silver-and-blue dining room of the Amalienburg in the gardens of Nymphenburg, outside Munich.

The blue smoke that hung over this scene, the sound of conversation, the hurry and the music, the shining glasses, and the happiness in the very young girls' faces made an exciting picture. The young people, men and women, were better-looking, better built, more fortunate of face, than any other race in the world. Some of the older of these Americans also had fine powerful heads, but best of all were the girls, with their young ready figures, their slender ankles, their lovely bosoms, their free graces. The faces of the boys were young and clean. There was little snobbishness in their behaviour, which showed the results of good kindergartens and schools. It was nice to see almost two thousand happy young people gathered together.

There was often trouble, of course. It started later, after supper, and could not be avoided, for, as in every large group of people, there were always several fools present. It was usually started by one particularly bad egg who managed to gather a few of his kind, and together they were brave enough to behave so that they had to be thrown out. That was one of the results of prohibition, for, though the boys were given champagne, they also carried hip flasks, out of which they and the girls drank awful liquor behind bowers and palms and under the stairways. And then the boys sometimes engaged in pranks that could be outrageously nasty, as when one of them, in what he and his friends thought was fun, horribly humiliated the inoffensive little man who took care of the men's room, making him cry.

We had a way of dealing with such young guests. It would have been unfair to let our men do it. They were here to serve; they would stay in this business many years; and the young men who performed such messy antics would grow up and inherit money, and, since they and the employees moved in the same places, sooner or later when they were drunk again, they would remember some humiliation at the hands of a servant and be in a position to pay it back. Luckily mostly nice people came to these dances, and among them were two young giants with big hands that hung down almost to their knees, icy bespectacled faces, and coiffures that were almost German – hair cut short and then worked back so that the top of it looked like a tight black shoe brush. They played football, in spite of which they hung much around the bar; but they could drink. We had promised them a bottle any time they wished to come into the hotel, if they would do certain little jobs of this sort for us. They enjoyed the work.

When a fellow got out of hand, we called these two. They smiled, said: 'Where?' and almost ran to their assignment. They would engage the troublemaker in conversation, hook their arms into his, and, with many pleasantries and wide smiles, carry him off. He couldn't do anything about it, for he hung in the air between them. Then he had a little ride in the elevator down to the basement. There they pushed him in the chest so that he sat up against the wall, and if he persisted in being fresh, they twisted his nose and arms and might even give him, if he had been particularly vicious, a thrashing that was a joy to watch. Then, if he was not quiet about it, we took him out to Officer Casey, who patrolled the street in front of the hotel and who did a little night-stick poking on his arms and back and the soles of his feet. Finally the young man was sent home in a taxi, and he usually stayed away from the next few parties.

It was remarkable how well the young men knew the hotel, better than the architect who built it. They would eventually find their way to the top floor, to the Budapest string quartet and the private bar for the older people, by riding up to the roof in the front elevator, crossing over through the maids' dormitory, riding down the baggage elevator, climbing up an outside stairway under the air-cooling equipment, coming through a door beside the ventilating ducts of the ballroom, and thus entering through the pantry. All at once a young man and his friend would be standing in the front of the bar, where he was not supposed to be. Then there would be two more of them, very polite, bowing to the old people, so that no one thought of throwing them out. Then there would be four more, then sixteen, and then they would get fresh.

Pommer, the bartender, was a strong tough man; he had to be. He had under his bar table a big wooden mallet with which he opened wine and whisky cases. This he would wave in the boys' faces, and tell them to go away, when they took glasses from the trays prepared for the older guests and held them in a ring in front of him. The young son of the host would be called and he would tell the bartender who he was, and order him to serve them champagne. Pommer would answer that he didn't care who the young man was; he had orders not to serve them. Then they would lie about their age, deny that they were as young as they looked, all the while pushing about the bar and egging on the son. The boy would threaten to go get his father, saying that Pommer would be sorry. Pommer would just look up at the ceiling and down again and tell them, please, to go away.

Once they pushed too hard and one of them reached over the bar and got hold of a bottle while the others kept Pommer busy. There was behind the bar a mop for soaking up spilled wine, whisky, and mineral water, and it was kept in a corner where the broken glass was pushed. Pommer was tired and nervous from the unbroken series of many parties; he grabbed the mop, swished it across the young men's shirt-fronts and faces, then took up his mallet and said he'd break their skulls if one of them came near. He looked so wild that they stood away out of his reach. The son called me and demanded that I immediately discharge the man. He shouted that he would tell his father about this, and then he would see what we would see!

When he brought his father back with him, he pointed at old Pommer and said: 'That's him, and there's the mop, and these fellows all saw it, and I asked to have him fired.' The father spoke to Pommer, shook hands with him, and gave him a twenty-dollar bill. The boys left.

Every morning, in the season, the house after such a party is strewn with wreckage, dirty dishes, and empty bottles. The party usually ends at five in the morning, and the musicians

COMING OUT

drink up the rest of the orange juice, tilting up the silver punch
bowl, as they talk and start to pack up their instruments.

    So I told the boss, do me a favour, put my name down
    Come on, you guys, break it up
    Hey, I got a car downstairs waiting
    I played for Whiteman, sure
    Why is an old maid like a tomato
    I know a better one
    I paid six hundred bucks for it brand-new
    She has one just like it
    I gave mine away
    I said to the old lady, what do you want to wear that
       one for, I'll get you a new one
    Well, so long
    Hey, coming, I got a car waiting

I'm going with him
Well, so long, if you want to stay all night
Come on, come on
High class
She has a sister works for the Standard Oil
No, I sold mine at 53

The keys of the piano are again sweaty when the lid is finally put down on it. The bass-fiddler goes up to put his instrument away in the locker which his union provides, along with an instrument, in every hotel, so that the musician need not carry the big fiddle around; and he takes the tape off his hands, for he seldom bows the strings for dance music, only plucking them. The lips of the brass-players are split. Even after the men are gone, the music still seems to go on playing.

Mr. Sigsag is busy collecting leftovers. No matter how tired his men are, they must help him save all the junk that can be rescued: cheesecloth draperies used in decorations, the stumps of candles, fancy lamps, Christmas ornaments, lost gloves and fans, branches of silver-sprayed smilax, empty cigar and cigarettes boxes and the tinfoil therefrom, champagne corks, flower baskets. Even the oranges that were wired to trees he collects at five-thirty in the morning. The cut flowers are placed in water in champagne tubs; the rest goes up to his museum, a room filled from floor to ceiling with boxes and shelves of junk.

When this is done, he leaves orders for the next day. The flowers in the champagne tubs are to be sent to friends, or given to the lady cashiers. In the middle of all this late work he sits down and writes out a rough draft of the bill, and checks over stubs, his face the colour of cold salmon. Under his desk, in a tub of ice, are some bottles filled with cocktails left over from dinner. He keeps them there for the scrubladies.

Officer Casey comes in to say good night, that is, to get a drink, his voice hoarse from his standing in the street. He is given a few packs of cigarettes, and he likes to go into the icebox with us when we get a little caviar for ourselves.

'Gee, look at that ham!

'Gee, look at that turkey!

'Gee, thanks.'

He wraps an extra slice of roast beef in a piece of bread and puts the sandwich away while his night stick hangs on the uppermost left button of his coat. Then he takes a second drink and goes home.

The doorman is the last person from outside; he has locked the doors and turned off the lights on the marquee. He gets a drink too, half a glass of whisky straight; he is cold from standing all evening in the slush and rain, the snow, or just the cold wind.

When he is gone, the old scrubwomen come out of the elevator; they live in a dormitory on the top floor of the Splendide. Mr. Sigsag has fallen asleep, sprawled over his bills and the next day's orders. One of the scrubwomen knows where he keeps the drinks for them; she reaches down between his chair and the desk, careful not to wake him, and pulls the bottles out of the ice. Then they rub their brushes on brown bars of soap, tuck up their shirts, take another drink, stick into their hair flowers that have fallen off young dresses, and sing Irish melodies while they start to scrub the marble in the ladies' room.

13. Cinderella and Santa Claus

MR. SIGSAG studied the New York *Social Register*, its changes in names, the people it dropped and admitted; he read with care the summer supplement of *Dilatory Domiciles*, and subscribed to a social journal called *Town Topics*. He had a copy of *Burke's Peerage* and the *Almanach de Gotha*. He wanted to become as proficient as Monsieur Victor, and held lectures on the importance of people, their names, their social position, and their connections; a fund of information he could lay aside the moment a fat Jewish wedding or a dinner for a society called the Manufacturers' Association came along. That's different, he said then.

CINDERELLA AND SANTA CLAUS

One can learn, he said, when he was in the *Social Register* mood, to tell people of quality the moment they walk into the room. They had to be treated differently and with the respect due them. And, as the sound of his name is music to every guest, so is the address by his proper title music to the Judge, the Senator, the Governor, and, in the case of foreigners, to the Count, the Baron, or the Prince.

Every Italian who entered the Splendide seemed to have a title – prince, conte, marchese, or at least commendatore. Even one of our dishwashers was a marchese, a real one. He was elderly and in very reduced circumstances, and his job was in the china department, where he carried plates from the big washing machine to shelves and arranged them there. He also unpacked new china out of barrels and checked it, made a list of the pieces that were broken in shipment, and put the pieces in a box. Along with all the other Genomies, about thirty of them, he lived in his Portuguese boss's boarding house, a condition of their employment. There they ate on their free days, drank their wine, and bought their cigarettes.

The Marchese arrived at the Splendide every morning and went home in the evening in a derelict fur coat, a garment lined with shabby rabbit and trimmed with Persian lamb, which was worn down to the grey skin at the wrists and buttonholes. The collar stood up around his ears, a smeary felt rather than fur, and he wore a beret. His suits were windy, dark, and beyond a tailor's help. The small narrow feet were stuck in cracked patent-leather shoes with cloth tops and little buttons. On the handle of his black cane was carved a yellow ivory borzoi with its front legs broken off; its rump was attached to the cane with a silver band.

He dressed in a little closet, away from the other men, between a column of china barrels and a partition. He sat on a homemade bench which he locked away with his clothes, and to keep his feet from getting cold he had a square piece of old ballroom carpet which he rolled up, tied with a string, and stowed away in his orderly locker together with his little bench. When he took off his trousers, he pulled around him a curtain he had made of discarded draperies; it hung from an old shower bath ring he had picked up from the rubbish in some corner. The little man never spoke of his past; he was never intimate and never leaned on anyone else with his troubles, or talked of politics, which was the main conversation of most of the men who worked here after they had lost money and position.

One day the City of New York gave a dinner to Count Galleroni, a visiting Italian diplomat, who brought with him a gift to the city, a great bronze reproduction of Michelangelo's *Moses*. It was very large and heavy, and many workingmen had to carry it into the lower entrance hall of the ballroom, where they placed it on a pedestal. The Marchese was very much excited; several times that morning he came up the circular backstairs to look into the ballroom. He watched the platform being built for the speakers' table, and the smilax crates being broken open; then he went down again, afraid of being ordered out. Soon afterward he was in the stair hall, reading the inscription on the statue, inspecting the seated Moses, and passing his hand over the prophet's drapes.

Later he came again to watch the silver, the glasses, and the linen being wheeled in. He had changed his day off with another man just to come in and see this. He helped a man outside stack the plates into the heaters, asked what the guests

would have to eat, and made himself thin among the rushing waiters, standing here and there, out of the way and behind the ovens, palms, and stacks of boxes of knives, forks, and spoons.

At two o'clock he appeared silently on the other side of the room where the wine was being taken out of cases and put to cool in large tubs. Asking for permission to examine the bottles, he read the labels carefully, held the red wine up to the light to look for sediment, and then carefully replaced each bottle. I gave him the seating list. He studied it with care as if it were for his own party, and asked where this or that table would be, and which person would be seated there, and he was happy, when the tables were finally set, to be asked to put the numbers on them and help in placing the cards. Then he got in the way of someone who ordered him out.

But he came back again and stood between a curtain and a

screen at the end of the ballroom, where I could see him in a mirror. The musicians had arrived and taken their places; some were tuning their instruments. A very smart police captain was pouring down a cocktail, after which he pulled on his white gloves. The chandelier and the lights all around the room were lit, the centrepieces had been carried in and a florist was sticking into each one little American and Italian flags. The Marchese stood looking on with folded hands, like a child that had been left out of the play of others. It was only then that I noticed that he was about the size and figure of Mr. Sigsag.

In one of Mr. Sigsag's dress coats, the Marchese with his shoes shined came into the ballroom with the rest of the guests in time to have a chat with several diplomats in the foyer.

I had put his name on the guest list and the seating chart, written a fine gilt-edged card for his place, and put him at one of the best tables. He looked around with the proper detachment, fished in the back pocket of his tail coat for a handkerchief, brushed his hair back with a narrow, elegant gesture, and regarded the other guests with the distance of a man of worth, fortune, and position. Slowly he came up the stairs, announced his name to the secretary, and saw it crossed off. The surprised maître d'hôtel who had driven him away earlier bowed from habit, made a face, and gave him the number of his table. I pointed him out and carefully pronounced his name and title to Mr. Sigsag, who bowed and repeated it saying, 'I know him, of course. I know him.' As he sat down, he pulled, as if he did it every night, his tails away from under him. He nodded to the other men at his table, studied the menu, and engaged his neighbour in casual conversation while he brushed his beard and played with his dessert fork, gestures I had never seen on him.

CINDERELLA AND SANTA CLAUS

He remained the evening through, to the end of the dinner. I was at times afraid he might get up and make a speech. He drank all the wines and the brandy. He applauded, but not all the speakers, with enthusiasm. He took only a small Corona, although three sizes were offered, and before he left he shook hands with, and spoke a few words to, Prince Potenziani. He took along with him the menu, his place card, and the two little flags out of the centrepiece of his table.

I passed his locker one evening shortly afterward. He was inside his shower curtain, whistling. I could see the little strings with which he tied his old-fashioned drawers running across the little carmine patch of ballroom carpet, and on the inside of the open door of his locker were fastened the menu, the place card, and, crossed under them, the little flags.

Just before Christmas, in the thickest part of the season, we served in our Orchid Salon, which now seemed poor and empty after all the great parties with their many orchestras, a dry, frugal dinner of some hundred covers. It was given by the head of a big financial house who lived in a suite up on the tenth floor of the hotel, with seven telephones, and two valets to put on his trousers and help him about. He was the fattest man I had ever seen and he bore the countenance of God the Father, a Falstaff god. His cheeks were rosy, his eyes blue; his hands, benevolently folded over his stomach, could barely meet, so that only the finger tips interlocked, presenting a row of wide fingernails. A white patriarchal beard surrounded this happy face, in which was a merry greeting, an advertisement of good cheer, peace on earth, and happiness for everyone.

That is, it was so when all went well. He had a thin sharp fellow inside him, who sometimes looked out through hardened eyes. Then the sun would go behind clouds; the thin fellow would rock the immense bulk from within and bend it forward. 'What did you say? A hundred dollars' rental? Why, you go right back and tell Brauhaus that I won't pay it, and that this dinner for seven-fifty is an outrage.'

There were then frequent trips up to the apartment, where the god could be seen being soaped in his bathtub, especially constructed for him, in his undershirt, in his bed. The rental charge was taken off, the dinner reduced to almost cost price. The godly Falstaff would then nod and beam with the double joy of a face that was twice as big as anybody else's, while he sat on the edge of his bed, his pants still unbuttoned, a valet putting on one of his shoes, a secretary fluttering about with data, telephones in his hands, and others ringing. One associates fat men with comfort and generosity, but this one was deceiving.

The estimates, the many changes in menu and their prices, are the preparation for a dinner which he gives annually to his employees. The floral decoration, two boxes of cut flowers ('Your men can arrange them in vases and put them around the tables'), are donated by a well-known florist who is a friend of his; another friend supplies a box of candies and assorted nuts from a chain drugstore. As for the drinks, 'Why, there's prohibition, isn't there? So let's have some ginger ale for everybody. How many bottles?' Before one can answer him, he has decided that one bottle is enough for two people. 'Put them on the table where they can be seen. Eight people to a table, that's four bottles on every table, and if any more are needed, then come to me, and I'll order them, but I won't pay for anything that isn't properly ordered. Tell your men not to accept orders from anybody, no matter who they say they are, you understand? I pay only for things I sign for.' After all the details are settled, the thin man inside goes – and God the Father from Wall Street is back again, smiling, asking a thousand questions and hardly waiting for the answers, about the number of waiters we employ, how many parties we serve, how old I am, what my salary is, and what I do to improve myself.

On the night of the dinner, he sits at the raised speakers' table in a chair especially constructed for him, between two high candelabra, and in the middle of a row of his executives. Before him is a gavel; he smiles down at all the tables, waving his hand to this one or that, and looks constantly around as he munches his donated nuts. The dinner is brief, and the least exciting fare we can offer. No cocktails, of course, and no hors d'œuvres; it starts with a glass filled with scooped melon, which is followed by a cup of hot consommé, a filet mignon with string beans and potatoes, a lettuce salad with Russian dressing, vanilla ice cream with marrons glacés, and coffee; a dinner ordered without care or imagination, and determined solely by him.

The dinner is served quickly; then the waiters clear off and leave the room while a man is stationed outside the service door to see that the pantrymen do not make any noise. There was a noise three years ago, and Falstaff has not forgotten it; if there is another, Brauhaus will receive a letter of bitter complaint the next morning. The host does not believe in dealing with any but the top people.

The speeches begin; they are full of advice and the promises of reward for honesty, hard work, and persistence. Mr. Sigsag, standing in a corner, listens with devout eyes. These inspirations last half an hour and are repeated by all the men who sit to the left and right of the god. It is a cheap, vulgar business meeting which properly belongs, if anywhere, to the paid working hours of these little people who sit beneath him, eat his miserable dinner, and have to applaud every one of his banalities. Toward the end of the dinner comes the event of the evening, the great Surprise, at which the god and his assistants have hinted during their speeches – the men who have this year sold above a certain amount of the god's commodity will receive a gold star, those above a certain lesser amount a silver star, and those who did well, but not well enough to earn either gold or silver, will get honourable mention and a few kind words of encouragement.

Each, as his name is mentioned, stands up, bows, and walks up to the dais in front of the Lord, an embarrassing procedure that makes a schoolboy of the man; he seems to stand exposed in his nightshirt. A few words are addressed to him, his reward is handed down, a sum of money in an envelope, all new, crisp bills. 'Don't spend it too fast, John, it's going to rain any day now.' Then come a few humorous observations on John's peculiarities, on his fecundity, for his wife is going to have another baby. The room laughs and claps hands; John looks down and grins, and then walks back amidst more applause. The boss picks up a few bread crumbs as his finger slides down the list for the next hero. 'Come over here, Harry, where we can hear you. Talk louder, don't be afraid.' Harry makes a speech of thanks, and a declaration of loyalty and admiration.

Printed sheets have been handed around; the pianist plays the office song, which has to do with the selling of their reckless commodity, to the tune of 'Smiles'. After this they have to sing others: 'There's a long, long trail', 'Pack up your troubles', 'Dixie'. One of the executives acts as leader and waves the time with the gavel. Half a gallon of orangeade is ordered to be served during the dancing. The authority to order more is transferred to the first executive vice-president. An unheard-of orchestra of six young boys appears to play abominable dance music, and the Lord, bowing, smiling, shaking a few hands, goes to the lift.

I took him to the express elevator, which was reached by walking through part of the pantry. There was no operator on this lift at night; anyone who needed it, ran it himself. That worried the Lord. He asked why I was running it for him, and whether I knew how, and whether the underwriters knew of this. He said he was going to look into it. I shot him up to the tenth floor.

He stamped his immense legs apart into the carpet of the long corridor, for he chafed easily; his valet was always powdering him. Because he was about to leave for his annual trip to a health resort in Battle Creek, he called me into his suite to settle the dinner bill right away, and ordered me to produce all his signed slips for checking. In advance he had set a limit of two gallons of orangeade.

A friend of his, who was going to Battle Creek with him, was waiting in the apartment, and while the Lord checked the bill, pencil in hand, the friend sat beside him on the bed and held the blueprint of a yacht. 'Two thousand tons,' he said, 'and I'll save a million by having it built in Germany. I'll never travel in a damned liner again, and have to get up at six in the morning to disembark in some lousy port. I'll make four extended cruises on her and call it a day, sell her to the highest bidder. No damned nonsense about captain's dinners and fellow passengers and getting up at all hours. I want my peace, I tell you. Four extended cruises and I'll be satisfied.' When I left with the signed bill, they were discussing this, both sitting on the bed, grim and unhappy, each with a glass of champagne in his hand.

14. The Ballet Visits the Magician

THE MANAGEMENT of the banquet department kept on file the addresses of a number of men who were magicians, fortunetellers, or experts with cards. One of these entertainers frequently appeared at the end of the small dinner parties which were given in the private suites of the Splendide in those days. Our entertainers had acclimated their acts to the elegance of the hotel, and the magicians, for example, instead of conjuring a simple white rabbit from their hats, cooked therein a soufflé Alaska or brought out a prize puppy with a rhinestone collar. When young girls were present, the magician pulled from their noses and out of corsages Cartier clips, bracelets, and brooches, which were presented to them with the compliments of the host.

Among the best and most talented of our performers was Professor Maurice Gorylescu, a magician who did some palmistry on the side. He came to the hotel as often as two or three times a week. After coffee had been served, he entered the private dining room, got people to write any number they wanted to on small bits of paper, and held the paper to their foreheads. Then he guessed the numbers they had written down and added them up. The total corresponded to a sum he found on a dollar bill in the host's pocket. He did tricks with cards and coins, and he told people about the characteristics and the habits of dress and speech of friends long dead. He even delivered messages from them to the living.

At the end of his séances he went into some vacant room near by, sank into a chair, and sat for a while with his hand over his eyes. He always looked very tired. After about half an hour he shook himself, drank a glass of water slowly, then ate something, and went home.

Professor Gorylescu earned a good deal of money. His fee for a single performance was a flat hundred dollars, and he sometimes received that much again as a tip from a grateful host. But although he worked all during the season he spent everything he made and often asked for and received his fee in advance. All he earned went to women – to the support of a Rumanian wife in Bucharest, to an American one who lived somewhere in New Jersey, and to what must have been a considerable number of New York girls of all nationalities to whom he sent little gifts and flowers.

When he came to the hotel during the day, he would hang his cane on the doorknob outside the ballroom office, ask me for a cigarette, and after a while steal a look at the book in which the reservations for small dinners were recorded. Very casually, and while talking of other things, he would turn the leaves and say something like 'Looks very nice for the next two months,' and put the book back. It took only a few seconds, but in this time his trick mind had stored away all the names, addresses, dates, and telephone numbers in the book. He went home with this information, called up the prospective party-givers, and offered his services.

There was a strict rule that no one should be permitted to look at these reservations, certainly not Professor Gorylescu, but I liked him, and when I was on duty in the ballroom office I pretended not to see him when he peeked in the book. I also gave him leftover petits fours, candies, and after-dinner mints, of which he was very fond. He waved good-bye with his immense hands, asked me to visit him soon at his home, and suggested that I bring along some marrons glacés, pastry, nuts – anything like that – and then he left, a stooping, uncouth figure bigger than our tallest doorman.

Maurice Gorylescu lived on one of the mediocre streets that run between Riverside Drive and West End Avenue. He had a room in one of the small marble mansions that are common in that neighbourhood. The rooming house in which Gorylescu lived was outstanding even among the ornate buildings of that district. It was a sort of junior Frankenstein castle, bedecked with small turrets, loggias, and balconies. It faced the sidewalk across a kind of moat – an air shaft for the basement windows – traversed by a granite bridge. The door was hung on heavy iron hinges that reached all the way across.

In character with this house was the woman who rented its rooms, a Mrs. Houlberg. She stood guard much of the time at the window next to the moat, looking out over a sign that read 'Vacancies'. She always covered three-quarters of her face with her right hand, a long hand that lay diagonally across her face, the palm over her mouth, the nails of the fingers stopping just under the right eye. It looked like a mask, or as if she always had a toothache.

Gorylescu lived on the top-floor front and answered to four short rings and one long one of a shrill bell that was in Mrs. Houlberg's entrance hall. Badly worn banisters led up four flights of stairs. From the balcony of his room one could see the time flash on and off in Jersey and the searchlights of a battleship in the Hudson. The room was large and newly painted in a wet, loud red, the colour of the inside of a watermelon. A spotty chartreuse velvet coverlet decorated a studio couch. Facing this was a chair, a piece of furniture such as you see in hotel lobbies or club cars, covered with striped muslin and padded with down. There was also a Sheraton highboy, which stood near a door that led into an adjoining room which was not his. From the ceiling hung a cheap bazaar lamp with carmine glass panes behind filigree panels. On shelves and on a table were the photographs of many women; in a box, tied together with ribbons in various colours, he kept packets of letters, and in a particular drawer of the highboy was a woman's garter, an old girdle, and various other obvious and disorderly trophies.

THE BALLET VISITS THE MAGICIAN

Gorylescu reclined on the studio bed most of the time when he was at home. He wore a Russian blouse that buttoned under the left ear, and he smoked through a cigarette holder a foot long. One of his eyes was smaller and lower down in his face than the other, and between them rose a retroussé nose, a trumpet of a nose, with cavernous nostrils. Frequently and with great ceremony he sounded it into an immense handkerchief. His cigar-coloured skin was spotted as if with a bluish kind of buckshot, and when he was happy he hummed through his nose, mostly the melody of a song whose title was 'Tu sais si bien m'aimer'.

At home he was almost constantly in the company of women. He made the acquaintance of some of them at parties where he had entertained. They brought him gifts, and if they were fat and old, he read their minds and told them things of the past and future. At other times he went looking for girls along Riverside Drive, humming through his nose, and dragging after him a heavy cane whose handle was hooked into his coat pocket.

He went to various other places to find girls. He picked them up at dance halls in Harlem, on the subway, on roller coasters. He easily became acquainted with them anywhere, and they came to his room willingly and took their chances with him. I always thought I might find one of them, dead and naked, behind the Japanese screen, where he kept a rowing machine on which he built himself up. For the space of time that I knew him, love, murder, and this man seemed to be close together and that room the inevitable theatre for it.

The Professor gave me a series of lectures during my visits to his room in which he detailed for me the routines and the mechanisms of his untidy passions. He insisted during these long études that the most important piece of strategy was to get the subject to remove her shoes. 'Once the shoes are off, the battle is already half won,' he would say. 'Get a woman to walk around without shoes, without heels – she looks a fool, she feels a fool, she is a fool. Without her shoes, she is lost. Take the soft instep in your hand, caress her ankles, her calf, her knee – the rest is child's play. But remember, first off with the shoes.' While he talked, he would scratch his cat, which was part Siamese. The lecture was followed by a display of the collection of photographs he himself had taken, as evidence of the soundness of his theories.

When the Russian Ballet came to town, Professor Gorylescu was not to be had for any parties at the hotel. He went to all the performances, matinées and evenings alike, and he hummed then the music of *Puppenfee*, *L'Après-midi d'un Faune*, and the various divertissements, and was completely broke. One day he was in a state of the highest elation because he had invited a ballet dancer to tea. He wanted me to come too because she had a friend, who would be an extra girl for me; both of them were exquisite creatures, he assured me, and I was to bring some tea, marrons glacés, petits fours, and ladyfingers.

I came early and I brought everything. He darkened the room, lit a brass samovar, laid out some cigarettes, sliced some lemons, hid the rowing machine under the studio couch, and with the Japanese silk screen divided the room into two separate camps. On one side was the couch, on the other the great chair. He buttoned his Russian blouse, blew his nose frequently, and hummed as he walked up and down. He brushed the cat and put away a Spanish costume doll that might have made his couch crowded. He arranged the petits fours in saucers, and when the bell rang four times short and one long, he put a Chopin record on his victrola. 'Remember about the shoes,' he told me over his shoulder, 'and always play Chopin for ballet dancers.' He quickly surveyed the room once more, turned on the bazaar lamp, and, humming, opened the door – and then stopped humming suddenly. He had invited two of the dancers, but up the stairs came a bouquet of girls, more than a dozen of them.

All at once it was the month of May in the dimmed room. The lovely guests complimented the samovar, the cat, the music, and the view from the balcony, to which they had

opened the door, letting much fresh air come in, which intensified the new mood. Gorylescu's voice became metallic with introductions; he ran downstairs to get more glasses for tea and came back breathing heavily. All the girls, without being asked, took their shoes off immediately, explaining that their feet hurt from dancing. They arranged the shoes in an orderly row, as one does on entering a Japanese house or a mosque, then sat down on the floor in a circle. One of them even removed her stockings and put some slices of lemon between her toes. 'Ah-h-h,' she said.

There started after this a bewildering and alien conversation, a remote, foggy ritual, like a Shinto ceremonial. It consisted of the telling of ballet stories, and seemed to me a high, wild flight into a world closed to the outsider. In all of these stories appeared Anna Pavlova, who was referred to as 'Madame' – what Madame had said, what Madame had done, what she had thought, what she had worn, how she had danced. There was an atmosphere of furious backstage patriotism. The teller of each story swayed and danced with hands, shoulders, and face. Every word was illustrated; for anything mentioned – colour, light, time, and person – there was a surprisingly expressive and fitting gesture. The talker was rewarded with applause, with requests for repetition of this or that part again and again, and there swept over the group of girls waves of intimate, fervent emotion.

The Professor served tea on his hands and knees and retired to the shadows of his room. He sat for a while in the great chair like a bird with a wounded wing, and then, with his sagging and cumbersome gait, he wandered around the group of innocents, who sat straight as so many candles, all with their shoes off.

The Ballet Visits the Magician

The room was alive with young heads and throats and flanks.

The Professor succeeded finally in putting his head into the lap of the tallest, the most racy of the nymphs. She quickly kissed him, said, 'Sh-h-h-h, daaaahrling,' and then caressed his features, the terrible nose, the eyebrows, the corrugated temples, and the great hands, with the professional detachment of a masseuse, while she related an episode in Cairo during a performance of *Giselle* when the apparatus that carried Pavlova up out of her grave to her lover got stuck halfway, and how Madame had cursed and what she had said after the performance and to whom she had said it. An indignant fire burned in all the narrowed eyes of the disciples as she talked.

Suddenly one of them looked at her watch, remembered a rehearsal, and the girls got up and remembered us. They all had

Russian names, but all of them were English, as most ballet dancers are; in their best accents, they said their adieus. With individual graces, they arranged their hair, slipped into their shoes, and thanked Maurice. Each one of them said 'Daaaahrling' to us and to each other. It was Madame Pavlova's form of address and her pronunciation.

All the girls kissed us, and it was as if we all had grown up in the same garden, as if they were all our sisters. The Professor said a few mouthfuls of gallant compliments, and when they were gone he fished the rowing machine out from under the couch, without a word, and carried it in back of the Japanese screen. Together, we rearranged the room. The marrons glacés and the ladyfingers were all gone, but the cigarettes were still there.

15. Kalakobé

THERE WAS only one Negro on the staff of the Hotel Splendide. He was a Senegalese, and very black, and his name was Kalakobé. He had come to New York five years before and had found work in the kitchens of the hotel because he was a Frenchman. Besides French, he spoke an African dialect and a few words of English, and he always insisted that he was not a Negro but an African.

Kalakobé was employed under the magnificent title of 'casserolier', a job for which it was very difficult to find anyone. The casserolier had to drag huge casseroles across the floor, and copper and iron pots that were sometimes four feet and more in diameter, lift them into wooden tubs, wash them, and put them back where they belonged. This work took a man of immense strength, and therefore everybody was glad that Kalakobé was so big and that he worked ten hours a day year in, year out and sang while he was working. He had shoulders like two shovels. He stood in a steam-filled room, a pantry all his own, and here he knocked the huge pots around and poured streams of hot water from one into another. He was bare to the waist and worked under a strong light that made him blue-black, except when he was scrubbing the outside of the casseroles. Then his body was red wherever the copper reflected. As he lifted the largest of the casseroles, a play of muscles started on his back, cords pulled, ridges rose, like oxen dragging a weight. It was a lesson in anatomy.

If Kalakobé was not in his pantry, there were four places where he could be found: in the silver room, under the stairs of the Jade Suite, in the ballroom, or at the uniform tailor's shop.

Under the stairs of the Jade Suite he had built a small jungle. Someone had given him a broken-down couch and he had hung up several carpets which were not in use; they formed the walls. In there he sat, ate, and sometimes slept by the light of candles.

He was at his most beautiful in the silver room.

After he was through scrubbing the casseroles that were used for cooking the midday meal for about eight hundred guests, he went to the room where the hotel silver was cleaned, and there he attended two Tahara machines, which are wooden drums that turn. Inside each drum are thousands of little pellets like bird shot. The drum is opened, a quantity of silverware is put in, and with it a large piece of soap the colour of strawberry ice cream. When the drum is closed and starts to turn, the pellets inside sound like the ocean far away. After a while the drum is opened, the silver is taken out, rinsed off, and dried. It is then as bright as new. The Hotel Splendide's silver passed through these machines almost constantly.

In this room Kalakobé stood against a background of champagne-coolers, soup tureens, rows of candelabra, trays, and dishes of every size. When these had been washed and dried, there were hundreds of forks, spoons, demitasse spoons, and silver knives for him to do. From all these objects a shimmering white light reflected, so that his body from the waist up was covered with silver scales. He had cut away from his shoes the part that covered his toes, and his trousers were held up with a red sash, and no matter where he stood, he was always a good portrait. The bare walls of the silver room were tiled, and against the precise divisions of the tiles one could measure him and even his movements – three tiles across for the shoulder, eight from the elbow to the wrist, and ten from the top of his head to the first ribs on his chest.

He was most happy in the workshop of the old tailor who made the uniforms for the hotel staff and pressed and repaired them. Kalakobé brought food to the tailor's cat and held it in his arms while he sat in a corner of the room, watching the doormen with envy as they were being measured for new coats. His dream was to be a doorman someday and wear a beautiful uniform. Occasionally he would get up and stand in front of the rows of closets in which gala liveries for footmen and elevator boys hung, or go through the drawers filled with epaulettes, gold and silver braid, crests, pale-blue silken knee breeches, fancy caps, and pumps with gilded buckles. When the tailor was not too busy, Kalakobé tried on various liveries. One day the tailor made him a present of a doorman's coat that was too far gone to be worn before the Splendide's elegant entrance and Kalakobé was beside himself with gratitude. He put extra buttons and trimming on it and then took it home with him, to use as a dressing gown or bathrobe.

When Kalakobé was through working and ready to go home, he dressed with extreme care. His plum-coloured suit fitted his athletic frame like a sweater; his socks were the colour of a wet frog. Into a neon-red tie he sank the point of an imitation-gold tie-pin – a crocodile with paste rubies for eyes and four false emeralds for teeth. Out of his pocket he brought a lapis-lazuli ring and a golden one with an obscure African arrangement of two nude ladies beaten into it. Then he slipped on a form-fitting mauve overcoat that reached almost to the floor. He left the coat open, and wore one yellow glove and carried the other in the gloved hand. As he came out of the hotel he lit up the entire street. The scene was like a Maxfield Parrish painting until he turned the corner.

Kalakobé was supposed to work only during the daytime, but when we had banquets in the ballroom he was paid a little extra to come up and get the casseroles used in the banquet kitchen and, with a long iron hook, drag them into an elevator and down to his pantry. At first he came only during the serving of the meal and left with the cooks, but then he found out that if he waited until the party was over and the tables were being cleared, the waiters would come back from the ballroom with a trayful of glasses in each hand, and in each of the glasses some drink would be left. After that he always stayed in the pantry and waited for the used glasses. He poured all the drinks – champagne, Moselle, Burgundy, Bénédictine, rye, Scotch, Irish

whisky, brandy, and kümmel – into one pitcher, added lemon and sugar and ice, and bottled the whole mixture. What he did not drink himself, he took home and sold.

He came up to the ballroom during the daytime whenever he could get away from his casseroles, and particularly after large balls, when the place was filled with leftover scenery and flowers. While the carpenters and the cleaning women came and went, he sat alone in a far corner of the room, in the dark, with a rose behind his ear, and only the glow of his cigarette giving away his presence. To protect himself against the cold draughts, he sometimes took one of the white felt covers that are used under tablecloths and wrapped it around himself like a robe. Then, with a bottle of his terrible drink on the floor beside him, with his feet spread, his arms loose and so placed that his two hands hung down over his knees, he sat there and made noises, sang quietly, hummed, or tapped his heel and toe, and watched himself in the many mirrors.

When Kalakobé wanted someone to talk to, he would come to see me in the assistant manager's office of the banquet department near by. The first day he came, only his head came into the room. He expected to be ordered out, and when I let him remain he came in altogether, sat down on a silken fauteuil, and told me all about himself. He said that he was a Frenchman and that he wanted to make a fine doorman, that he was six and a half feet tall and would make a fine doorman, that he looked very well in uniform, and that perhaps I could fix it up so he could be a doorman at the Hotel Splendide. In the tailor's shop there was one unused doorman's uniform that fitted him exactly. Also a cap. Perhaps only as a night doorman to start with. He would learn English rapidly, immediately, he said. He could speak a little now – enough for a doorman.

I told Kalakobé that he would make a wonderful doorman, but all our doormen were Irish or English and, as far as I knew, all the doormen in the large and fine hotels in New York were either Irish or English. He said that this might be so, but that Goldfarb had a doorman who was not Irish or English. 'But Goldfarb is a florist,' I told him. He said that was all right, a florist then – anything so he could be a doorman, any job where he could wear a uniform and advance himself in the world.

I inquired about jobs for him and even sent him to one place which needed a doorman, but although he was acceptable, the uniform that went with the job was dirty, plain, and several sizes too small for Kalakobé, and he came back again.

KALAKOBÉ

This was about the season of the year when society moves to the South, and there was, as always, a lull in the business of fashionable hotels. Kalakobé had more time and he came to see me very often. In the dim light of the reception room, he would sit and talk to me. He spoke very slowly and what he said was simple. His voice was soft, like a deep reed instrument. His thoughts crept around like rainworms, plain and with both ends the same – you could see where they were going and where they came from. His ideas were his own, free and private – it was not the usual tip-hungry conversation of hotel employees. He spoke of the city, of Africa, of trees, animals, an overcoat he wanted, or a Great Dane. His French was exquisite and induced a pleasant drowsiness, like a sleeping tablet, and after a while the hypnosis worked and I was completely rested and asleep but heard every word he said. He knew a wonderful story, which I asked him to tell over and over. I cannot reproduce his imitation of the voices of the animals as he spoke; but this was the story:

Long, long time ago, the Elephant was the King of the Animals; but the poor King was so old, so old that he no longer could do his duties or even think about them. He went about the whole day long with his mouth open, like a small child with the pain of its first teeth. A useless ruin of a King. The animals, however, went on acting as if they thought he left his mouth open because he was smiling, and all of them said: 'Oh, see what a good King we have, he is always smiling, he smiles without interruption!'

The dry season came, no rain fell, all the grasses were burnt by the sun. The Hare searches for fodder and finds none; no salad, no cabbages, nothing, absolutely nothing. But you know the Hare is filled with cunning and malice. When he sees the King's open mouth he jumps into it, and he crawls down into his stomach and gets busy eating the bowels. The Elephant feels nothing, his mouth stays open, he smiles without interruption. The Hare is a wicked animal. When he has eaten enough bowels, he goes up and gnaws the King's heart. Now the old King stops smiling, he closes his mouth, and he dies.

As soon as the Hare has eaten enough he wants to get out. Impossible; the door is closed. What is he to do? He returns to the stomach and sits down and thinks.

Outside the King, the animals in the meantime have discovered that he is dead. They are sad, they cry. The Ape goes to the young Elephant who will be his father's successor, and he says: 'Lord, to lessen our sorrow somewhat, permit that we bind the body of your father the King in scented grass, lemon twigs, ferns, and palm leaves. What a terrible loss we have suffered!' And all the animals repeat in chorus: 'Yes, Lord, yes – let us protect his body so that it may stay as long as possible free of decay.'

The Ape then says to the other animals: 'Go search for herbs and grasses. I will keep with me the Rat, the Mouse, the Worm, and the Centipede, to empty the King's body.'

The Hare, who heard all this inside the King, wrapped himself quickly in what was left of the intestines, and the Ape had them taken out and thrown away far from the tree under which the King had died.

The Donkey and the Parrot came and held long speeches beside the grave. The Hare acted very sad. He threw himself down on the ground and lifted his eyes to heaven, and he cried:

'Woe – woe – woe unto us, how cruelly have we been stricken! And I was not here to close his eyes! My poor brothers, how will we bear it? We have lost the best of Kings. I was away on the island, visiting my wife's uncle – who also is near death – and when I came back I heard everyone say that the King, our good King, is dead. Let me weep! All of you share in this sorrow, my brothers; you all know what we have lost. But no one, no one but me, can know what a good heart, what an excellent heart, our King possessed.'

16. The Hispano

THE BEST source of information about the guests of the Hotel Splendide was not its credit department or the manager's office but the couriers' dining room. Under the heading of couriers came the chauffeurs, valets, butlers, nurses, and footmen who were not employed by the hotel but travelled with the guests as their personal servants. To them were assigned small rooms on the air shafts; they were fed a table d'hôte menu in the couriers' dining room. This apartment was a market for scandal, a place to which they all rushed and in which they lingered over the second and third cups of coffee, comparing notes, exchanging griefs and complaints. In English, French, German, Italian, and Spanish, and in all the various dialects of these languages, the infirmities and vices of the great were laid bare. The choicest filth was on tap in the couriers' dining room, and from there it flowed out through the hotel; the best items travelled all the way up to the roof, where the Splendide's florist presided over his hothouse, and all the way down to the fourth basement, where the plumbers had their workshop.

One rainy April afternoon the telephone rang in my office. When I picked up the receiver, Pacifico, the valet of a Cuban marquis who was staying at the hotel, asked me whether I'd like to buy a car, a fine car, very cheap. If I wanted it, he said, would I buy it right away?

'This afternoon, please,' he urged. 'I will sell it at any price. I want to be rid of this car.'

The Marquis's entourage occupied an entire floor. He was a small man, fat, and smelling like a box of candy. He wore high heels and his blue-black hair was glued to his head with pomade. Through the gossip of the couriers' dining room, I had heard all about him. I knew that he was kind to Pacifico one day, embraced him, gave him watches and rings, sent him to the theatre, and beat him the next. I knew also that the Marquis had a wife and many children in a place in Havana, that he had a house in Paris, that here in New York he resided with a young girl he had brought along from France.

Her name was Nicole, but the Cuban's servants called her La Platina because of her bleached yellow hair. She was a routine French mannequin, nice enough, with a sweet face, a small mouth and nose, and the glossy eyes of a Pomeranian. On the street, smartly dressed in fine furs, her eyes shaded by her hat, she was quite exciting. But in the corridors and restaurants of the Splendide, where women of fortunate faces and figures were as common as champagne bottles, no one turned around to look at her.

The Marquis never let her out of his sight. Half Indian, dark as the fine cigars he smoked, he danced around her with unending clumsy caresses. He held on to her, softly pushed her before him, stroked her, sat her down, stood her up, and often left one hand in her lap while he ate with the other. Pacifico said the Marquis even undressed and bathed her himself.

The Platina was fond of tuberoses but could not stand their

scent. The house florist had been instructed by the Marquis to fill her rooms with them and to cover them with glass cloches.

The Marquis had two cars. On cold days, when he wanted to use the closed car, a Minerva, Pacifico telephoned the temperature of the Marquis's apartment down to the doorman, who then conveyed this information to the chauffeur. The Minerva had a small thermometer on the instrument board. When the Marquis and the Platina got into the car an hour or so later, they always found that it was the same temperature as their rooms.

The Marquis's other car, an open Hispano, was painted café au lait, to match the Platina's two Afghan hounds, who always rode with her. The Marquis hated dogs, but he put up with the hounds because the Platina loved them. The Hispano was long and low. Its tonneau was built by the Carrosserie Saoutchik. It had won the Prix d'Élégance at the Automobile Salon in Paris and later a race at Monaco. The seats were upholstered in leopard skin, and whenever the car was parked anywhere it was hidden in a few moments by a throng of curious people.

The Marquis was a devout Catholic and every Sunday was driven in one car or the other to High Mass and to confession on Saturdays. The object of his special devotion was the Madonna. On a chest just outside the Marquis's bedroom stood an altar, and on it, in a small bed of Spanish lace, reposed an exquisitely dressed, much-blessed statue of the Virgin – antique and jewel-studded, with the Christ Child in her arms. There were other statues of the Virgin all over the apartment, and into the dashboard of the Hispano a miniature tabernacle had been built. There, behind glass in a tiny grotto, stood a silver statue of the Madonna, a few inches high. When the driver pushed a small button, the Madonna turned her back on the occupants of the car, so that she could not be offended by whatever went on in the deep, soft seats of the elegant vehicle.

On the day before Pacifico phoned and offered to sell me the Hispano, the Platina had been driving it in city traffic. She had come up behind a truck loaded with steel girders that stuck far out in the rear. It was assumed in the couriers' dining room that instead of putting her foot on the brake, the Platina had pushed down on the accelerator. Anyway, the car shot ahead, and the girders, smashed in on her, almost severed her head from her body. When the car was brought back to the hotel there were bloodstains on the leopard skin of the driver's seat. The windshield was broken; so were the headlights. The radiator was pushed against the engine.

The Marquis wanted to kill himself. He had cursed the Madonna and then he had begun to weep. He had prayed on his knees all night. At daybreak he had instructed his servants to pack and had obtained passage on the next boat for France. Then he had told Pacifico to have the dogs destroyed and to get rid of the car. He never wanted to see the Hispano again.

The best firm of undertakers in New York City prepared the Platina for a voyage to Paris. They sent out for all the tuberoses that were to be had in New York, and a few hours after she was in their hands, with her eyes closed, Pacifico told his friends in the couriers' dining room, she was prettier than she had ever been before.

All such things are not as important and terrible as they would be outside a large hotel. In a hotel too much is happening – the guests eat and drink, laugh and complain as at any time, the orchestras play in the restaurants, the hum of conversation

is not a shade lower. Whatever is unpleasant is done quietly. When someone has died in a hotel, two men carry a plain basket out of a side door early in the morning.

I did not want the Hispano. I knew that it was an expensive toy to keep, that it used too much gas, that replacements were costly. I did not like its colour or the leopard-skin upholstery. But Pacifico offered it to me for almost nothing – the repairs would cost more than the car – and so I bought it.

The next afternoon Kalakobé came to visit me in my office. I told him about the Hispano. Immediately he wanted to see it, and so I took him over to the Splendide's garage and showed him the car. He turned the pink palms of his black hands toward it and said, 'Quelle merveille!' At last he saw his chance for a job that required him to wear a uniform. Kalakobé said he would get one after the car was repaired and painted, and on his days off be my driver. In his free hours he would take care of the car and shine it – all out of love.

I could not get Kalakobé away from the Hispano until I agreed. He begged me to keep the leopard skin – just to have the bloodstains taken out. He straightened a rug and tried the emergency brake, which was on the outside of the tonneau. He went through the luggage compartment. He turned the Madonna around several times. In the glove compartment he found a tortoise-shell mirror and a cigarette case with emerald initials. He opened the cigarette case and discovered that inside there were rubies worked into the design of a tuberose. The case was worth more than the car.

During the next week, Kalakobé spent a good deal of time in the chauffeurs' dressing room of the Splendide's garage, and he stood outside the hotel and watched the guests' cars arrive. Every day he came to me with new ideas for uniforms. He made designs with crayons until he got one that he liked, and he was unhappy when I told him that it would not do. He had created a pale-blue Cossack coat with mustard piping, a bright colour, and gold buttons. I told him that nobody wore such uniforms, but he could not understand why, if he himself bought the outfit, he could not wear it. So I gave him a ticket to see *Othello* and told him to miss the first act and stand outside the Metropolitan, on the Thirty-Ninth Street side, and watch the fine cars arrive. He came back from this performance and agreed in principle; but he said that one car had arrived with two chauffeurs, both wearing wide fur collars and fur hats. I explained to him that it was probably the car of some parvenu.

Finally he consented to a plain gun-metal gabardine coat and breeches, a black cap, black shoes, and puttees. The Splendide's uniform tailor made it for him at cost. Kalakobé looked very well in it.

On the day the Hispano was ready to run again, Kalakobé suggested that we go driving. With everything on him neat, his puttees shined, Kalakobé walked in front of me, now and then looking back to see if I was still following. At the car he smiled, stripped his lapis-lazuli ring and his gold ring from his fingers, and slipped his hands into tight black gloves. He walked once around the car, opened and closed the doors, and looked at the tires. Then he polished the already gleaming windshield and the headlights, which were as big as snare drums. Finally, without looking at me, he informed me that the most elegant way was for me to do the driving while he sat beside me. It was very chic, he said, for the boss to drive – he had seen it many times. Besides, he added, he didn't know how to drive.

So that was what we did. Whenever we took the car out, I drove and Kalakobé sat beside me. He opened and closed the doors, handed out fares on ferryboats and tolls on bridges, paid for the gas, lit my cigarettes, and let people stare at him while he waited with the car. He called the car a convertible rooster, and told its pedigree to the crowds that gathered. His uniform was always pressed and spotless, his visor shined to its brightest possibilities.

17. The Magician Does
a New Trick

ONE DAY Professor Gorylescu came to see me at the banquet office. He hung his cane on the doorknob as usual, skimmed again through the reservation book, and asked me if I knew anything about dogs. He wanted to get a dog, he said, and he had seen one he thought he might buy. It was in a shop on Forty-Ninth Street only a few blocks from the hotel and was very expensive. He wanted a dog because he had decided he could use one in his sleight-of-hand performances, and he wanted me to come with him and look at the one he had found and see if I thought it would be a good dog for that purpose.

I took down my hat, put on a coat to hide my uniform, and we walked to the pet store. The dog of Professor Gorylescu's choice was a toy griffin; he sat in a garden of excelsior in the shop window and at frequent intervals was half smothered under the pink-and-black bellies of some fox-terrier puppies who seemed to move always in an avalanche. His name, we learned, was Confetti. Between avalanches, Confetti would right himself and look thoughtfully at the floor, as if he were trying to figure something out. He did not want to play. The proprietor of the shop asked fifty dollars for him and Gorylescu bought him for thirty-five, with a leash and collar thrown in.

We took Confetti to the hotel and I gave him part of a dish of lamb hash which I had ordered for my lunch. He pushed the saucer under my desk, and clattered around with it, and the Professor went out to buy a currycomb, some dog biscuits, and a dish for food. Confetti came out from under the desk and I got acquainted with him. He was a weird dog. He had a loose coat somewhat like the plumage of a grouse and his four legs were stuck into him without much care for design. He walked sideways with a sort of hop. He looked a hundred years old, and a hundred years of worry were in the misery of his lips and eyes. The end of his tongue stuck out between his teeth, and when he wanted to show affection he exploded with the sounds of a bronchial catarrh. Freezing and jittery, full of little fears, suspicions, and nervous twinges, he seemed to me to be the perfect dog for a sorcerer. He was exactly suited for Gorylescu and I was glad I had advised Gorylescu to buy him.

I saw Confetti again a few weeks later when Gorylescu asked me to come to his house. Gorylescu had taught Confetti the first simple tricks, and before showing them in public, he wanted a few friends to come and see how clever the little dog was and how fast he had learned his lessons. I took a bus up to his château country in the Seventies. The street scene seemed always the same, an identical arrangement of people and things. There was invariably at one end of the block a man walking a chow dog, at the other end a woman carrying a hatbox, and between the two a Wanamaker truck, with two men carrying a couch either into a house or out of it. In the Hudson, sometimes, was a battleship. I went to the door of Gorylescu's castle and rang the bell. Mrs. Houlberg stood at the window, as always, looking out into the street with one hand held diagonally across her face.

Gorylescu had not come in yet and I sat in the entrance hall of the house and waited for him. Mrs. Houlberg told me why she always looked out into the street. It was, she said, on account of her husband. He suffered from a serious heart condition and she waited for him in fear every evening, worried that he might not come home, or, if he did, that people would be carrying him. He kept a card in the outer pocket of his coat on which she had lettered instructions where to bring him in case he was suddenly stricken. As she spoke, she turned her face in my direction only for brief moments, keeping her eyes the rest of the time on the street outside.

'He'll go,' she said, and snapped her thin fingers. 'He'll go just like that. One day they'll carry him in here – dead.'

The Magician Does a New Trick

Mr. Houlberg, I learned, had a button-and-ribbon business somewhere in back of Lord & Taylor's, and he worked too hard.

Mrs. Houlberg did not approve of Gorylescu's way of living. He had too many girls, she said. She needed his rent money badly or she would long ago have asked him to move out. She said that the visits of women all day long, and at late hours even, gave the house a bad name. As she spoke, the door opened and a girl with a small bag came in and went upstairs without saying anything. 'That's what I mean,' said Mrs. Houlberg, nodding at the girl's back. 'That's one of them. That's the latest one. She has a key and she's going up to his room now.' The girl was young, had a run in one of her stockings, nice legs, thick lips, and blue-black hair. Polish, I thought – perhaps from Scranton.

As for the dog, Mrs. Houlberg liked dogs, she said, and she did not mind feeding Confetti. But she wished that Gorylescu would keep him upstairs. Ever since the Professor had brought him down and shown him off, Mr. Houlberg and the little dog had been inseparable friends. They played together, the man at the risk of his life. 'He's not supposed to bend over or run up and down the stairs,' she said. 'He's supposed to sit still and be quiet and not get excited. There he comes now,' she said, and opened the door. Mr. Houlberg looked as I feared he would. He sat down and asked how Confetti was, and then he leaned back and looked at the ceiling with his mouth open.

The Professor, who had been out airing Confetti, came in a moment later and Confetti ran to Mr. Houlberg as soon as he saw him, hopped into his lap, licked his hands, and tried to reach his face. Mr. Houlberg petted him and talked to him in German. There is a curious phrase which all people who speak

German use when talking to a dog. They say, 'Ja wo ist denn das Hunderl? Ja wo iss er denn? Ja wo iss er denn?' This is repeated as long as the conversation lasts and is altogether meaningless, the translation being, 'Where is the little dog? Where is he? Where is he?' This goes on while the little dog sits right in front of them. Mr. Houlberg said it over and over, and then the Professor and Confetti and I went upstairs. The Professor kissed the hand of the Polish girl, who said she was Spanish, that her name was Mercedes, and that she was a dancer. Two more friends of the Professor's came in, a theatrical agent and a man from a magicians' supply house, and the Professor got ready for his performance.

He went back of a Japanese screen and put on a tail coat, a garment especially made for his act with Confetti. It had trick pockets all over it, big enough for Confetti to get into. The performance went very smoothly. Confetti disappeared slowly and came back again. Then he disappeared fast, both from in front and in back of the Professor and while the Professor was sitting, reclining, walking, standing, or turning around. The dog folded himself up silently and went into a pocket under the lapel or into one of the tails of the dress coat. After that was over, the Professor asked Confetti questions on international affairs, on the marital problems of movie stars, and even on what the future held for various politicians in the highest offices. Confetti answered with a nod of the head for 'Yes' and shook his head for 'No'. The Professor explained that he was trying to teach him to shrug his shoulders in answer to the more delicate questions.

After the performance the little dog hissed and coughed and scratched the floor, bowing to our applause. Then the Professor said good-bye to all of us except the Spanish dancer, and as we left Confetti squeezed out of the door and ran downstairs to his friend Mr. Houlberg. He had smelled Sauerbraten and was going to get some.

A few days after all this, Gorylescu took the dog with him to Florida. He had made arrangements to appear with Confetti and an orchestra at some night club in Palm Beach. He came back to New York at the end of the season and stopped by the hotel as soon as he got off the train. We had written to him about an important engagement for the day after his return and he now asked double the price he formerly got and said that half of his fee was for Confetti, who was a sensation. He asked me to come along to his house and see for myself.

As we went out through the lobby of the Splendide, he waved

to a girl who was waiting there, the dog in her arm. It was the Spanish dancer. She came along with us. Outside was a taxi with a theatrical trunk strapped on the back, a trunk, Gorylescu explained, that he never let out of his sight.

'Never take a dog to Florida,' the Professor said to us on the way uptown, 'on account of ticks. It's full of ticks down there. Look at him, he's full of them.' Confetti scratched himself all the way up to the Riverside Drive castle.

For once, Mrs. Houlberg was not at the window. We went upstairs, all of us helping to carry the trunk. The Professor unlocked the door to his room, quickly looked through the accumulated mail, sorted letters from bills, and sniffed at several of the smaller envelopes. The girl silently unpacked the trunk. First she took out a collapsible chair that had a box under the seat instead of legs. Next she produced a nest of black and gold Chinese lacquer boxes. Then she laid out some tiny black garments which turned out to be full evening dress for Confetti.

While the Professor dressed the dog, he explained the routine. The first trick, he said, went like this: On one side of the stage, or the room, the dog sits on a chair facing the audience. On the other stands the Professor. He asks a lady in the audience for the loan of a diamond bracelet. 'One, two, three,' and the bracelet is gone. Next, 'One, two, three' – the dog is gone. An attendant brings in a Chinese lacquer box, gold and black. The Professor opens it. Inside is a smaller box, inside that another one, and in the third box, unharmed and wearing the diamond bracelet around his neck, is Confetti.

'Now watch it closely,' said the Professor. He buttoned a high collar around Confetti's neck. The dog pulled his mouth sideways in annoyance, sneezed, and then tried to get some comfort by turning his head from side to side. Standing behind him, the Professor made a neat knot in the white tie under the dog's chin. 'Now,' he said, 'watch it closely!'

Confetti sat on his chair facing us. There was no bracelet, so the girl gave the Professor her wrist watch instead. 'One, two, three,' the Professor said, and the wrist watch was gone. Then, 'Fffft' – the dog disappeared. The girl brought in the Chinese boxes and put them on the chair. Then she sat down beside me and chewed gum. 'Now watch me closely,' said the Professor, and he took out the first box, then the second. Then he smiled, raised his eyebrows to a high degree of fake surprise, and reached into the last of the small boxes. His face changed suddenly and he was really surprised now. The girl stopped chewing. The box was empty. No dog, no wrist watch.

The Professor started several sentences of alarm and explanation while he looked behind the Japanese screen, under the couch, and into the trap door that was built into the chair. Having searched the room, he went out into the hall to whistle for the dog. On the stairs he saw the wrist watch, and now he knew where Confetti was – down looking for his friend Mr. Houlberg.

We went down to the basement, where the Houlbergs lived. The place smelled of flowers, there was a shabby palm in the hallway, and from the Houlbergs' parlour shone an uncertain, flickering light. It was the light of candles. The mourners sat in a circle which was open toward the door, and in a casket, as his wife so often had predicted, lay Mr. Houlberg. The little dog, in his dress suit, sat behind a row of relatives, all properly dressed in black.

Just as we came up to the door, Mrs. Houlberg saw the dog. She picked up Confetti and threw him at Gorylescu.

'You have a sense of humour all your own,' she said with a dry throat, and then she screamed, 'Get out! Get out!' the way bad actresses scream in rotten plays.

18. My Valet Lustgarten

THE MANAGEMENT of the Splendide felt that all its employees must be carefully dressed. The uniforms for the bellboys and footmen, the doormen and elevator operators were supplied by the house at a cost of tens of thousands of dollars in tailoring and in upkeep. The executives were fashion plates and most of the maîtres d'hôtel had their clothes made in London.

Dress was most important in the banquet department. The functions that took place there – weddings, balls, diplomatic dinners, concerts, coming-out parties – demanded that the permanent staff present an elegant appearance.

Clothes had not only to be of fine cut and the latest fashion; they had also to be forever pressed, the boots shined, the linen fresh.

During the season there was only a brief time, while the guests of one party were leaving and before those of the next arrived, for going upstairs to dress. We changed four or five times a day – from morning coat to cutaway, to dinner coat, to tails, and always in a hurry. The worry about having enough clean linen, the fiddling with buttons, cuff links, and studs, pulling them out of one shirt and sticking them into the starchy-edged holes of the bosoms and cuffs of a new one, taking trees out of one pair of shoes to put them into another, looking for white waistcoats, was annoying; so was putting on high collars, tying thin cravats into bows, with nervous fingers, sometimes three times during a long night.

The cleaning and dressing of clothes was attended to by the house valets. Each of them was assigned to a floor of the hotel, to attend the guests, and they were supposed to come down in the afternoon to do some hurried pressing and cleaning for the staff, for which they were paid by the hotel. They were all English valets, and they felt it to be beneath their dignity to look after us; they gave us the most hurried, careless service possible. They would never bother to lay out our clothes, or put studs and cuff links into shirts, and of course we could not expect them to be there in the middle of the night when we needed them most. We tried several other arrangements, such as having a bus boy take the things to an outside tailor and trying to train him to arrange the studs, but they all had fat dirty fingers or were clumsy, and sometimes the clothes did not come back in time, and it never worked out right. It was a mess until I found Joseph Lustgarten.

One afternoon, when there was only a lecture in one of the smaller ballrooms and no dinner scheduled for the evening, I left an old waiter in charge and went for a ride in the Hispano. One of the ballet dancers I had met at Gorylescu's tea party, named Lydia, went along.

We drove up Riverside Drive and on to the Dyckman Street ferry. On this ferryboat was a musician, and after the engines started pounding and the boat had left its slip, he began to play on a three-quarter violin. The weather had worn all the patina off his instrument; it looked as if it had been sandpapered. In the bad light of the gangway in which the car stood, the man's threadbare overcoat, the fiddle, the face, the hat, and the patched shoes, were all one colour – a dull green. The thin fingers were blue and they walked up and down over the strings like the legs of a bug. There was a drop on the end of the man's nose. It was cold and windy. He played Kreisler's 'Liebeslied' – he played it very correctly, and Lydia said how surprising this was. She knew the music – she had danced to the melody – and she said he played it without any melancholic liberties, without the usual whining. He came to the car after he had ended the 'Liebesleid', and I gave him a bill.

He took it and walked to the edge of the ferryboat and unfolded the bill. He folded it carefully – unbuttoned the overcoat, another coat, pushed a sweater up, and then slid the bill into the pocket of his vest. Then he looked at the river, at Lydia, and again at the Hispano and at me, and I felt that it was wrong to have given him the bill, that it would have been better just to have given him a quarter. I was upset because the man seemed very unhappy about it; he fingered his instrument and blew warm air on his hands.

I got out and spoke to him. He clicked his heels and made a bow and he told me that he was not a professional musician, but a tailor out of work; that he came from Graz, and had served in a Viennese regiment where he had been orderly to a colonel, who was a baron. His conversation was still infected with this experience. When I spoke to him in German, he answered in precise military language somewhat softened by his Austrian dialect. He addressed me by several titles – 'Ja, Herr Graf, Jawohl, Herr Baron' – and when I asked him to play some Heurigen music, he again clicked his heels, wiped his nose on his sleeve, and said, 'Zu Befehl, Exzellenz.'

Here stood the complete solution to our valet problem. When he finished playing 'Sweet Rosmarin', I told him to get into the car. He protested, but when I promised him a job, he sat down gingerly on the leopard skins in the back. We covered him up with a rug, and he ate with us at West Point. The next day he reported at the hotel. His name was Lustgarten, 'Joseph Lustgarten, Your Excellency,' he said, and stood at attention.

Lustgarten was immediately engaged to press and take care of our clothes, lay out the linen, shine the shoes. He ate in the hotel and helped out with other work on occasion. He made good money and von Kyling, the director of the banquet department, gave him a castoff cutaway and striped trousers. Others gave him a dinner coat and civilian suits; and it turned out that my old shoes fitted him. After he was properly dressed and warm, his white hair combed, he looked very distinguished and historic, like Metternich.

My Valet Lustgarten

I soon found out why he had appeared to be so upset on the ferryboat. There was a contradiction between the expression on his face and the emotions he felt. When he was happiest – and the five-dollar bill had made him very happy – he looked as other people do when they cut themselves or swallow something bitter. His laugh was a string of indrawn muted cries, and the more he laughed the sadder he seemed.

He had an annoying habit, when nervous, of pulling his fingers out of their joints and snapping them back again, but otherwise he was without fault. He was happy with his job, never tired, needed no sleep, was full of warm little talk and restful. He had a quiet, kindly humour and he loved to read.

We all had dressing rooms in one of the noisy sections of the hotel. When we worked very late it was our privilege to ask at the desk for a room to sleep in; during the season we worked late almost every night and never left the hotel for weeks at a time. The room clerk would give us the key to a vacant suite – the Splendide had no single rooms – and, in return for some cigarettes or an occasional bottle of wine, he saw to it that the rooms were the best and that we were not disturbed the next morning. We got to bed about four or five, sometimes six in the morning. When the exciting parties ended, the music seemed to keep on playing – the bass fiddles and the big drums beat on and on, and I rarely got more than two hours' sleep.

At about midnight Lustgarten would go to the front office and get the key to the room where I was to sleep. Then he packed the clothes for the next day – the linen, the shoes, the tie, toilet articles, and pyjamas – into a black bag. From one party or another there was always champagne and caviar left over. He would put some caviar in a dish with ice, take a bottle

of stale leftover champagne, a toaster, and bread. After plugging in the toaster and cooling the wine, he sat and waited for me.

We were in a different room every night, but every night we ate caviar. I ate it in bed with a soupspoon, drank champagne, and wrote plays. At that time I wanted to be a playwright. Lustgarten read my manuscripts back to me. I wrote about one play a week. None of them seemed very good. I never could let go of a character. There were always two of them – a good one who was dumb; a bad one who was intelligent. The dumb one began by asking the other a question, and then the other answered for an hour. Lustgarten sat on the edge of my bed and gave me the day's accumulated scandal about the hotel guests and employees. He darned socks, bit off thread, sewed on buttons, and whistled Viennese music. He slept on the divan in the living room.

There came several nights when the hotel was filled and no room was available for us except the Adam Suite. This apartment was the quintessence of elegance. It was leased by a multi-millionaire and was on the highest floor of the hotel; its ceilings were sixteen feet high, the furniture museum pieces. On a small dais in one bedroom stood a canopied Napoleon bed. The bath was sunken, the fixtures gilded. There were Aubusson carpets and tapestries in the living room. The silver, the glasses, the china in the dining room were all antique and priceless. The library held first editions and fine bindings, also a Bechstein piano, on which stood a group of photographs – among them Queen Marie of Rumania, two members of the British royal family, Mary Pickford, and Bernard Shaw. All the photographs were signed, and some had a few words of friendship added. The tenant of the Adam Suite was in Europe most of the time, in the care of a specialist. He travelled with a doctor and two nurses from Baden Baden to Bad Gastein to Paris. The Suite stood empty the better part of the year.

We moved in very carefully at first. Every night Lustgarten packed the little black bag and every morning he brought it down to the ballroom again. When the room clerk, after a gift of a box of cigars, said that it was all right to stay there, Lustgarten at first left only our toothbrushes and the packed bag. But eventually, when I came in after a party one night, I found all my clothes hanging in the closet. Lustgarten clicked his heels, said, 'Zu Befehl, Exzellenz,' and established us there for good. It was better for him, too, because there was a second bedroom and a bath, and a pantry where he could keep cold food, a few bottles of wine and cold meats, sturgeon and other leftovers, and the caviar.

Lustgarten now bloomed into the perfect servant. He not only put buttons and cuff links into the shirts, mended socks, and shined boots, he knew remedies for sore throat, tired eyes, hangovers. He always arranged his face into agreement; he played nice music; looked out of the window in the morning and announced the weather, always with consideration – 'A very nice rainy day, Your Excellency,' he said. 'Just a little wind, a lovely high wind.' He never wanted a day off. We often went to the theatre together; we saw most of Eugene O'Neill that way. 'You write much better, Herr Baron,' Joseph often said to me.

For six months we lived undisturbed in the Adam Suite. Lustgarten loved to sit on the floor and play the violin. Gorylescu, the magician, came up on Sunday evenings with his trained dog. Kalakobé visited us. I took up painting again, and the models joined us for little cold suppers and music on the violin and the Bechstein. When there was nothing else to do, there were two Renoirs and four Toulouse-Lautrecs to look at. In the library were Werfel and Thomas Mann in first editions, and Voltaire in the original text. And there were the millionaire's subscriptions to magazines: *Vanity Fair*, *La Vie*

Parisienne, Judge, the *Atlantic Monthly, Punch,* the *Sphere,* the *Tatler, Simplicissimus,* and *Town Topics.*

One night I brought to the apartment a Bavarian who had been a cavalry major in the German Army. His troop had been stationed in Regensburg. His name was Count Hugo von Trautmansdorff and he had known my grandfather well and had been a steady customer in my grandfather's brewery in Regensburg. He had come to America after the World War.

Lustgarten fell all over himself with attention. For the first time he failed to call me Herr Baron, Herr Exzellenz, and Herr Graf. All his efforts were directed toward von Trautmansdorff. He followed the Count all over the apartment while von Trautmansdorff looked at the Bonaparte bed and the Toulouse-Lautrecs and the collections of photographs on the piano. When the Count had seen the whole apartment, Joseph settled him in a chair in the corner of the library, near a big window, where he could look out over the city. The Count told me that he still had some family jewels and a small income, but it was not enough so that he could live like a gentleman. To marry an American woman, he said, was a terrible way out, and it was probably impossible, since he was too old and had asthma. To do exhibition dancing was also impossible, for the same reason. His one hope, he said, was to have a little riding academy. It was that or good-bye, beautiful world. He got up then and stood for some time looking down at the street, which was thirty-one stories below.

From that time on, I had trouble with Joseph. Although the season of balls and banquets was over and there ought to have been less work for him to do, he seemed always busy. The reason for this was that he broadened his activities and began soliciting

215

business among the captains in the various restaurants, the room waiters, and all the employees who had anything to press or repair. Over the tub in his own bathroom he hung a long pole, and uniforms dangled from this, with tickets on the sleeves. He engaged a bus boy to work for him in his free hours, and the boy was continually rushing in and out of the apartment, hunched under pressed and unpressed uniforms. From the bathroom came the hissing of steam and the smell of moist clothes, and the apartment took on the odour of a tailor shop.

Lustgarten had no time to run errands for me or to sit on the edge of my bed and talk. He was too tired, or too busy, to play the violin or read my plays. He was so busy that he did not even go down to eat. His meal was a dreadful half-hour in the Adam Suite. At five o'clock in the afternoon he sent the bus boy out to a delicatessen on Third Avenue. When the boy arrived with a paper bag and a bottle of beer, Joseph turned his tailor's iron downside up and boiled himself two potatoes on it. He was fond of smoked herring and especially a very fat kind that was imported from Germany and was calling Bückling. With his pocket-knife, he scraped the metallic skin off. Then he cut six slices of pumpernickel and smeared them thickly with Liederkranz. Next he covered the Liederkranz with chopped chives, and finally, when the potatoes were done, he opened the bottle of beer.

At the beginning of the meal he would lean on the Bechstein piano, look at the photographs and the distinguished signatures, and eat the herring very daintily, his lips pulled back from his teeth and his little finger stretched away from his hand. But when he came to the Liederkranz sandwiches he turned his back to the photographs to concentrate on his dessert, and his face took on its most bitter lines of happiness.

Eventually Joseph added Count von Trautmansdorff to his list of clients. The Count lived in a small furnished apartment on Sixtieth Street east of the Park, in a rooming house filled with others like himself. He had entrée into the best society, and he used to dine out occasionally with the hope of getting someone interested in his riding academy. Beforehand he would bring his tail coat up to the Adam Suite, and Lustgarten would work on it until it was wearable again.

When he and Lustgarten were together, it was like being around the stables of a cavalry regiment. They spoke of horses, drills, terrain, manœuvres – the Count with telegraphic briefness, as if issuing commands; Lustgarten standing before him with his hands flat on the seams of his trousers, his face miserable with joy. In the late hours, Lustgarten would permit himself to sit down, and then he and the Count talked of ancient Hapsburg scandals: the Affaire Mayerling, the idiocies of the archdukes, and the mad Wittelsbachs. Fritzl, the homesick bus boy, sat silent, his eyes wide. Occasionally he tried to get the conversation around to Regensburg, where he came from, but it didn't work. The Count detested Regensburg.

Until the pressing shop was set up, Lustgarten had never given me any cause to complain, and I stood it a long while; but at last I told him that it would have to stop, that he would have to eat out in the pantry with the door closed, and that above all he would have to get rid of the smelly waiters' garments in his bathroom. He promised to do so.

One evening a few days later I came in and found the suite again smelling like a tavern. The bus boy rushed past me on his way out, and from the bathroom – 'fhhhs, fhhhs' – came the sound of pressing. I opened the windows and called Lustgarten, and this time I spoke to him in anger. I had never spoken to him that way before. He smiled, and his servant's face became very tired. He tried to speak, and then after a moment he excused himself and left the room.

That night he packed quietly and left. In a day or so I had a letter from him, postmarked 'New York City'. It began, 'Sehr geehrter Herr und lieber Freund', and was full of Austrian misspelling of German words. He would never forget my many kindnesses, the letter said, and he would always look back upon this year as one of the happiest. He had been able to save up a little money, especially during the last few months, and as soon as the warm weather came, he and His Excellency, Count von Trautmansdorff, were going to open a riding academy in Central Park. They were only going to have two horses at first, but there would be more later, and they hoped to have my patronage.

The idyll of the Adam Suite came to an end soon after.

The millionaire to whom the suite was leased had written to the manager that he intended to give it up, to sublet it, if a suitable tenant could be found. Mr. Brauhaus, the manager, had an inquiry for just such an apartment, and one morning, while I was still in bed, he showed the suite to two ladies.

An entire procession came into the living room: Mr. Brauhaus, the two ladies, Fassi, the assistant manager, and Madame de Brissonade, the housekeeper. They all stood at proper distances from one another, according to rank. The ladies inspected the furniture, the view, the layout, and asked questions.

Mespoulets, who stayed with me after Lustgarten left, came

into the bedroom shaking all over. He looked at me as if I knew the solution to a great mystery, and he stammered that Cheeses Greisd was outside.

Mespoulets looked as if he were going to cry, and hid behind a screen. The door was opened by the assistant manager and when he saw someone asleep in the bed he said, 'Pardon me,' and closed it again. The visitors were ushered out of the apartment, but the assistant manager came back to the bedroom and walked over to the bed, and then he went out and got Mr. Brauhaus. They talked in whispers because I was asleep. Fassi pointed to the champagne stand and the empty bottle. He lifted it out of the melted ice water and fished out the label so that Mr. Brauhaus could see that the wine was of good vintage.

'They are fine dogs,' Fassi said, hoarsely. 'The gentlemen of the banquet department, they know what they like.' He held up the empty box of caviar. 'Monsieur Louis here also drives a Hispano,' he added. He loved the 'fine dogs' and repeated it several times in describing the elegance with which we lived in the banquet department.

Mr. Brauhaus looked very angry while he listened but he told Fassi to let me sleep. He had read the report of the banquet the night before and seen that we had gone to bed at six in the morning. He told the assistant to have me report to his office as soon as I woke up. 'Diss time I'll fire him, Gotdemn it, Cheeses Greisd,' he whispered, and carefully closed the door.

19. The New Suit

FRITZL, WHO was always homesick for Regensburg, did not go to Europe the next summer; he worked one more year at the hotel, and what the banks say in their advertisements is true. When you save your money and regularly deposit small amounts, you find yourself in possession of a respectable sum. With frugal living, with an occasional tip on the market, Fritzl found himself the owner of three thousand five hundred dollars.

At the end of the season, in June, when the last wedding was over and the ballroom cleared for painting and repairs, he said that he had succeeded in finding a ship on which he could work his way over, and that he would meet me in London. He wanted to go to London to have the suit made in which he would arrive in Regensburg.

The problem of outfitting himself for his homecoming had been with him constantly for months. The suit was the only good suit he ever wanted. After that he did not care what he wore, he said. He said that he wanted to arrive in Regensburg 'looking like a gentleman'.

In pursuit of this project he had combed advertisements in the papers, looked into all the clothing store windows. He had also spent hours leaning over Miss Tappin's desk. Miss Tappin had tried to discourage pinchback suits and pinstriped double-breasted flannels. She had stopped once in front of Brooks Brothers' and almost agreed that what was in the window was right and good, but then she had begun to reminisce about British tailors and told Fritzl what a pity it was that he could not have a suit made in London, at a shop such as that where her father and her brother-in-law traded; at John's and Pegg's in Clifford Street, or at Anderson and Sheppard's. The suit would be about a hundred dollars but it would be right.

Fritzl, though he counted every penny, did not seem to mind that expense. When I told him I would not go to London just to get him a suit, that he could get one which would still be a sensation in Regensburg for half that money, here in New York, he moped down in his washroom, but finally he went with Miss Tappin and they ended up once more at Brooks Brothers', buying two suits: one – against Miss Tappin's advice – a light grey flannel, double-breasted, with white stripes; the other conservative and dark grey. After the tailor had made the alterations, Fritzl came back and walked up and down in front of all the ballroom mirrors and looked at himself from every angle.

He sat with a new suit in the banquet office and pictured his arrival in Regensburg – his mother's and his father's pride, and how mad everybody else would be. That part gave him the most pleasure. He took hold of the sleeve of my coat and said, 'Ludwig, can you imagine Professor Hellsang? Can you picture him? Can you see his face when he sees me in this suit? Maybe he will be at the railroad station. Sunday afternoons he always eats out in the restaurant of the depot and then walks up and down watching the trains arrive. I hope he'll be there—'

His joy was trebled when I told him that we would not arrive at the railroad station, because I was taking the car.

'Ah,' he said, 'they'll be twice as mad. We'll pass the Professor in the street, most probably, several times a day.'

He packed the suit away carefully and did not wear it again until we were in Europe. He wore the dark one. The light grey he wanted for his entrance into Regensburg.

'I don't think a Hispano-Suiza has ever been seen in Regensburg,' he said on the road from Nancy to Strasbourg. And later on he said, 'The Duke of Thurn und Taxis has only a Mercedes. Perhaps in Munich there might have been one, but I hardly think so.'

Fritzl's hopes were fully realized when something happened to the car. It had got stuck several times, but never in a better place than on the Sunday morning when we drove into Regensburg. It stopped, being out of gas, precisely in front of the main portal of the cathedral, just as High Mass came to an end.

The New Suit

It was a bright morning. The post office which stands directly opposite the cathedral was newly painted. Between the high crosses on top of the spires the sun shone down on the long low car, and out of the cathedral came the last strains of the High Mass. Down the stone steps poured the Regensburgers. They were, by a benevolent arrangement of lamp posts, buildings, statuary, and a barricade around a torn-up portion of the square, forced to thin out and pass the car in line, to the left and right.

The children pointed at the Hispano, soldiers and servant girls walked slowly by. The beau monde tried to pass quickly – and only when they were at a safe distance did they turn to look in such a fashion that their field of vision included the church, the lamp posts, and part of the post office, so that one could not say that they were staring at the Hispano.

The uppermost class – the Burgomaster, the Rector of the Lyceum, at which we had studied, and their friends and relatives – did not even look that much. They betook themselves to the windows of a corsetière and a bookshop, and studied the scene in the reflection of the glass with their backs toward the cathedral and the car.

When most of them had gone, I drove Fritzl across the stone bridge to Reinhausen and I went back to the brewery that had belonged to my grandfather and waited for Fritzl to come back to join me.

I stopped for a while in the long entrance hall of the brewery – a tunnel that went through the main building and opened out into a garden filled with old chestnut trees, iron tables and chairs, a bandstand, and stacks of barrels.

All this was as familiar to Fritzl as it was to me. Fritzl, when he was a little boy, came all the way to the brewery every

evening, barefooted, and solemnly carrying a beer jug in front of him; a stone jug that broke if it ever was dropped. He came for beer for his father, not the regular beer, but a beer that cost only three pfennigs a quart.

This beer should really have been thrown away, but many people would not have had anything to drink at all then, and the brewers of Regensburg set the low price of three pfennigs a quart, so that it did not become a begging matter and the poor could drink a lot. Its alcoholic content was as high as that of good beer.

The place where beer was served was a vaulted hall between

the tunnel and the restaurant. It was badly lit day and night, its stone floor always wet. This room had an entrance from the restaurant and another from the tunnel.

Against one wall a wooden platform of heavy rafters was built. It inclined somewhat and on it stood the beer barrels. Every time a barrel was tapped some beer was spilled and flowed down into a basin that stood on the floor. More beer was spilled when the brewboy who served it filled the glasses. This spilled beer was caught in a brass sink and also flowed down to the basin. The waste beer caught in that basin was called 'Convent' beer on account of the poverty of the nuns.

The good beer was passed to the waitresses across a counter. This counter was covered with a sheet of hammered pewter and it had always looked to me, as a child, like a drawing of the sunrise. In the centre was the sun, a funnel-shaped opening. From this, small gutters like sunbeams reached to all the corners of the counter. All around, where the rays stopped, brewers' symbols and tools were stencilled into the metal. Over the sun was my grandfather's name: Ludwig Fischer; under it the Bavarian coat of arms, and across the outer edge the legend: 'Hopfen und Malz, Gott erhalts.' Two beer barrels, on the left and right sides of the lower edge, completed the design, and the righthand barrel had the date of the founding of the brewery.

When the mugs of beer were placed on this counter the foam was brushed off them and it ran down the side of the steins, liquefied, and collected in the gutters running down to the centre and into the funnel. A pipe drained this also into the basin which stood under the barrels.

At about five, the children waited outside the tunnel. At that time hundreds of beers were served and the Convent beer

became a little more alive than during the quiet hours. The children handed their mugs through a side window, and out of the goodness of his heart, and because a brewer needs good will among the poor, he put a good shot of real beer on top of the stale soup and handed it back. With most serious faces the children streamed out into the night. The little bare feet of boys and girls went like machines under them because their fathers were connoisseurs of this mean brew. They could detect time lost looking into a shop window. When they got home too late with it a thrashing awaited them.

I remembered all this as I sat in the restaurant, and thought how things stand still – the same smell, the same pot of Convent beer, the same noises and the same faces all about me.

After a while Fritzl came and sat down with me and ordered a beer. When he had got used to the light, he nudged me and pointed to a table a few feet away and said, 'Look! There he is – it's Hellsang.'

The New Suit

I looked and recognized Professor Hellsang. We nodded and he nodded sharply. Fritzl and I had been in his class and his appearance brought back more memories of the unhappiness of German youth.

Fritzl had been recommended by the priest of his parish as a smart and good boy, and the city fathers had made it possible for him, along with a dozen other poor boys, to attend the Lyceum. But they should also have fed and dressed him.

Fritzl had always been hungry. He had had to wear his brothers' suits after they had outgrown them; he was the smallest of the four. His little pants had stood up almost by themselves; they shone like antique tiles that once had been green. There were patches on the knees and on the seat, patches on the elbows of the coat. These terrible little suits exhaled years of little boys' untidinesses; the spilled beer, unmade beds, and the closeness of low rooms.

We had sat together on the same bench in the Regensburg Lyceum. I did not mind Fritzl. He was my friend and I was used to the smell. But Professor Hellsang used to object to Fritzl and to his suit. He called him 'Cabbage Soup'. He stopped at his place as he paraded up and down between the rows of pupils, sniffed the air, asked a boy to open a window, and said: 'The eternal cabbage soup!' He looked down at Fritzl and advised him that when he ran home with his father's beer he might try falling near the Artillery Armoury, where the stables are; it would be a holiday for him, a change for once from the smell of eternal cabbage cooking.

Such suggestions were routine to us, they no longer hurt. But once Hellsang stopped and carefully started to examine Fritzl. He looked at him very closely, went over him inch by inch; the boy's hair was brushed, his ears were clean, his neck washed, scrubbed. Then he examined Fritzl's clothes. Finally he found something. The sleeves were like the edges of an old carpet, all tassels and stuck-together fringe.

The Professor picked Fritzl up and stood him on the bench so that he faced the class of well-dressed boys, and then he reached into several pockets until he found a pair of scissors. With these he carefully trimmed the ends of the sleeves and brushed the cut threads into his hand; he burned them in the oven and then very deliberately went to the washstand, pushed back his sleeves, took off his cuffs, and made a careful and long job of washing his hands.

While he dried them, he came back and with mock solicitude patted Fritzl on the head and said that it was a pity about the cabbage soup; that he would be glad to have the suit cleaned for Fritzl, if only he had another to wear in the meantime. 'A few more patches and then we'd be almost elegant, eh, Fritzl?' He addressed the class then and asked them whether one of the boys could not ask his parents for an old suit for Fritzl.

In the courtyard of that school a door led into a woodshed where we sometimes played and hid during recess. There I found Fritzl.

He was sitting in a corner weeping. It seemed as if some invisible person continually kicked him. His face was hot and dirty, smeared with tears. He looked up and tried to form words with his shapeless mouth, and between sobs he said: 'I'll pay him back – oh, I'll pay him back for this. Oh, wait till I grow up, I'll pay him back.' Then he turned his face away, bit his hand, and began kicking the ground with his legs.

This happened not so many years ago – and here across the

room sat the Herr Professor. He hadn't changed much since those terrible days.

Fritzl got up and walked over to the Professor's table, clicked his heels, and bent low. The Professor put down his paper, greeted him, and asked him to sit down. I wondered what would happen. There was some conversation and for a while I was fearful, but both smiled and presently Fritzl bowed and got up again. He came back to get me, and as we sat down with the Herr Professor, Fritzl said that he had wanted to invite the Herr Professor for dinner at the Hotel Maximilian but that the Herr Professor had a meeting at the Ministry of Culture in Munich the next day and could not come.

The best restaurant in Regensburg, one that a professor never could afford, is the restaurant of the Hotel Maximilian; but there are much better ones in Munich, said Fritzl, and so we ended up by offering to drive the Herr Professor to Munich – and to have dinner with him there.

We returned to our table.

'Just wait,' said Fritzl. 'Just let me alone. I've got it all planned. I'll pay him back. I have a little speech to make – and he'll have to listen to it.'

We were a little late starting the next morning. It was always hard to get Fritzl out of bed. When we were ready and had had our breakfast, the problem of getting money came up. Professor Hellsang was sitting downstairs in the lobby of the Maximilian, with a small bag, waiting. The headwaiter of the hotel said we might get a cheque cashed at the Dresdner Bank, but on account of the inflation it was hard to get any large amount, or rather any amount we might ask for would be too bulky to manage. 'Large' meant one or two billion marks. He said we might get it because we had American Traveller's Cheques. I went to the bank and tried to get a hundred-dollar cheque cashed. The Dresdner Bank called up several other banks and finally, with the aid of someone who wanted foreign exchange, we got it. I had to call Fritzl to bring a travelling bag to put in the packages of money. Two employees at the bank were busy counting the bundles and packing it away.

The Professor stood and watched. Some were old fifty-mark bills, and on each bill '500 MARKS' had been printed across the old amount. Other bills were for a thousand, and one package was made up of ten-thousand-mark bills. There were some left over and we put them into the glove compartment of the Hispano. And then we got in, the Professor seated between us, and we raced all the way to Munich.

No one said a word. I knew that Fritzl was rehearsing his speech – he sat silent, his lips compressed, and looked straight ahead. We dropped the Herr Professor at the Ministry of Culture and arranged to meet him there again later, and then we went out to Nymphenburg.

Fritzl still seemed preoccupied. When I looked at him and said, 'Well, what are you going to say to him?' he smiled and said, 'Just wait – you'll see.'

The Royal Palace in Nymphenburg was deserted. We drove back into Munich, past the railroad station to the Ministry, and waited. The Professor came and Fritzl helped him into the car, addressing him by his title, with great ceremony, as always. We drove off to a small, distinguished, hidden restaurant that stands on the Platzl right next to the Hofbrauhaus.

This restaurant has two public rooms, one for the well-to-do middle class, the other for the rich. Built into both rooms is a square, ample oven made of grass-green tiles. Both rooms are panelled in almost black stained oak. Nibelungen scenery fills the space between panelling and ceiling in the lesser room.

The room into which we went, the one on the right, offers antlers, a portrait by Kaulbach, and over the door a nude with her backside turned to the room. The door under this picture opens out into a dimly lit passage with a stone floor. When it is open, the scent of stale beer, latrines, and carriage horses comes into the room. This aroma, the smoke of expensive cigars, and fresh bread, identify the excellent South-German restaurant.

The car outside was surrounded by people. Fritzl brought the Gladstone bag filled with money into the room. The proprietor advanced with two deep bows to every step he took. He pushed his help around, hissed at the waiters, and three chairs were pulled by three of them. Three menus, each one as wide as an American newspaper, were put into our hands. Everything on them was crossed out and all the prices covered with stickers. Only in the centre of the printed card was a vacant column with lines left for handwritten special dishes. This was half filled; the plats du jour and their prices were there.

The piccolo swished flies off the tables with his napkin. Professor Hellsang, very shortsighted now, held the card close to his nose, and in the fearful and ancient gesture with which he corrected our lessons, his finger wandered down the list on the side where the prices were.

Herring filet in wine sauce, eight hundred thousand marks.
Homemade Sulze, five hundred thousand marks.
Noodle soup, three hundred thousand marks.
Kraft-suppe mit Ei, four hundred thousand marks.

Ragout mit Spätzle, one million marks.
Paprika Schnitzel mis Reis, one million five hundred
  thousand marks.

'I don't know what to choose,' said the Professor.

Fritzl announced to the Professor and me that we were his guests. He put the big menus away and called the proprietor and explained to him that we wanted a good dinner. We wanted some caviar, some truites au bleu, and a poularde rôtie, with some compote.

'Ah, yes, but certainly,' said the proprietor, 'but the price, mein Herr?'

'The price,' Fritzl explained to him, 'usually appears on the bill at the end of the meal.

'After the poularde,' Fritzl continued, 'we want some asparagus with hollandaise.'

Now the proprietor clasped his hands together hard, and let them remain in the position of prayer. Asparagus, he said, a thousand apologies, asparagus he had not, he could not afford to keep it.

Fritzl complained about the kind of restaurant he was running. The man looked stupid, hopeless, and embarrassed, and I told him he could send someone to Dallmeyer's, Munich's de luxe delicatessen store which is located close to the Feldherrnhalle, and ask for the best they had; large, fat, white Belgian asparagus – enough for three people.

The proprietor almost kicked the piccolo through the door, to hurry him to Dallmeyer's shop. In the meantime we ate the caviar, very small portions of it.

Professor Hellsang sat between us, silent and uncomfortable. He looked into the wineglasses as they were filled and then he moistened the tip of a finger and with it picked up bread crumbs that lay about his butter plate. He wolfed his food down and nibbled clean every bone of the poularde, holding a leg in his hands. When the asparagus came, we each had six stalks, nice and white and large, with excellent hollandaise of just the right consistency. The Herr Professor ate one, then one more, and after a while a third.

Suddenly he paused and looked around. Fritzl looked at me. Now, I thought, the time is ripe. Fritzl leaned across the table and said, 'Herr Professor—' He repeated, 'Oh – Herr Professor,' and reached to touch him. But Professor Hellsang did not hear him.

The Herr Professor tried to catch the eye of a waiter; then he asked to be excused. He walked to the kitchen entrance, and as he took two steps up to the service door, I saw that the Herr Professor had holes in his socks, and a disorderly pair of trousers with frayed cuffs. Fritzl looked after him and said to me, 'My God, this cannot be – look at Professor Hellsang, a German professor, with holes in his socks and torn trousers.'

The Professor had disappeared into the kitchen. Presently he returned with a piece of wrapping paper. He sat down at the table and his eyes were on his three remaining asparagus stalks. He took them one after another, and carefully wrapped them up in the paper he had brought. Then he tucked them away inside his coat.

At last he said, talking down to the table, without raising his eyes, in a toneless voice and with much clearing of his throat, 'This asparagus is for my wife.' . . . He said too that neither Frau Professor Hellsang nor he had had asparagus since before the war, or for that matter coffee or tea . . . that this little gift would make his return from Munich a double joy . . . that she would be so grateful to us for having made it possible.

We ordered coffee and cigars. Out of his waistcoat pocket the Professor produced a pair of scissors and offered to clip the ends of our cigars. He smoked his own very slowly, and we sat and waited until it was time for his train to Regensburg.

20. Teddy

FRITZL'S HOMESICKNESS was cured after his visit, and by the knowledge that he could go back any time he wanted to. He became interested in things American, and pleased Mr. Sigsag by subscribing to a course in the correspondence school. Mr. Sigsag presented him also with a limp art-leather copy of the *Autobiography of Benjamin Franklin*.

Mr. Sigsag was one of Mr. Franklin's apostles; I thought he was more like Uncle Wallner in Regensburg. Lustgarten came back to the hotel, the riding academy failed, and the millionaire's apartment was not rented, so we moved quietly back into the Adam Suite.

On one of the evenings when there were no parties at the Splendide and the ballroom remained dark and empty, Lustgarten and I went to the theatre.

We went to see *Lysistrata*. During the second act a loud rain began to fall outside in the street and after the curtain went down people jumped over puddles and ran, bent over, to the opened doors of taxicabs.

In a niche of the theatre building, to the right of the door, pressed against the wall, stood a small boy and a larger one who held him by the neck of a torn sweater.

The little one's face was wet and smudged. He looked up at the older boy. Under his arm, tightly squeezed, were several mussed copies of the *Daily Mirror*.

The rain came down in a curtain of strings and splashed on the sidewalk. Lustgarten unfurled an umbrella and stood on his heels, and when the umbrella was opened the larger boy moved under it, letting go of the small one. The little fellow sold me a paper. Immediately after he had received a nickel, he jumped out into the water and ran across the street to the second-balcony entrance of another theatre. Lustgarten was pushed out into the rain as the larger boy chased after the little one. It all happened very quickly and when we got to the other side of the street, Lustgarten was almost thrown into the gutter as the bigger boy came rushing out of the balcony entrance and raced down toward Eighth Avenue.

We found the little one with two unsold copies of the *Mirror* sitting on the stairs with one shoe off: He told us that the other boy had stolen his money: the nickel he had had in his hand and, besides, the day's earnings of sixty-five cents which he had hidden in his left shoe. The thief had slashed down the front of the shoe where it was laced, pulled the shoe off, taken the money, and run.

'The dirty lousy bum,' growled the little boy, and picked the stubs of his shoelaces out of their eyelets. He said, with a nod in the direction of Eighth Avenue, that now he could not even go home, as a beating awaited him if he returned without money. He said that in a casual, tired fashion and when I asked him where he would sleep, he shoved his filthy cap back, pushed his lower lip out and shrugged his shoulders.

I decided then to take him home to the hotel.

Lustgarten pulled at my sleeve and shook his head. He whispered, 'Give him some money, fifty cents or a dollar, and send him off – send him home in a cab if you must, but don't bring him into the hotel. Look at him. No joy will come out of this, and besides I wouldn't be surprised if the boy isn't covered with lice . . .'

A cab came along and I told the driver to take us to the hotel. Lustgarten sat in a corner and the boy, with his two copies of the *Mirror*, sat on the floor. I asked him how old he was and he said that he was eight. He answered my questions in a voice too old for a child, too young for a man; a soft husky talk like that of a young streetwalker. He smelled like an animal, like a dog. His face was a mixture of fatigue and impertinence.

Whenever we had reason to enter or leave the hotel unobserved, we used, instead of the front-entrance door or the employees' entrance, an auxiliary ballroom door at the side of the hotel on a street where the least traffic was.

It was like all the Splendide's doors, a revolving door, cumbersome to open. Revolving doors are locked with two long plunger-like rods that go up into the ceiling. The locks are high up, near the top of the door. While I lit a match, Lustgarten had to reach up and find the keyholes, turn the door, let us in, and then lock the door twice from the inside. He was annoyed that he had to do all this on account of the boy.

Teddy came into the ballroom with no manifestation of awe. He held on to his newspapers and sat in the ballroom office waiting for Lustgarten to bring him a glass of milk and a sandwich. He drank the milk, ate the sandwich, wiped his mouth with the napkin, and then we took the service elevator up to the apartment.

After he entered the living room he walked to a large sofa, put his papers on it, placed his face on them, and then he fell instantly asleep.

TEDDY

Lustgarten wanted to get him to take a bath but I said to leave him alone. The boy slept all night.

'You must listen to reason, Herr Graf,' said Lustgarten the next morning, sitting at the side of my bed. 'Who is this boy? Where does he come from? Who is going to take care of him? What if anything happens to him? What about his parents? What about if the management finds out that he is here? We'll all be thrown out. I had a brother once who took a boy like this off the street, the trouble he had! I don't even want to tell you. Give him his breakfast, give him money, give him anything you like, but send him away or you'll be sorry. No good ever comes of this kind of charity.'

Teddy told me that his name was Iswolsky, that he was of Polish parentage, that he lived on Tenth Avenue and Forty-Fourth Street, and that he attended a Polish parochial school in which English was taught two days a week and Polish the rest.

The boy who took his money, he said, regularly waylaid him but never had come as close to Broadway as last night. He usually waited for him down near the river.

Teddy was silent whenever Lustgarten came into the room. When I asked him whether he would like to stay with me he said, 'Sure.'

He was still wild and hungry-looking after he was washed. His face was old, he had a certainty to all his motions. In standing, sitting, running, there was never any play, any foolish posture in his limbs, no repetition of meaningless phrases or nonsense in his talk, no loud laughter and no song. He had a bitter logical mind, and he never cried.

There was some trouble with the Polish principal when I took him out of the parochial school and placed him in a public school. The teacher came out into the street with some neigh-bours and shouted after the car in which I drove away with Teddy.

There was more trouble when Lustgarten had to go to a store with Teddy and buy him shoes, a turtleneck sweater, some clothes and linen. Lustgarten did not want to go with Teddy and Teddy did not want to go with Lustgarten.

A week after he was in the new school I received a card and the teacher said that she regretted to have to inform me that Teddy had appeared only twice. At the hotel he came and went very freely. He sometimes arrived at two in the morning, and several times he did not come home at all.

He had a pocketknife and besides always carried a string with a piece of lead attached to the end of it. With this apparatus he fished coins out of subway gratings. To pick up the coins he attached chewing gum to the lead. He travelled all over New York on the rear bumpers of automobiles and on the ends of trolley cars, and once he pushed some bricks from the roof of the hotel down into the street. There was a commotion but nobody was hurt. He denied doing it, but one of the maids, who was drying her hair on the roof of the hotel, told the engineer and the house detective who came up to investigate that she had seen a little boy with black hair on the roof just before the bricks fell down. He spent most of his time in cheap movies, seeing the features twice. I took him along to better pictures occasionally, but he hated Chevalier, and of *Nanook of the North* he said, 'Nothing but snow and whiskers.' He did not enjoy the hotel's cooking and subsisted on hot dogs and hamburgers which he bought outside the Splendide.

'He is going to end up in jail,' said Lustgarten. 'On the gallows that boy is going to end. Just wait, your pet will make you a lot of trouble. I would like to be in charge of him. First thing every day, a good licking, whether he deserved it or not, and instead of pocket money I'd give him a slice of black bread and a smack on the head. Wait and see, you're going to be sorry.'

Lustgarten wouldn't listen to any explanations or understand that to beat children is a completely European fashion of education.

Lustgarten came into the room with a triumphant face when he could at last report that a pair of studs were missing, golden ones. He said that Teddy must have stolen them. He came next with stories that small change was missing out of a box where he kept it.

The week after the report I was short a five-dollar bill. Next, two bottles of wine disappeared and a bottle of excellent Scotch. We did not know exactly when it was stolen because we had not checked up on our stock for a while.

Lustgarten came and made a speech and begged to throw Teddy out, but I told him to have patience. I explained to him that a child that has led a life like Teddy's can't be cured with a lecture or a thrashing. 'First we must get his affection,' I said, 'then we can work on him.'

Lustgarten folded his hands and shook his head, and once when he buttoned Teddy's shirt he shook and choked him. And he looked at the bottles every day.

'Aha,' he said the week after we had discovered the first series of thefts and again with pleasure he announced, 'Look, two more quarts of champagne, Krug 1928, extra dry, are gone. They were here yesterday.'

'What interests me,' I said to Lustgarten, 'what I should like to know is how does he get them out of the hotel? He's such a small boy; the bottles are heavy and awkward to hide ...'

'He doesn't have to take it out,' said Lustgarten. 'Most probably he sells it down in the basement. Your pet is all over the house like a mouse. You can see him in the cellar, on the roof, in every elevator. He's the butcher's and cook's friend. They make hamburgers for him. As for the wine, he sells it perhaps to a bus boy or a waiter, who in turn sells it to a captain, who sells it finally to a customer for twenty dollars a bottle. That's why we have Prohibition.'

'Why can't we put a lock on the closet where the champagne is kept?' I said.

'Because the closet is a very antique and shaky Sheraton sideboard.'

'Then why can't we move the champagne to a closet which can be locked?'

That is where the argument ended. Lustgarten walked away mumbling. He retired into himself for a week and he never looked at Teddy.

Toward the end of Lustgarten's silence, a man in a cheap overcoat and a derby came into the hotel and was shown to the ballroom office. He sat in a chair when I went to see him, opened his mouth and closed his eyes like a bird.

In a hotel, people like this usually have a cigar between their fingers and start their conversation with 'How much do you want for the use of the Hall?' but after the rental figure is quoted them, they get up and ask for the address of the Hotel Commodore or the Pennsylvania.

But this one announced that he was a detective. He asked me whether a small boy by the name of Teddy Iswolsky lived with me. He opened his mouth again, made an effort to speak, and then said, 'Where's the boy? Where is he now, I mean?'

I told them that I did not know where he was, that perhaps he was upstairs. We took an elevator to the top floor and walked down to the apartment. Teddy was not there.

'In case he comes in while I am here,' said the detective with closed eyes, 'in case he comes, you just sit there and listen. I don't want you to do any talking or make any signs to him, you understand? You just sit here, and I'll be here, you understand that? I'll ask all the questions.'

I gave the detective a drink and talked with him and after about ten minutes Teddy came into the room.

The detective called him, placed him in front of himself so that the boy's back was turned in my direction. He took hold of both the boy's arms and he closed his eyes again and after a while he said:

'What's your name?'

'Teddy Iswolsky.'

'What's this man's name?'

The boy told him my name.

'What do you call him when you talk to him?'

'I call him Chief.'

'What does he call you?'

'He calls me Teddy.'

'Where does he sleep?'

'In there.'

'And where do you sleep?'

'In here on the sofa.'

He asked a few more questions and then he said, 'All right, sonny, run along now and play.'

The detective picked up the phone and called a number. He gave his name and said with closed eyes: 'I'm here on case number so and so, and this man doesn't seem to be either a criminal or a pervert. I'll hand in my report tomorrow.

He hung up. 'Sorry, Mister. I think you'll hear from the Society,' he said to me. 'You know, you can't just pick up a stray boy and keep him. There are formalities, papers to sign, but if I were you, I'd get rid of the kid. I've never seen it work out. Good day, sir, and thanks for the drink.'

Lustgarten said: 'For God's sake send that boy away. If the

management hears of this – a little boy who is already a bootlegger, a thief, and you think you can do anything with him. Before anything serious happens send him away.' I walked out into the foyer on my way down to the ballroom. Teddy stood next to a portière, his cap in hand, the little old face pale, the mouth clamped into a straight line. I think I wanted to say something to him, and he wanted to say something to me. I had the doorknob in my hand for a while longer than it was necessary, but then I went to take the elevator to the first floor of the hotel to see that the plates for five hundred people were in their places and the waiters' fingernails clean.

I thought during the serving of the dinner that it was best to send him home. I thought that when the banquet was over, if it were not too late, I'd take him home myself. I thought about this after the soup was served. I walked out into the pantry.

Teddy stood on top of the service stairs, as he always stood at entrances, afraid to come into the room, and he sent his hungry look down at me.

The guests went home early and when I got up to the apartment, Teddy was waiting again.

I asked him to sit down next to me, and I asked him about his father and mother. He did not answer. He sat staring and then he said that his father was in prison. He said that his father was in Sing Sing.

His father, Thomas Iswolsky, he said, had killed a man. He said that he had wanted to ask me for some money so that his mother could visit. It would take five dollars, he said. He confessed that he had taken some money to help his mother. She needed it, he said, for lawyers and to visit his father. His face was pale, his eyes large and fixed on a place he had picked to look at while he talked to me, a point somewhere between the half-open doors that led to Lustgarten's pantry.

He ran home with the money about eleven o'clock.

The next evening I had to see a man who wanted to give a dinner at the hotel and who had very definite ideas about the decorations of the room and the menu. He had an office downtown and worked late. I drove down to see him at 111 Broadway. Lustgarten and Teddy waited in the car. It was about eleven at night when I got through and we drove uptown again.

We passed Madison Square at the moment when the clock on the Metropolitan Building struck eleven. Teddy sat between Lustgarten and me. Suddenly he clawed himself into my coat and screamed: 'Now they're cutting his trouser leg, now they're taking him in, now they're turning on the juice. It's all over,' he whimpered.

It is difficult to console anyone, and more so to help a child. After Lustgarten understood that Teddy's father had been executed in the electric chair, he felt sorry that he had ever disliked the boy. He talked to him, took him on his lap, and when we got to the hotel he cheerfully unlocked the revolving door and took Teddy upstairs. He put him to bed and afterward walked around half the night accusing himself. He apologized and said he was sorry to have been so mean and that God would reward me for my goodness of heart. He suffered a complete emotional reverse.

Teddy was gone most of the next day and he came back and said that his mother needed a little more help. She had a small amount of insurance money coming to her, but bringing the body down from Sing Sing cost a lot of money. There were

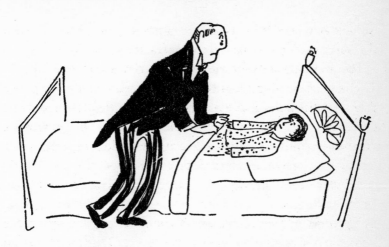

burial expenses and she needed money to put the children into proper dark clothes. She needed another twenty-five dollars, to which Lustgarten contributed an extra five.

Two days later he came and told us that the dead father had arrived. He smelled, he said, of burns. When one stood at the head of the coffin, the hair, what was left of it and not completely singed away, smelled of vinegar. He explained that they use a sponge with vinegar on it to ensure quick execution.

He was dressed in a cheap suit, the dead father, a cheap suit made in prison. He described the candles and the flowers in detail.

I told Teddy that I would take the afternoon off and go home with him and see what I could do for his poor mother. At this he suddenly protested.

'Oh – please, Chief – please – don't do that. You won't like it. It's terrible,' he said. 'The burns, the smell, and all the people crying . . .'

I held him by the hand because he wanted to run away. I had to hold on to him all the way to the address he had given the investigator. He wanted to jump out of the taxi, and while I paid, he tried to pull himself away.

It was a windy day. Open newspapers floated down the street and ashcan covers banged.

In the hall of the house where he lived he kicked and bit, but I took him along up three flights of stairs.

There was a kitchen with laundry hanging from the ceiling, a leaden children's bathtub hung on the wall. A box filled with old shoes stood under a table and two dirty little girls searched in it for a pair to wear.

In the living room of the flat, very happy, big and alive, an honest enough man, with a black curly moustache that supported two red cheeks, sat Mr. Thomas Iswolsky, Teddy's father, eating sausages with his fingers and drinking beer. On the mantel in back of him was a kewpie doll, an American flag, a papier-mâché shepherd dog with rhinestone eyes, and several empty bottles of our wine.

In an adjoining room, graced with a crepe-paper alter, and in bed, was Teddy's mother. The father explained happily that they were soon to be parents again.

Teddy was very quiet and well behaved and I left him there.

21. Mespoulets's Promotion

MESPOULETS HAD finally won a promotion to a situation that no one else wanted. He had been upped to the new position by force. He was in charge of a club that took up quarters in the suite of small dining rooms that was on one of the upper floors of the Splendide.

The members of the club were young men engaged in the real-estate business. The group called themselves 'The Mid-Manhattaneers' and the club 'The Mid-Manhattan'.

The president of the club was the scion of a firm of real-estate people whose FOR RENT and FOR SALE signs hung on most of the buildings in the midtown zone of Manhattan. This firm also managed the real-estate part of the hotel's business. The hotel stood on rented ground. Many of its apartments were rented over a period of years. All this and the Splendide's taxation problems were taken care of by Drawbridge and Company.

'How would you like to put on a black tie and be in charge of "The Mid-Manhattan"?' said Mr. Sigsag to Mespoulets after the club had been running for a month. Mr. Sigsag tried, by this device, to get out of having anything to do with the club, and, particularly, with its president.

'Pardon, Monsieur Sigsag,' Mespoulets had said. 'I appreciate the honour, but I am not at all the executive type. I am quite content. I like my little corner here in the restaurant and my tables close to the kitchen. I have my friends down here. Last and least, I do not like to give orders. A promotion from waiter to head-waiter, alors, holds nothing for me, as far as the finances go. What I gain in salary, I lose in tips, but thank you very much for asking me.'

Hamilton Drawbridge III was a young man, small, and curiously sedate. He was the fulfilment of all the hopes a real-estate father could have nursed. He wore sensible suits made of grandfather cloth, always with a vest, and a neat golden watch chain on which hung a fraternity key and a watch at which he frequently looked. He was as humble as a clerk, but determined. He was untiring and filled with a constant, commercial enthusiasm that played in his face, was in his quick handshake, and in his walk. He was not just setting one foot in front of the other – he was going somewhere with intent and always inspecting things on the way. As he moved along, his eyes were on lighting fixtures, the paint on walls, carpets, fire department violations, doors and windows. He was also alert to kitchen smells.

When he talked to someone, he played with the watch chain, or swung his key chain, or looked down at the floor. When he did that, he pushed an imaginary pebble this way and that with the toe of his right shoe, like a juvenile actor in a rustic play.

He had been voted as most likely to succeed at the University and fulfilled this high promise when, only one year after graduation, he was elected president of 'The Mid-Manhattaneers'.

He had a father-and-son luncheon with the elder Drawbridge every Thursday. Then, both sat together in dark suits and smiled quietly as they buttered their bread and ate the sixty-cent special.

Hamilton Drawbridge III was also in society and, during his college years, he had come to most of the debutante parties that took place at the hotel during Christmas vacation.

At these parties he had danced little but had gone about in his investigating mood and observed. He had occasionally stopped Mr. Sigsag and spoken to him and to von Kyling, asking questions and informing himself concerning the cost of various items. He did it always quietly without comment, seeming at times a little hungry, and as if looking in through a window from the street and not himself part of it.

He left the parties as soon as it was polite to go home. He was one of the few young men who said good night to the hostess and her daughter, and thanked them. He never fell or staggered. He was never known to be particularly elated even on the gayest occasions, and when he went downstairs to the coatroom he put on a daytime hat, and a grey coat over his tails. Then he sat down to put his shoes into rubbers and he wrapped a muffler around his throat. Thus protected, he went out into the cold.

To masquerades, he came as a French chef with a moustache painted on, or in a similarly economical getup.

Mr. Sigsag was drawn to him. At many parties they stood together up on the ballroom balcony looking down over the banister at the crowd, exchanging observations. Mr. Sigsag was proud to answer his questions and he fitted the young man in among the things he considered worth-while, like the books of Elbert Hubbard, and the *Autobiography of Benjamin Franklin*, which he was reading with religious fervour then.

'There is a man to watch,' he said when Hamilton Drawbridge III passed us – but that was before 'The Mid-Manhattaneers' had been formed and moved into the hotel.

'It's very easy,' said Mr. Sigsag to Mespoulets, ignoring his protests. 'You will be in complete charge up there. Nobody will bother you. You just stay up there and see that everything is all right, that the waiters' jackets are clean and that the food gets there in time. You stick around the entrance and get to know the various members and their faces. That's the only important thing – to learn their names. Remember, a man's name is music to his ears. When they come in, you say: "Good morning, Mr. Drawbridge" or "Good morning, Mr. Ashland" or "Good morning, Mr. Asphalt".'

Mespoulets grudgingly bought himself a black tie, had the spots taken out of his tail coat and, with a slight increase in salary, he stood, stooping, at the door of 'The Mid-Manhattan' and bowed. He made the members very happy as he pronounced their names in his elegant French accent.

After they were all in the dining room, he walked about through the rooms, rubbing his hands, looking appropriately worried. When this or that one waved him to his table and, pointing to the menu, asked what, for example, was 'chicken hash Parmentier', Mespoulets gave a minute, correct description of the hash, its ingredients, the process of making it, and of the garnishing, which, in the case of 'Parmentier', is one of potatoes. He added a brief history of Parmentier, the man who was responsible for the introduction of the potato to Europe. All this with the sixty-cent lunch.

'I am not complaining about the work,' said Mespoulets, after the first few weeks. 'I must say the position is one of dignity. My hours are especially nice, but I find this clientele extremely depressing. For example, listen to this luncheon conversation which took place only yesterday at table one – the choice table that I always reserve for Monsieur Hamilton Drawbridge. This son of a multimillionaire comes in with the son of another multimillionaire, Artemus Ashland, who is also in the real-estate business. They are one year out of Harvard and Yale. They sit down and order the sixty-cent lunch, the oxtail ragout, and then, with the coffee, one says to the other sadly:

'"Ham, I don't know what is the matter with me. I haven't rented it yet!"

'The president of the club seemed to know what the other was talking about. It concerned the renting of an apartment. He looked grim for a while and he swung his key chain and then he said: "I'll tell you how to rent this apartment. The next time you show it, show it to a woman. Take her up there around five-thirty or so, when she's tired and when she can't see how bad the light is in the living room. I'll bet you'll rent it like that."

'The other snapped his fingers. He looked at his friend with admiration and said: "I bet I will, too!"'

A week after that conversation took place, Mespoulets reported that the apartment had been rented by the device the president of the club suggested.

'Let's you and I have a drink on this,' Hamilton Drawbridge III had said to his friend, and fished the key chain out of his pocket.

They walked together out into the pantry and opened one of a row of small closets. From this, the president took a bottle of bourbon and held it against the light to see if anyone had broken in and taken a drink.

Satisfied that the contents had not been tampered with, he asked for water and ice, for which the hotel made no charge, and after he measured two drinks into small glasses, he slapped his friend on the shoulder and both showed their teeth in great merriment. The president slammed the cork back into the mouth of the bottle and they walked into the dining room and sat down to lunch together.

'I couldn't sleep all night thinking about it,' said Mespoulets

On Saturday at luncheon time, I walked down the corridor of the floor on which the club was located and saw Mespoulets standing at his post, a small box in his hands for which he had just signed a receipt.

'The quarter I gave the boy who brought it comes out of my

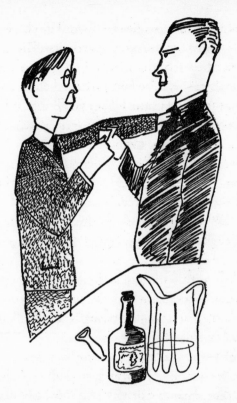

pocket,' said Mespoulets. 'Monsieur Drawbridge is married and he has designated Saturdays as Ladies' Day. This bouquet of flowers came from the flower shop of a department store. Here is the ticket. Imagine ordering flowers where you buy shoes and socks, and, what is even more unfortunate, the store has an order to deliver a bouquet of these violets every Saturday until further notice. And do you know who he is married to? He is married to the sister of the other one, the sister of Monsieur Ashland, the one who rented the apartment with the dark living room. It is all extremely sad.'

Mespoulets handed the box to one of the waiters who was just putting silver buttons in his newly laundered white mess jacket, and told him to put it on ice.

'Good morning, Mr. Drawbridge,' he said a moment later, as the president appeared in the corridor.

Mr. Drawbridge hung his hat on a rack and, with a voice that seemed to come out of the telephone, said:

'I'm expecting Mrs. Drawbridge. Did the flowers get here yet?'

'I have had them put into the refrigerator, Monsieur,' said Mespoulets.

'Good,' said Hamilton Drawbridge III, and went to wash his hands.

He came out with both hands in his pockets, and stood and looked at a board which was hung up every day and, after lunch, put away. This board, which was covered with billiard cloth and made by the hotel's carpenter, showed the names of those members who owed the club money.

Hamilton Drawbridge III scrutinized this board every day. Almost all the members of 'The Mid-Manhattan' were employees of the two large real-estate firms of Drawbridge and Ashland. All of them were college graduates and most of them had been in the same class with Mr. Drawbridge or Mr. Ashland, and while there was a kind of camaraderie in their greetings of the rest of the members, and some laughter, the air changed after either of the two rich young men had entered the club.

After Mr. Drawbridge had gone into what he called the 'clubroom', an ordinary member arrived who carried a suitcase.

Mespoulets, after he had bowed him into the clubroom, said,

'This one goes hunting in Connecticut on Sundays – on a horse – in a pink coat. The pink coat is in the suitcase here.'

'Good morning,' said Mespoulets to a pretty and sweet young woman who came down the corridor.

She asked for Mr. Drawbridge.

'Hiya, Margie. Come on in,' said the president, after Mespoulets called him out. Mrs Drawbridge had a small package in her hand which she did not give up.

Hamilton Drawbridge III came out after a while with the small package. He handed it to Mespoulets, smiled at him, and in his metallic voice he said firmly:

'I think it would be nice if, on Ladies' Day, we'd have a few stands with some after-dinner mints around the tables in the club-room. Maybe a few candies too – and here are four packs of cigarettes. Will you have them opened and placed about on some of those silver seashells you have downstairs.'

Mespoulets sent down for the silver seashells and then he telephoned Mr. Sigsag and Mr. Sigsag had to go to the chef and argue about the mints and the candies. Eventually, a waiter was sent to the pastry cook and he brought up three dishes of the white and green mints and the chocolates. It was no use charging them because Mr. Hamilton Drawbridge III crossed out such items out and then wrote letters explaining that this was part of the service of a club.

On such occasions, Mr. Sigsag deeply repented and said that he should never have taken 'The Mid Manhattaneers' into the hotel.

Mespoulets only pointed to the coat-rack.

'Look at it,' he said. 'Do you remember Mr. and Mrs. Dreyspool – where the portrait of the life they led and of the sauces and pastries was in the laughing knees and the spilled ankles? Well, here it is in these battered office hats and the windy coats. That's how thin they are. That's the way they look to me. Just the hat and the coat – no face, no fat, no life. Here, take one of these grease-stained hats and look at the label. It's of a college town. In every hat is such a label. It's very sad also.'

At the very beginning, when 'The Mid-Manhattan' was started, Hamilton Drawbridge III had come with the fewest demands one could expect. He seemed to be well acquainted with the layout of the rooms before he spoke about renting them. He also seemed to know about the problems that serving luncheon up there entailed. He had his answers and suggestions ready. He stood with his hands in his pockets, or played with the watch chain, and pushed the pebble about as he proposed the club.

'It's found money, Mr. Sigsag,' he said. 'The rooms are there anyway – they're empty. I happen to know that you never serve lunch up there, yet you have to keep the rooms in order for private dinners. Now, we'll pay you a rental of, say, three thousand dollars a year – well, it's just so much gravy.'

The three thousand a year threw everything out of focus for Mr. Sigsag, and from then on, whenever difficulties arose, Hamilton Drawbridge III mentioned this sum.

'What is three thousand a year,' said von Kyling to Mr. Sigsag, 'for all the trouble they're going to give us? I wash my hands of it. Take care of them if you wish, but don't come crying to me – after.'

The chef had refused the idea completely.

'Non, non, non, ça ne va pas du tout,' he cried when he listened to the proposed menu for fifty cents a head.

'Not even for seventy-five saints is it possible,' he protested. 'I make the kitchen with butter.'

To which Mr. Sigsag had answered:

'Let's give them small portions and use leftovers.' He added: 'And remember, they come every day. It's a steady thing.'

'Small portions for young men you cannot give, and leftovers I have not in my kitchen. Let them go to Childs', or to the Automat,' said the chef.

Mr. Sigsag had told Hamilton Drawbridge III about the chef's decision and the young man had just listened and smiled quietly and pushed the pebble around.

He had left and later came with his father to see Mr. Brauhaus. They told him about the group of young men who were just trying to get a start in business and had little money – how it was good for the hotel, that they would pay it back later in patronage, etc. – and Mr. Brauhaus told Sigsag to give them anything they wanted.

A compromise was reached and the chef agreed to a sixty-cent luncheon, consisting of a plat du jour and a cup of coffee. If they wanted anything more, they had to pay for it at the regular prices.

An old vegetable cook was dressed up in the high white hat of a chef and put up there to dish out the food. The portions were large, because the miserable 'commis voyageurs' or travelling salesmen, as the chef referred to them, were hungry from running all over the city and climbing up and down stairs in unfinished buildings whose elevators were not yet installed and in which they had to rent apartments or office space. Also, they lived in the suburbs and had to run to catch the trains.

The chef could not see anyone hungry, and the first days

when he went up there, he took the ladle out of the cook's hand and shovelled out portions that would have been an insult to the guests in the restaurant below.

In the second week, the club's president had a neatly written list of complaints which he called 'suggestions' about the kitchen smell in the corridor, about the waiters' insolence and dirty jackets. He also requested the printing of menus and of stationery for the club by the hotel's printer. He wanted to have a series of small lockers made, too, in which the members could keep under lock and key the bottles they brought into the hotel. There was a footnote about the monotony of the menu. 'There are too many ragouts, hashes, stews,' it said.

'What does he want,' said the chef, 'Faisan Souvaroff, capon under glass, or partridges?'

Mr. Sigsag was called up to the club every day at luncheon time and told about some need for improvement. Therefore, he eventually got the idea of making Mespoulets the manager.

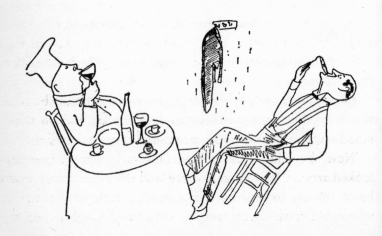

MESPOULETS'S PROMOTION

Mespoulets listened to Mr. Drawbridge and nodded, agreeing with him on everything, but then he went out into the kitchen where he and the cook ate something especially good that they got up from downstairs for themselves. With that, they drank a bottle of wine, smoked a cigar, and talked of France.

Eventually the president lodged no more complaints with Mespoulets, and since Mr. Sigsag did not come when he asked for him, he waited until he saw him.

He found him in the ballroom taking care of a party to which Hamilton Drawbridge III had been invited. He observed the room again and then cornered Mr. Sigsag and asked him a few general questions. Suddenly he began pushing the pebble about, looking down at the carpet.

'We've got a nice little club up there' was the phrase with which he usually started. 'Now, Mr. Sigsag, we've got something special coming up tomorrow.' He smiled as one in possession of a great and happy secret. He continued pushing the pebble.

'You've heard of Joseph P. Day,' he said, 'the great real-estate man. Well, he's coming tomorrow and he's going to give us a talk. We'd be happy to have you come up and listen if it interests you.'

He looked up and beyond Mr. Sigsag to the ballroom balcony, which was festooned with garlands of smilax and on which stood several tall vases of rust-coloured chrysanthemums.

'Now,' he said, 'I just got an idea as I came in here and looked around. The flowers there, and the smilax, they won't be of any use to you tomorrow. Now, I thought that maybe you could have them sent up to sort of brighten up the clubroom a bit. Mr. Day would appreciate that no end. My father will be there and some other people from downtown, a sort of representative gathering. Now, I wonder if you could see your way clear to do that for the club.'

'Certainly, we'll send them up first thing in the morning, Mr. Drawbridge,' was the only thing Mr. Sigsag could say.

The tired flowers and the smilax were there the next day, and also Mr. Sigsag, who listened carefully and learned about the problems of the auctioneer of real estate in New York.

Soon after that, Mr. Drawbridge came with another pebble.

'We've got a great little club up there,' he started again. 'Everybody in town is talking about it.'

'Now,' he said, 'we're thinking about admitting some older members. Mr. Ashland and I have drawn up a list of people prominent in various walks of life. Mot of them must be familiar to you. The list has already been okayed by Mr. Brauhaus. Everybody seems to want to get into this club,' he said with a chuckle, giving Mr. Sigsag a copy of the list. 'We'll try and see how it works. We thought of having a special luncheon next Wednesday, if that is all right with you. Now, we'll have to have an extra waiter or two and a few tables and chairs.'

'Only one thing,' he said, coming back after he had said good-bye and was half out of the room already. 'We have to do something about that coatroom situation. Now, I don't mind about hanging up my coat and hat and none of the other junior members do, I am sure, but you can't expect older people, men of distinction, like we have on that list there, to do the same. There should be somebody in the foyer to take people's hats and coats and put them away and hand them out again as they leave. Now, who could take care of that?'

'The concessionnaire,' said Mr. Sigsag, 'the man who has the hat- and coat-checking privileges all over the hotel. He'll be glad to put somebody up there.'

'Now, that, I'm afraid, wouldn't do at all,' said Hamilton Drawbridge III, leaving the pebble alone. 'That means tips.' He was playing with the change in his pocket. 'You see, Mr. Sigsag,' he said, 'in a club like ours people just don't expect to be held up every time they check their hats and coats.' He looked worriedly at the ceiling, and then he said:

'How about Mespoulets?'

'Mespoulets is the manager,' said Mr. Sigsag.

'The club manages itself by now,' said Mr. Drawbridge.'
Mespoulets is a nice enough fellow but he's got nothing to do.
He just stands there and says good morning. Now, he could sort
of receive the guests and, as an act of courtesy, help them off
with their hats and coats and hang them on a rack, and then,
when Christmas comes, you know, we could sort of take care of
him through the Christmas fund, take care of him that way
with something extra. How about that?'

'I'll see what he says,' said Mr. Sigsag.

'No, not me – ah no – I'm not the type for this at all,'
protested Mespoulets. 'Please let me take off that black tie and
resign. I would be happy to get down to the restaurant again or
in the ballroom and be an extra waiter.'

'You can't let me down now,' said Mr. Sigsag, and he talked
until it was almost time for the luncheon.

'Do it just for today,' said Sigsag, and ran.

'If I do it today, I will do it tomorrow, and then I will do it for
the rest of my life, and then there will be canes and umbrellas –
and in the winter lost galoshes and gloves – no. No, I will not
do it.'

At that moment the first distinguished guest came down the
corridor, accompanied by Mr. Drawbridge.

'*Bonjour*, Monsieur Drawbridge,' said Mespoulets out of
habit.

Drawbridge handed him his hat and then the hat of the
senior member and then the coat. Mespoulets disappeared into
the coatroom, where he held the distinguished hat at arm's
length from himself, then stove it in as hard as he could. He
hung it up after that.

The distinguished men's hats were almost all good, well-

MESPOULETS'S PROMOTION

shaped hats and new. Mespoulets pushed them all in and
stepped on some of them.

The next day Mespoulets was down at his old post again.

'Ah,' he said, 'here I breathe much easier.'

22. *Otto Kahn's Top Hat*

AS HE had promised himself for long years, methodically and with much pleasure, von Kyling got ready to leave the Splendide.

He drove to his farm on week ends, taking along pieces of old carpets and outworn draperies and, stacked under these, bottles of the rare vintages which he had carefully selected over the years.

The property he had acquired was up against a cliff in a stone-covered territory near Poughkeepsie. The old one-story house overlooked a pond and its only decorations were two trees in front of it, standing just far enough apart to hang a hammock between them.

The cellar was the most comfortable room of his house. Von Kyling sat there among his bottles a nearly completely happy man. He had no problems. He wanted no one to wait on him, he made his own bed, he cooked for himself, and he unpacked his bottles and arranged them nicely. He pulled the corks carefully and poured the wine into a fine glass for himself to drink.

He spent his evenings by the light of a petroleum lamp cutting towels apart with an old razor blade, removing the strip on which the hotel's name and crest appeared, and then stitching them together again. He wanted nothing to remind him of the Splendide in his retirement, he said. He also told Mr. Sigsag to go find himself an assistant, because soon he would be the manager.

The candidate for the important job of Mr. Sigsag's assistant soon appeared in the person of Robert, the young man who had been the brave commis years ago and who had been fired because he had studied boxing and had knocked one of the guests to the floor.

Robert had since become serious and forgotten his dreams about becoming a prize fighter. He had applied himself to the restaurant business and gradually advanced to the position of assistant maître d'hôtel of a small but very distinguished French restaurant.

He returned to the Splendide highly recommended. Because he came from the same city in France as the chef, he got along well in the kitchen. The guests also liked him because he was quick and always in good humour. The ladies were particularly fond of him because he was tall and elegant and always immaculately dressed. Only von Kyling had doubts.

'He's like a new tennis ball,' he said, 'he bounces too much. Wait until the end of the first season.'

Mr. Sigsag said that Robert was the right man for him and he spent hours sitting with him on the small sofa in the green ante-chamber between the office and the ballroom, teaching him the catechism of the banquet department.

'How many people does the ballroom hold for dinner?' Sigsag would ask.

'Six hundred,' said Monsieur Robert promptly.

'Good. And how many for a bridge party?'

'Twelve hundred,' said Monsieur Robert.

'Very good.'

Next he drilled him in the prices that were charged for various entertainments, dinners, suppers, balls. After he knew these by heart, he had to stand by and watch how wedding rehearsals were conducted. He was also allowed to engage entertainers and orchestras. As he progressed, he was given complete charge of small dinners.

At some of these dinners he met the magician and soon a friendship developed between them which became so deep that the magician found himself booked at every possible party and Robert took up residence with him in a new house along Riverside Drive to which Gorylescu had moved after Mrs. Houlberg had thrown him out.

Robert soon shared his new friend's interest in the ballet and found his enthusiasm rewarded when Nadya, one of the most beautiful of the Nymphs, detached herself almost completely from the rest of the disciples and gave all of her free time to him.

He constantly hung on the phone down in the ballroom lobby where the waiters called up their brokers. He sent bus boys with flowers and baskets of food, fruit, and candies to the girls. While he was on quick sorties from the hotel to the backstage of the Manhattan Opera House, or in a taxi cruising through the park with Nadya, the secretary of the banquet department, the maîtres d'hôtel, and even the cleaners and telephone girls covered up for him and told Mr. Sigsag that Monsieur Robert was out getting an estimate for place cards or wax candles or that he was showing the Jade Suite to two old ladies or that they had seen him in the ballroom only a minute ago.

The splendour of the girl who was almost as tall as he, pale, with green eyes shaded by long black lashes, and hair that seemed aflame in the spotlights on stage, fired Robert's ambition anew. He no longer was content to be a maître d'hôtel. Neither did he want to be a prize fighter any more. He had a bigger and better dream, the inspiration for which had come to him in the ballroom of the hotel as he had stood watching Maurice and Walton, a pair of exhibition dancers, perform to great applause and for a very large fee.

'You are absolutely right,' said Mespoulets, to whom Robert confided his plans. 'Five thousand a week, pleasant work. You are tall and good-looking. You can do it. Just watch.'

From then on, the two stood in the shadows and followed

the cone of the spotlight as it lit up the various dance teams that glided over the smooth parquet of the Splendide's ballrooms.

'Robert and Nadya' sounded as good as 'Maurice and Walton' or 'Vernon and Irene Castle'. Mespoulets found a teacher of ballroom dancing and Robert hung on the phone telling Nadya of the plan.

She had some doubts at first. She said that the rest of the girls were horrified when she told them. They thought any dancing but the ballet kind was cheap; they carried it so far that they did not even like to go out dancing for an evening. She said she did not dare tell Pavlova about it.

The magician, who blessed the plans, said that it was only a matter of time and she would change her mind.

'Now,' he advised, 'Say nothing about it when you meet her, but be a little cool. Withhold your caresses, but be nice and perhaps a little sad and suddenly one day, when she has some trouble with the girls, or when Pavlova will scold her, she will come to you. In the meantime, you take lessons. She doesn't need any. She can teach you when the time comes. In the meantime also get yourself a tailor – and order a good tail coat.'

'You are so right, so intelligent,' said Robert, thanking the magician. Gorylescu was right; Robert called him a few days later. 'Today she has asked me when we would start to rehearse!' he said. 'Immediately,' said the excited magician – 'in one of the ballrooms.'

The rehearsals were arranged early in the morning while the rooms were cleaned. The Genomies swept part of the ballroom and rolled the carpets back. Music came from a portable victrola. Robert imitated Maurice and danced with gliding pantherlike steps and too much of a crouch, which Nadya corrected. She also persuaded him to abandon an acrobatic number during which he swung her in circles holding her by one ankle and wrist, her face close to the floor.

They rehearsed for two hours every morning. At noon, the carpet was put down, the victrola put away, and Monsieur Robert walked to the office and worked.

Mr. Sigsag, who arrived at one, was particularly happy now and well satisfied with his choice of assistant. Looking through the time cards, he could see that Monsieur Robert reported every morning at nine regardless of how late he had stayed the night before. Looking at Monsieur Robert, he could see that he was pale and tired and already fully dressed in his tails although luncheon had not even started.

He took him aside. 'Take it easy,' he said. 'No need to get here so early. Take a few hours off in the afternoon, lie down.'

A young man with a purpose is able to do many things at once and to everyone's satisfaction. During his hours on duty, Robert was the lithe, untiring, and resourceful assistant that Mr. Sigsag had seen in him. No detail was too much for him. He gave his most painstaking attention to every plate, glass, and client.

'You see,' said Mr. Sigsag to von Kyling, 'I know how to pick men!'

And von Kyling, looking at the swift Robert passing by, said, 'Well, maybe I was wrong.'

Whether crossing the lobby and running to the front office to get the department's morning mail which, every day, contained a letter from Nadya, or chasing after a waiter who had forgotten to bring the sauce for the pudding at a midnight supper, every step that Robert took was now exercise for the dance and part of an endless rehearsal. He danced on the telephone. He danced to the rhythm of his fingernails tapping at the side of the filing cabinet. He tapped his way up from a conference with the chef on the iron backstairs and along over the linoleum-covered floor of the service corridors. The tiled walls carried the sharp echo of a machine gun ratatat that he drummed on the floor as he crossed the maître d'hôtel's dining room after he had eaten his plain meals of milk and vegetables. When he thought himself alone, he danced before the high mirrors of the ballroom, and when he was certain that all the doors were closed and no one was watching, then he held out his arms, picked up a chair, and waltzed with it as if it were Nadya.

Her picture hung on the wall of his dressing room and around it he pinned sketches she sent him from various cities. They were of ballroom dresses which she had designed for herself. 'Dearest and best,' she wrote from San Francisco, 'Madame ignores me completely since I have told her about our plans, sweet darling. She yelled at me in front of the entire company: "All right, go and sell your flesh, you devil, and after all I've done for you!" And the girls cried, but I am firm and I told them that I would leave at the end of the New York run and dance with you, my love.' On the cold morning that the train with the company and Nadya got into New York an hour late, the magician stood on the platform with Robert's large bouquet and explained that Robert had had to run back to the hotel to take care of a party.

Nadya and the Nymphs also rushed away to the Manhattan Opera House where the scenery for *Les Sylphides* was already up for the night's performance.

Otto Kahn's Top Hat

At the hotel, Mr. Sigsag sat with Robert on the small sofa and made him acquainted with the details of that night's party, a dinner by the Foreign Relations Committee, an affair which, from the standpoint of the General Welfare, was altogether uninteresting but which had to be carefully handled on account of the eminence of the guests who attended it.

Von Kyling had never stayed for it but always turned it over to Mr. Sigsag, and now Sigsag turned it over to his assistant. He and Robert went over the dreary menu which was served at the special rate of seven-fifty a plate:

> *Fruit Cocktail*
> *Potage Mongole*
> *Poussin aux Primeurs*
> *Bombe Alaska*
> *Pralines*
> *Demitasse*

Mr. Sigsag took his hat and put some bottles into a bag. He was driving up to von Kyling's farm.

'Remember,' he said, 'when you make out the bill – no rental, no flowers, no wine, no cigars, and ten per cent for the service – and good-bye! See that nothing goes wrong!'

Almost down the ballroom stairs he shouted back:

'And see that the flags are hung right – and don't forget the green table for the hats and coats for the distinguished guests.'

A green table was always placed in the antechamber so that the distinguished guests who sat at the speakers' table didn't have to check their hats and coats with the rest of the guests in the common coatroom below and also so that they could get them immediately at the end of the dinner without standing in line in the cold entrance hall where the general coatroom was located.

Robert was left in complete charge. He called the carpenter and ordered the American and British flags hung. He inspected the seating arrangement and visited the chef for a last-minute checkup. He conscientiously saw to it that the red runner was tacked down on the speakers' platform so that none of the distinguished guests would trip as they took their places.

Nothing ever happened at this party. Everybody arrived on time, ate, listened to many long speeches, and left soberly.

This time, as usual, the guests came promptly at eight. The twenty distinguished ones assembled in the antechamber, placed their top hats and evening coats on the green table, warmed their hands at the fireplace, and walked into the ballroom to the dais after the rest of the two hundred guests were seated.

Robert gave a nod to the maître d'hôtel in charge of the service and then also nodded to a chasseur who pulled the eight green curtains on the four doors of the ballroom. The waiters marched in carrying the fruit cocktails. Everything started off right and as it should.

As the soupspoons began to clatter, the magician, dressed in top hat and a black cape, carrying an ebony cane in one white-gloved hand, and waving an envelope in the other, came running up the stairs. In the envelope were tickets for the ballet, and the magician had a taxi waiting below.

'But I can't go,' said Robert. 'I'm in charge.'

'We'll be back here before this is half over,' said the magician, 'and nobody will know the difference.'

'But I can't go like this,' said Robert. 'I have no hat or coat.'

'Try on one of these,' said the practical magician, pointing to the evening coats and top hats that were spread out on the green table in the antechamber.

After some hesitation, Robert put on the first hat. It was Nicholas Murray Butler's and sank down over his face. So did Dr. Finlay's. The hat of the guest of honour, an Englishman, was too oval, but the fourth fitted perfectly. The coat that went with it was a little short.

'Good enough, let's go,' said the magician, and they ran down the stairs to the waiting taxi.

The disaster of that night was brought on by a mixture of happy and adverse circumstances. Nadya danced beautifully,

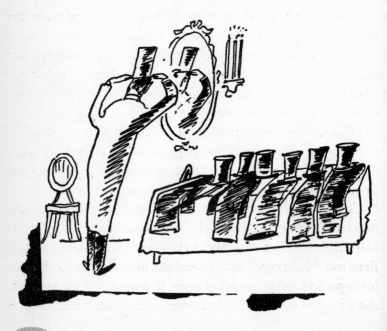

the enchanted Robert and the magician stayed to the end of the ballet and went backstage after. There the time passed too quickly, and later their taxi crept uptown through slush and after-theatre traffic. And while everything with them went slowly, that night the speech of the visiting Englishman had been brief. When they got to the hotel, the ballroom windows were already dark and everybody had left, but in the foyer they heard Mr. Brauhaus's voice:

'Gotdemn, Cheeses Greisd!' he screamed. 'I will fire everybody in this department here. Where is Zikzak? Where is the overgoat and dopphad of Mr. Gahn?'

Up on the balcony stood Mr. Brauhaus, Otto Kahn, and a few employees. Below, Robert handed the hat and coat to the magician.

'Here,' he whispered, 'is your chance to do a real trick,' and ran upstairs.

He stood there quietly while Mr. Brauhaus, with raised fists, poured his wrath on him. Robert was confident that at any moment his friend would settle the matter to everyone's satisfaction and amusement.

When nothing happened for a while, Robert attributed the pause to the time it took the magician to select from his great variety of tricks the one that would particularly please Brauhaus and Otto Kahn and fit the situation.

'Don't stand there, Dummkopf, go find the goat,' said Brauhaus. Robert tried to smile. Any moment, he thought, the soft thud with which opera hats open would be heard and Brauhaus would reach up and find the missing piece rocking on his head and the coat would come floating on to Otto Kahn's shoulders. Something like that, only funnier, was sure to happen.

But that night the magician performed with heavy hand. He just hung the hat and coat on a hook in the coatroom and sneaked out of the hotel, and the next day Robert was fired again.

'I told you so,' said von Kyling to Sigsag as Robert left. 'He had too much bounce!'

23. A Night in Granada

THE ANNUAL Quat-z-Arts Ball was to be given at the Splendide that year. All the public rooms of the establishment had been engaged for this affair. It was to be known as 'A Night in Granada'. Weeks before it took place a large committee of patronesses arrived with two interior decorators, an orchestra leader, and a costume designer, and started to make plans for transforming the vast rooms into a replica of the city of

Granada. Since Granada was at one time a Moorish city, I thought that both the party and Kalakobé would be benefited by having a black doorman in costume that night, and I suggested this to the energetic lady who was arranging the pageant and the tableau vivant. There were already close to a hundred people involved in one or the other, but when she saw Kalakobé she took hold of my arm and said he must not be wasted out on the street. He was so handsome, she said, that she would put him in the centre of the festivities. In the triumphal march, Kalakobé should carry Isabella into the ballroom.

The costume designer and a couturier who was making the dress for Isabella came the next day and vaguely asked for Kalakobé. I sent them down belowstairs, where they saw him in the silver room. They came up full of praises and the day after were back again to work out a costume for him. One of them looked at Kalakobé and said that he saw the whole thing in chartreuse. The other wanted a full-skirted effect, with a harem hemline, done in postman's blue, a hooded silver-sequin burnoose over the shoulders. They disagreed, snatched swathes of material out of each other's hands, and became frigidly polite. Chartreuse won, and the costume designer knelt in front of Kalakobé and, with his mouth full of pins, draped him from the waist down in soft chartreuse flannel, while the chef phoned up for his casserolier and complained that the pots were mounting.

On the day of the party, while the decorations went up, Kalakobé was excused from his casseroles and appeared in the ballroom at about nine in the morning. The wide foyer of the Hotel Splendide had been transformed into Bib Rambla Square, and everywhere stood the pomegranate trees that grow on the outskirts of Granada. The ballroom itself was the Plaza del Triunfo and the balconies had been decorated to resemble Granada's most frequented promenade, the shady Alameda. Every window and door was now Moorish in architecture. The smaller rooms were lined with jasper and coloured marbles. In the ballroom, a stage and a triumphal stairway had been built for the tableau vivant. In an antechamber that was to be used as a dressing room the costumes for the pageant were being unpacked.

The main characters were Ferdinand and Isabella, Gonzalo de Cordoba, Diego Hurtado de Mendoza, Alonso Cano, Mohammed Ebn Al Ahmar, and Boabdil, and there were also many lesser figures out of the turbulent history of Granada. Isabella's gown was the most elaborate. It had been copied, rather freely, from a portrait of Ferdinand and Isabella by del Rincon, and was to be worn by Mme. Julian Alexander Garrand. Mme. Garrand, one of the hotel's best clients, was an elderly, asthmatic patroness of the Quat-z-Arts Ball who from year to year braced an uncertain social position by her appearance as the central figure of these spectacles. She had the breakable face of a porcelain puppet, that can risk neither to laugh nor to frown; the kind of face that one observes frequently in the shop windows of opticians, a lithograph reproduction of an oil portrait whereon it is evident that the artist has been instructed to stress refinement and culture. On these portraits one sees the kind of glasses that Mme. Garrand wore, rimless, and attached to the end of a thin platinum chain, which hung across her left cheek. Without them, she was almost blind. She was distant and correct, and seemed nice until she spoke. The voice was a giveaway. It came out between the baby lips a cold ill wind, and to the trained ears of hotel employees it was the voice of a foe if anything went wrong.

For the supper that was to be served after the bacchanal, Mme. Garrand had engaged a large table in the centre of the room. She tried her costume on several times. It was of golden brocade with a rhinestone brassière, out of which her old arms hung, heavy with bracelets. She was going to wear a diamond choker, and a large diamond diadem in her hair. A mantilla of old Spanish lace was tried and discarded; it hid her face.

Kalakobé was dressed at three in the afternoon. Except for a brief parade through the kitchens below, where he stopped all work, and a visit to the tailor, he never left the ballroom. In back of the scenery he had a bottle of his mixture, and from time to time he went there to refresh himself.

A pianist came about four and there was a short rehearsal. Kalakobé was placed in the centre of the tableau vivant, with Mme. Garrand on his shoulder, and the pianist played Ravel's 'Pavane for a Dead Infanta'. After they had held the pose for a while, Kalakobé carried Mme. Garrand down the stairs. He did it with much grace and without effort, for she was small and light. He was told to make a few turns, as if dancing, to put her down gently on the throne, and then lay himself at her feet. The music for this was L. von Meyer's 'Marche Marocaine', arranged by Berlioz. After all the participants in the pageant were seated in a circle, a troupe of hired Russian dancers were to dance a bolero. Then Raquel Meller would sing a few songs. After this, supper and dancing until three.

The energetic lady director screamed and pushed people into the formations she wanted, the two decorators argued about the lighting, several costumes were found to be missing, and a scenery man turned his ankle. Otherwise everything went very nicely. The florists folded their ladders and took them out; the coatroom girls came on duty, bringing their towels, soap, and check stubs; the first musicians arrived and tuned their instruments; the ticket-takers slipped on their gloves; and the house detective picked his teeth and talked with the doorman. I went upstairs to change, and when I came down the orchestra was playing and the first guests were dancing.

At midnight the pageant began. The tableau vivant started off smoothly. Mme. Julian Garrand was carried down the stairs as if she sat in the saddle of a prize stallion. Kalakobé made so festive an entrance with her that the thousand-and-some guests applauded. Mme. Garrand, without glasses, smiled to the audience and bowed left and right. All the spotlights were on them. The sixty musicians fiddled and blew the last strains of the 'Marche Marocaine' and began the first bars of the bolero. The Russians came into the clear space in the centre of the ballroom, and Kalakobé, with Mme. Julian Garrand on his shoulder, was in their midst. Perhaps he forgot, or perhaps the uncorked bottle and the loose music had worked on him. He refused to sit down or to put Mme. Garrand on her throne. The Russians made faces at him as they danced and told him to set her down, and for the first time a number of the guests laughed. Most of them were too startled to do anything but watch as Kalakobé's body became rigid and a strange set of motions took hold of him. He started a wild stamping, and went on dancing more and more wildly. The Russians left the floor to him. In desperation the orchestra followed his stamping and he conducted with his head, his legs, and arms. He obtained his best effects by throwing his partner into the air, as far as his and her outstretched arms would let their bodies part. Then he jerked her back again, passed her through his legs and up over his bent back, and decorations and jewellery fell out of her as out of a shaken Christmas tree. Once she got away from him and, with her mouth wide open, her beer-blonde hair streaming after her, fled toward the ring of people, but he caught her as one does a fleeing pullet and danced on. Up she flew and around

and around, half mermaid, half witch, her legs bare, one shoe lost. The crowd roared at the end.

As we led Mme. Garrand to the nearest elevator, Kalakobé was surrounded by admirers. He was soaking wet. His chartreuse flannel trousers were sticking to his limbs, his abdomen weaved in and out, and Raquel Meller sent someone for a drink and a towel. Mme. Garrand didn't come down for supper.

The next morning Kalakobé sat alone in the ballroom. The kettledrums were still there, looking a little like his copper pots downstairs. He sat on the north side of the Plaza del Triunfo, his feet away from him, his hands hanging over the knees. His eyes clung to each piece of scenery as it was carried out. While I was talking to him a bellboy came with a message from the manager.

'Gotdemn Cheeses Greisd! She's going to sue us for a million – the old pitch,' he said to the hotel's lawyer as I came in the door.

24. The Murderer of
the Splendide

MESPOULETS FELL apart both professionally and personally as the years went by. He was again in charge of the monkey house, the dismal corner of the restaurant where the carpet was patched, where the service doors banged, where draughts of cold air came down from the ventilators directly overhead, and cooking smells, mixed with the vapours of dishwater, came in warm waves from the kitchen. There, in the shadow of a dying palm tree, he functioned loudly and ineptly, breaking plates and glasses, spilling soup on people's sleeves, mixing up orders, and talking back to the guests. He was tired and miserable. In a dress suit shiny with the drippings of every soup and sauce on the menu, he could be seen leaning on a banister, biting his nails, looking into space, and waiting for the occasional undesirable customers whom Monsieur Victor sentenced to his tables. He made barely enough to live on and had moved from his furnished room in Chelsea to a cheaper one in Brooklyn. It was hard to find anyone to work with him; no bus boy wanted to share the meagre tips or suffer the abuse of Mespoulets. Once kind and patient, he had become like a mean old dog. I was afraid that Mespoulets would be fired any day.

The firing of employees usually took place about nine in the morning. At that time every day Monsieur Victor arrived in a short black coat and striped trousers, sat down at a table in the empty dining room, drank a cup of English breakfast tea, ate a brioche, and smoked a few Dimitrinos. His secretary brought him the mail and sat at a table near by, ready to take down whatever orders he might have to give. His first assistant hovered around respectfully. The manager of the banquet department and myself were responsible directly to Monsieur Victor, and it was our duty to hover around also at this hour. Captains, waiters, and bus boys who were in trouble were called in and made to stand before Monsieur Victor, and a kind of court-martial was held. Victor, an expert at inflicting pain, moved his chair back and announced his findings slowly and usually with a smile. He treated the culprits to short, exquisite essays on promptness, on the relations between guest and waiters, on service, and on the particular circumstances of their cases. He loved to do this with deliberation. His essays nearly always ended in discharge. His judgments were absolute and final. He wished no advice, no defence of his victims, no recommendations for clemency, and, above all, no explanations.

It was no surprise to me when one morning while Monsieur Victor was opening his mail he smiled, looked up at me, and then, as he started to read a letter, said, 'Go call Mespoulets. I am going to fire your friend. He is—' But there he stopped. He put the letter he had just opened into his pocket and abruptly dismissed all those present. I started to leave the restaurant and he got up from his table, ran after me, took my arm, and said, 'Come here. Have a look at this.' Behind a screen near the sickly palm under which Mespoulets's tables stood, he showed me the letter he had put in his pocket. It was a sheet of yellow paper decorated with daggers and skulls and a bleeding heart. Under this was printed in crude letters, 'YOU ARE DOOMED, MONSIEUR VICTOR'. Monsieur Victor looked doomed; he no longer smiled; his voice had changed. He read the words over and over, looked at the drawings, held the paper against the light, and then looked at the envelope. It was postmarked 'Brooklyn'. 'What do you think of it?' he asked me. 'Should I call the police? My God, I have never – what do you think?' I said that I thought it was a joke. At that moment Mespoulets came in with an armful of tablecloths and began to put them on his tables, smoothing them out with his hands. He made a deep bow and said, 'Bonjour, M'sieur Victor.' Monsieur Victor, who hardly ever spoke directly to an employee except to reprimand him and answered all greetings with a curt nod of his head, said, 'Bonjour, Mespoulets.' I thought he might be in the proper mood for leniency, and I asked him if, as a favour to me, he would let me take Mespoulets back into the banquet department, where I could give him a simple job in which his shortcomings would not be noticeable.

'Of course, of course,' he said. 'But about this – about the letter – should I call the police? Don't you think it would be better if I did? No, no,' he answered himself. 'I think you are right. It's a joke.' He tore the letter up. Then he put the pieces together and read the message once more, shoved it into his pocket, and went to his office. Two more letters with the same decorations, the same warning of doom for Monsieur Victor, and the same Brooklyn postmark arrived that week, and Monsieur Victor remained nervous and subdued. No one was fired for days, and Mespoulets became a waiter in the banquet department.

The waiters who are engaged to work at banquets need not be as swift, as intelligent, or as presentable as those who serve in the restaurants of a hotel such as the Splendide. Their duties are much simpler. At a banquet, each waiter has one table. At that table are seated eight guests, who naturally all eat the same things at the same time. A signal – usually a green light some-where near the ceiling – is given by the banquet headwaiter when the guests are to be served a new course, and the signal also tells the waiters when the plates are to be changed for the next course. Banquet menus are, with rare exceptions, unimaginative and repetitious. The waiters are a kind of conveyor belt that runs from kitchen to guests and then out into the pantry, loaded with dirty dishes. They line up in front of the various counters, in turn, outside in the banquet kitchen; at one counter they get the fruit cocktail, at another the soup, then the fish, then the roast, the vegetables, the salad, and finally the dessert, the petits fours, and the coffee. Captains stand everywhere to keep them in line and tell them where to go. It is all cut and dried. The people on the dais, at the speakers' table, or, in the case of weddings, the immediate family, are served by a few well-trained men. The rest are extras hired for the night. Although Mespoulets was worse than most of the extras, I put him on the regular pay roll and assigned him to a table in the ballroom, where the big banquets were held. His table was just a few steps away from the pantry. He was teamed up with a younger waiter, another Frenchman, named Ladame, and it seemed to be working out about as well as I had expected.

Every large hotel has among its waiters a group of mal-contents. They congregate in groups in the pantries while they wait to serve; they stand in the kitchen or pantry and discuss the state of the world. In those days the Germans argued about their German problems; the Italians, in another group, waved their napkins in the air and shouted and made wild-eyed predictions. Mespoulets was soon the leader of the discontented Frenchmen. He was articulate, he had Communistic ideas, and in his harangues he rescued a few ominous bons mots from his failing memory. 'Ecrasez l'infâme!' he would shout. The nervous French waiters who were in his group sometimes thought him too violent. The Germans and Italians would come up and listen to him. The pantry rang with his eloquence, and often I had to send a captain to tell him to be quiet, because the noise could be heard inside the ballroom above the voices of the speakers. Even the waiters sometimes said, 'Sh-h-h! Quiet, Mespoulets.'

When the signal to serve was given, Mespoulets usually came down from his pulpit, the second step of the pantry stairway, and ran to get a tray of dishes. Trembling, mumbling, and excited, he walked into the bathroom and served the guests. Then he retired to a corner, wiped the sweat from his forehead with a napkin instead of his handkerchief, and bit his nails until the little green light gave the signal to clear off. He would not see it, but his partner, Ladame, would say, 'All right, Mespoulets, clear off,' and Mespoulets would clear off.

Mespoulets was moody. For several days at a time he would seem to be happy, almost elated. Around his mouth played a smile of self-satisfaction, and he talked confidently to the other waiters. From this mood he would sink into a torpid, sullen state and complain of severe headaches. One time, after a long speech to the other waiters, he fell on the floor of the pantry in a faint. He lay with his eyes wide open and his hands turned into claws. When he came to, I got the house physician to look at him. The doctor said he just needed a few days' rest. I sent him to his room in Brooklyn in a taxicab and told him to stay there until he felt well again.

About a week later he came back. After what had happened, I could no longer employ him as a waiter, but he could be used on other, easier jobs. I made him a captain. I thought there could be no waiter so dumb or so old that he could fail as a captain in the banquet department. A captain in the banquet department has a black tie in stead of a white one, and, for the rest, he nods to guests as they come in and smiles and shows people where the ladies' and gentlemen's rooms are – 'Downstairs to the left, Madame. Downstairs to the right, Monsieur.' He is engaged chiefly for decorative purposes, and the only other thing he has to do is pass the cigars while the coffee is being served. Mespoulets, however, proved he could not be trusted even with these duties. He did not take any cigars for himself, but he became absentminded and passed them to the ladies. He gave both ladies and gentlemen the wrong directions. He also had more time for his speeches now, and kept the waiters out in the pantry instead of at their stations. So this appointment, too, was proved a mistake. I had to take his black tie away from him and give him a job in which he did not come in contact with the guests.

He was assigned to order rolls and butter when they were needed and to see that the musicians got their water, coffee, and sandwiches. The rest of the time he was an unofficial watchman at doors through which people could crash a party.

On one such watchman's assignment he stood up on a balcony overlooking the ballroom. On this balcony was a door which could not be locked, since it served as an emergency exit in case of fire. This was a favourite door for crashers, and also for dishwashers and other employees who were curious, who wanted to listen to music or occasionally to the speeches. It was the watchman's duty to see that no one came in through that door.

A dinner was given one evening for a distinguished French author, an Academician whose writings were of a political character. The ballroom was filled with very important guests; some of them had come from Washington. At the speakers' table presided Dr. Finley of the *Times*. In the audience were Otto Kahn, Barney Baruch, Secretary Lansing. French and American flags were on the tables, an orchestra was engaged to play during the reception, ending with the anthems of both countries. Dinner was at eight sharp, speeches after the coffee, everything over by midnight.

Just before the speeches began, I walked up to the balcony

to see if Mespoulets was watching his door. He was leaning against it and biting his nails, and when he saw me, he pointed below and said, 'Give me two machine guns, one on this side and the other over on the other side. I'll cover the doors and get them as they try to get out, just like with a hose up and down – brrrrrrr – and the other gun can spray the speakers' table – brrrrrr – brrrrrr – brrrrrrr, Table No. 1 – brrrrrr, Table No. 2 – aim for the plates, shoot through the table, hit them in the stomach so they suffer a while. Here are our enemies. Ecrasez l'infâme,' he almost shouted. 'Liberté, égalité, fraternité! Ah! What has become of you? What mockery! Look there! They're all crooks!'

'All right, Mespoulets, go home,' I said, and put another watchman in his place.

Since Mespoulets was a good penman, I gave him a job we had open for a man to make out lists of material that had to be ordered for banquets – long sheets of paper on which were printed the many things one needs to serve a mass of people. The lists started with demitasse spoons and ended with how many buckets of fine ice and cube ice had to be ordered to cool champagne, to shake up in cocktails, at what time all this had to be delivered, and to what pantry. Besides this, cheques had to be sent out for various supplies which the department bought. To this job we assigned Mespoulets, and he did his work to everyone's satisfaction. He seemed very happy to have escaped into a job in which, he said, he was a gentleman and could use his mind. He kept clerical hours now, washed his hands at five, and at five-thirty went home. There was peace for a while in the ballroom. Below, in the restaurant, the letters on yellow paper decorated with daggers, guns, and bleeding hearts, and more recently with bombs blowing up tables and chairs, kept arriving regularly.

Monsieur Victor had begun to get used to them, but he was still a little nervous. Von Kyling, the banquet manager, had shown them to the police captain of our precinct, who said that they were clearly from a dangerous man. The police captain asked if any of us had any suspicions as to who the writer of the letters might be, and von Kyling said that it could be any one of a thousand or so employees whom Monsieur Victor had fired, or even one of the innumerable undesirable guests of the hotel whom he had insulted in the course of many years. The police captain said in that case he could be of little help. Monsieur Victor continued to examine the letters and show them to us when they came in, but none of us could think of anything to do about them. His secretary kept on filing them away.

Late one afternoon, Ladame, the French waiter who had been teamed with Mespoulets in the ballroom, came to me with the face of one who is burdened. He twisted and squeezed a napkin in his hands and moved a chair and finally asked for a few words with me alone. He asked for my strict confidence, and then, looking around several times and leading me to a dim corner of the ballroom, told me that he did not wish to turn informer but he felt he had to tell me, and that he told me because I was a friend of Mespoulets and had always helped him, and so on, and that he told me only because he was worried. He finally whispered that Mespoulets had said if he, Ladame, would bring him his telephone and gas and electric-light bills, he would see to it that they were paid. Mespoulets had explained that he was the secretary of the banquet department now, and sent out cheques, and that he would arrange to mix these bills with invoices and have them O.K.'d and paid. It was perfectly all right to do this, Mespoulets had said, because the hotel oppressed and exploited its employees. Monsieur Victor, who was rich, was particularly tyrannical and this was just one little way in which he could make things even. To how many men Mespoulets had offered this assistance, Ladame did not know.

When I went to look for Mespoulets, I found he had gone home. I asked the night auditor to come over and we went through the invoices. We found several irregularities – cheques Mespoulets had sent out for small sums, like two dollars and thirty-five cents, a dollar eighty, and the highest for four dollars and thirty-six cents. I asked the auditor to keep the matter quiet for the time being.

Early the next day I looked for Mespoulets again. I could tell that he had come to work because his hat and coat were in the employees' cloakroom, but he was not at his desk.

I walked all over the hotel in search of him. He was not in any of the large rooms, or down among the waiters' dressing rooms, where he sometimes hung out. He was not in the employees' barber shop or at one of the tables in the staff dining room, where he now took his meals. I looked for him in the private dining rooms, the pantries, and in the Jade Suite. He was not there either.

The architectural waste that goes with the building of the elaborate public apartments of a luxury hotel creates many odd corners. A semicircular dining room, a flight of stairs from one elevation to another, rotundas and balconies – in, under, and around all these are vacant spaces which are used as lockers for brooms, vacuum cleaning equipment, extra tables, and spare pieces of furniture. We had dozens of these closets. Mespoulets was in none of them.

At the south side of the ballroom, under the stage, was a long corridor. The electricians went in there sometimes to replace fuses or to connect cables for projection machines when movies were to be shown. The parts of a long horseshoe table were stored in there as well. On one side of this passage were switches and boxes with fuses, and on the other was a row of steel doors, behind which the elevators passed up and down, sucking in air and rattling the doors. The place was filled with the breathing of the heavy machinery, a mechanical intake and outgo, and a machine somewhere far below pounded in even rhythm like a beating heart. I walked in there and saw Mespoulets at the other end. He was leaning against a steel door, holding his head with both hands and howling like an animal. He had not heard me come in and he did not see me go.

It all fitted together now – the speeches, the feeling of persecution exhibited in the petty embezzlements, the resentment of Monsieur Victor, the fainting spell, the periods of elation and depression, and now this hysteria. I remembered all the way back to when I was his bus boy and how I went home with him one day and saw him cut his canary's head off. Mespoulets lived in Brooklyn, and he was obviously the man who had been writing the letters.

I went to Monsieur Victor's secretary and asked her to give me the letters. A new one had arrived a few days before. On the yellow paper there was again the bleeding heart, the dagger filled in with red ink to the hilt, and a scene in which a bomb blew up tables and chairs. The chairs in the restaurant of the Splendide were of peculiar construction, very costly, and styled unlike the chairs in any other restaurant. Even in the crude fashion in which the chairs on the yellow paper were drawn, they clearly resembled our chairs. Someone who knew these chairs well and had worked among them was writing and illustrating the letters. Every protecting doubt vanished. The last letter was signed in something of a brownish shade. It was more violent and confused than any of the others had been.

Without telling either Monsieur Victor or von Kyling I took the packet of letters and went to see the head of the psychiatric department of one of the city's largest hospitals, a man who often came to the hotel and with whom I was acquainted. He looked at them carefully and began to read them. Soon he became interested and started to nod his head. He thought that the last one was probably signed with blood. He swung his chair around and said, 'This man is a killer.' I asked him if anything could be done about the situation, and he said, 'Sometimes – if there is a close relative willing to sign a commitment to an insane asylum. Has this man any relatives?'

'He has, as far as I know, a daughter who lives in France – Marseille,' I said.

'There you are,' he said. 'Without a relative, you can do very little. If you had a business out and away from everywhere, then, between you and me, I'd advise you to run him over with a truck and make it look like an accident. As it is, there's nothing much you can do. The laws governing the legal commitment of such people are themselves psychopathic. Why, only last year, twenty-one such cases were brought to me right here in this hospital. I had to release every one of them, identical cases, exactly like this one. Up to this moment seven of them have done murder, and I am waiting for the others. Under the law, you need a relative to commit them. It's practically impossible to have them put away without a relative. The law is on the side of these maniacs. If they go before a lunacy commission, they usually blossom out and talk like philosophers. This man is safe as long as he can take it out in writing letters, but God help you if he runs out of red ink. Whatever you do, don't annoy him, and for heaven's sake don't fire him.

'There's always this comfort. Last year one of these fellows chased me all over the lobby of a hotel in Milwaukee. He fired four times and missed me three. The fourth shot was only a flesh wound.' The doctor pulled up his right trouser leg and showed me a scar just below his knee. 'They get into a high state of excitement, and the motor reactions are interfered with, and for that reason he may quite possibly miss you.'

The psychiatrist gave me back the letters, and at the elevator he said once more, 'And don't forget, whatever you do, don't fire him, and try not to provoke him.'

I went back to the hotel as quickly as I could and ran up to the ballroom. As I passed through the outer office, I saw that Mespoulets's desk was still vacant. But instead of the usual disorder, the ink, pens, and blotters were neatly arranged, and the books and various forms he used for ordering material had been put away. I asked von Kyling where Mespoulets was, and he said that Monsieur Victor had found out about the cheques and had fired him just before lunch.

'How did he take it?' I asked.

'He didn't say a word – just nodded, and went and got his hat and coat and left,' said von Kyling.

I went over to the restaurant and asked Monsieur Victor to come to the ballroom, where we could talk privately. I gave him back the letters and told him what the doctor at the hospital had said. Monsieur Victor sat down. His face twitched and he said, 'Oh God, oh God, oh my *God!*' He wanted to call the police, but, afraid of the bad publicity this might bring to the Splendide, he instead gave orders to the timekeeper not to let Mespoulets into the hotel. He stationed a maître d'hôtel at the entrance to the lobby and another in the pantry, and before he went to his office he called up his secretary and asked, 'Is everything all right over there?'

'Yes, everything is all right over here,' she answered.

He looked around corners as he left the office, slowly walked out into the open ballroom, ran down to the restaurant, and, in spite of all these precautions, complained of a headache and went home right after lunch.

He came to see von Kyling and me the next morning in the ballroom office before he had his brioche and tea. He said that he had not been able to close an eye all night.

Von Kyling told him that he had privately consulted the police captain again, and he had said that they might pick up Mespoulets and hold him for a while for leading a Communist demonstration, but that eventually they would have to let him go. The man, he said, had his constitutional rights. Of course, after he had shot somebody, they would move right in on him. 'But that,' said Monsieur Victor, 'would be small consolation to my family.'

He had a drink, then called up his office, and asked, as he had the day before, 'Is everything all right over there?' and his secretary answered that everything was all right. He took one more drink and went over to his office.

Von Kyling and I sat down. Von Kyling was a quiet man and

always did the thinking when we were in any difficulty. He was bald on top of his head and over each ear was a patch of grey hair which he let grow very long. When he thought hard he twisted these hairs into curls. He had not slept either.

'Before we do anything,' said von Kyling, 'we want to find out how Mespoulets feels about this. We'll get hold of Ladame and send him over to Mespoulets's house. Ladame is to tell him that he is very indignant at his discharge and he is to try and find out how Mespoulets feels about it.'

We sent Ladame over to Brooklyn. He came back and said that he had found Mespoulets sitting at a table, talking to himself and drinking brandy. He had bitten his fingernails, refused to answer questions, and looked out of the window.

When Ladame had left, von Kyling said to me, 'Listen carefully and tell me how this sounds to you. The telephone bills and the gas and electric-light bills were paid with company cheques. You go over with Ladame and see Mespoulets. He trusts you. You tell him that you have come to warn him. Say that the company has put the whole thing into the hands of the police and that the police are on the way to his house, but because you are his friend, you have come to warn him and help him to get away. We have to get him on a boat, get him out of the country. Once he's out, he can't come back. He's not even got his first papers.'

For the next hour, von Kyling was busy telephoning. With the aid of the hotel's steamship agent, he found the office of a travel bureau which specialized in trips on tramp steamers. Their downtown office informed us of four boats that were leaving at dawn the next day. The most suitable of these seemed to be the twelve-thousand-ton cargo boat *Sadi Carnot*, sailing from Brooklyn for Marseille. There was no time to lose. While von Kyling arranged for the passage, Ladame and I went to see Mespoulets in his rooming house. We found him bent over a table in his room. He listened quietly. We did not mention the letters and neither did he. He thanked us for our efforts to save him from the police, we helped him pack, and then we sent a cable to his daughter Mélanie to meet the boat in Marseille. We took him out to a late dinner, gave him more to drink, and put him on his ship toward morning. In his stateroom, we helped him into bed, left him some money, and sat with him as he fell asleep. We left him just before the boat sailed at sunrise.

As soon as Monsieur Victor walked into the hotel that morning, he called von Kyling up and asked whether everything was all right, then asked us to come over to his office. He listened quietly to our report of what we had done with Mespoulets. When he had been troubled, he had become cordial. Now he was himself again. He spoke in the pompous, somewhat mincing tones that he affected with his guests; he divided his attention between the telephone and a list of reservations besides which he was writing table numbers. He had realized that we might ask him for a contribution toward the cost of disposing of Mespoulets, so now, without asking what this sum was, he suggested that it might be broken up and charged against sundry operating expenses. He hummed softly to himself and disappeared among his tables, placing reservation cards here and there.

Monsieur Victor's reprieve from anxiety was brief. A week later, at the customary morning court-martial for employees about to be fired, Victor was opening his mail and prolonging

the sentencing of a bus boy with a little essay on service when he flung down a half-opened envelope. Protruding from an envelope was the familiar yellow paper, and when we unfolded the letter, there was the bleeding heart once more and the warning,

'YOU ARE DOOMED, MONSIEUR VICTOR'.

The letter had been mailed the night before, in Brooklyn.